PENGUIN Ⓟ CLASSICS

MENANDER: PLAYS AND FRAGMENTS

ADVISORY EDITOR: BETTY RADICE

Menander (341–290 B.C.) was the most distinguished author of Greek New Comedy. An Athenian of good family, he wrote over a hundred plays, although only one survives intact today: *Dyskolos* or *Old Cantankerous*. This won the prize in 316 B.C. and was recovered from an Egyptian papyrus as recently as 1958. Many more fragments of his plays have since been discovered, and some sizeable pieces from *The Rape of the Locks*, *The Arbitration* and *The Girl From Samos* have been known since 1907. These confirm Menander's skill in drawing humorous or romantic characters and making good dramatic use of a limited range of plots with stock scenes of disguise and recognition. Menander's plays were revived in Athens after his death and some of them were adapted for the Roman stage by Plautus and Terence, through whom they strongly influenced light drama from the Renaissance onwards.

Norma Miller was educated at the universities of Glasgow and Cambridge and spent her professional life as a teacher of Greek and Latin languages and literature at the Royal Holloway College. She is now Reader Emeritus at the University of London having retired a little early in order to concentrate on writing. Most of her published works are on Tacitus, but she has taught Greek Drama for many years, and has reviewed books on Greek Drama for the *Literary Review* and the *Journal of Hellenic Studies*. In 1985 she lectured in Greek Drama at the University of Trent in Ontario, and also at the University of Toronto.

Menander
Plays and Fragments

Translated with an Introduction by
Norma Miller

PENGUIN BOOKS

For
the Departments of
Classics
and
Drama and Theatre Studies
at
Royal Holloway and Bedford New College,
University of London

PENGUIN BOOKS

Published by the Penguin Group
Penguin Books Ltd, 27 Wrights Lane, London W8 5TZ, England
Penguin Putnam Inc., 375 Hudson Street, New York, New York 10014, USA
Penguin Books Australia Ltd, Ringwood, Victoria, Australia
Penguin Books Canada Ltd, 10 Alcorn Avenue, Toronto, Ontario, Canada M4V 3B2
Penguin Books (NZ) Ltd, 182–190 Wairau Road, Auckland 10, New Zealand

Penguin Books Ltd, Registered Offices: Harmondsworth, Middlesex, England

This translation first published 1987
9 10

Printed in England by Clays Ltd, St Ives plc
Filmset in 9½ pt Linotron 202 Bembo

CONTENTS

PREFACE

'It is difficult to decide,' Paul Jennings once wrote, 'whether translators are heroes or fools.'[1] Most of those who attempt to translate a literary text will probably agree that they more often feel they belong in the second category. I should like to explain some aspects of my own foolhardiness.

This is a prose translation of a verse text, because I felt that the problems of trying to turn Menander's elegant and economical Greek into the all but uninflected English tongue were merely compounded by trying simultaneously to fit the translation into a metrical frame. References to gods, and oaths, have all been modernized, except where the reference to a particular deity is necessary for the sense; the audience is addressed as 'ladies and gentlemen', although the Greek says simply 'gentlemen'; and references to specific sums of money have been avoided where possible, but where the reference is inevitable, the sums are translated as, say, £5 or 500 drachs, whichever sounds more natural in the context. These and similar devices are simply attempts to avoid jarring the modern ear where Menander did not intend it to be jarred. I have transliterated most Greek names (for example, Knemon, Nikeratos), but have preserved the traditional 'ch' in names like Moschion, because it looks more natural in English.

I have based the translation on the Oxford Classical Text of Menander (edited by F. H. Sandbach, Oxford, 1972), and I owe a particular debt of gratitude to the commentary on it by A. W. Gomme and F. H. Sandbach (Oxford, 1973), and to the works on Menander by Professors W. G. Arnott and E. W. Handley, some of which appear in the suggestions for further reading (p. 18). Occasionally, I have borrowed from them the translation of a word or phrase which I thought ideal, as, for example, Professor Arnott's brilliant *dolce vita* in *The Arbitration* (l. 680). I have included in the translation what remains of all but two of the plays which have survived on papyrus; a selection of the longer passages preserved for us by quotation in other authors; and some papyrus fragments which may not be by Menander, but which are certainly from Greek New Comedy. Where evidence is scrappy, every scrap is precious which helps to illuminate range of material, variety of style, names or themes. The plays are presented according to their state of preservation, from virtually complete text to possibly non-Menandrean fragments. Missing or mutilated text is always indicated: this makes for a less easy read, but I think it important that readers should know what we actually possess of what Menander wrote, and understand some of the difficulties of interpreting a fragmentary text. The Introduction is intended to be precisely that, and I hope that interested readers will go on to some of the works listed under Further Reading and to the bibliographies which they contain.

Finally, I wish to record my thanks to the late Betty Radice, who as Editor of Penguin Classics encouraged me to embark on this voyage round Menander; to Trent University in Ontario, where my Ashley Fellowship in 1985 provided me with an agreeable context in which to complete the translation; to the drama students of what was then the Royal Holloway College, for trying out some of the translation in their workshops; and to four friends who have read different parts of the typescript and offered valuable comments upon it – to Robert Gordon, Eric Handley, Leslie Styler and David West. I have incorporated many of their suggestions, and where I have intransigently preferred my own views, I may yet prove to have been indeed foolish.

N.P.M.
July, 1986

INTRODUCTION

1. New Comedy For Old

To the student of European Comedy, the hundred years between 421 B.C., when Aristophanes produced *Peace*, and 321 B.C., when Menander probably produced *Anger*, present one of the most remarkable developments in the history of that dramatic form. Comedy, developing from origins that are both complex and largely conjectural, had its first official production in Athens in or about the year 486 B.C. Sixty years later, Aristophanes was producing plays which stand at the peak of that particular development of the comic form. They are extravaganzas, in which wild fantasy (to make a private peace with Sparta, to fetch a poet back from the world of the dead), politics (issues of peace or war, the jury system of the Athenian lawcourts) and personalities (Socrates, Cleon, Euripides) are presented with (occasional) bawdiness of speech and indecency of dress and gesture, the whole blended with song, dance and a poetic text which shows a bewildering mixture of accomplished metres and a wide range of imaginative vocabulary; the structure is loose, and the setting can be in Athens, Heaven, Hell or any station between.

A century later, the plays of Menander present a very different picture. Comedy is now about a very limited range of domestic or personal issues. It is about relations between fathers and sons or husbands and wives, about love affairs or about children lost and found – in various permutations and combinations the elements appear and reappear, and it is remarkable how varied the plots contrive to be. In such dramas, neither fantasy nor politics has any real place; characters are no longer caricatures of real people, no longer called by comic-characteristic names like Justice-for-the-Community or Son of a Twister: instead, they have names like Chremes and Demeas, which are the fourth-century B.C. Greek equivalents of John Smith or Mr Hardcastle. The singing and dancing is reduced to a performance which acts as a kind of living curtain that separates the five acts of a tight plot structure in which it plays no part. The language of the text, while still metrical in form and elegant in style, is now much closer to reflecting the spoken language of the day – both in structure and vocabulary, it is much simpler than the

3

language of Aristophanes. Bawdiness of language and crudity of gesture have all but vanished from the text, and contemporary illustrations in the form of terracottas, sculptures or mosaics, show that the actors, though still masked, now wear ordinary Athenian dress. Both visually and conceptually, we are in a different world. What has happened to Comedy? And why?

Basically, what has happened is that the Greek world has changed – changed quite drastically – and Greek drama has changed with it. Politically, during that hundred years, Athens had first of all been defeated by Sparta, and then taken over by Macedon. Alexander the Great died just about the time Menander started writing, and struggles between and with his successors dominated Athenian politics during most of the playwright's life. Athens was no longer always mistress of her own city, and certainly had no longer anything resembling an empire. Public life was often bitter and bloody: Macedonian and anti-Macedonian governors, Athenian nationalists who tried, with any available assistance, to 'restore the democracy', all tended, on taking over power (and they were constantly taking over from one another), to demonstrate the newness of their regime by executing or exiling anyone suspected of contact with the other side. Menander himself, as a friend (probably from student days) of Demetrius of Phaleron, who governed Athens for Macedon from 317–307 B.C., is said to have been in some danger when Demetrius was expelled in the power struggle of 307 B.C.[1] Such politics were not a suitable subject for Comedy, and to try to make them so would often have been dangerous.

Intellectually, philosophy had become much more the basis of education, and therefore more widely understood. Menander was a pupil of Theophrastus, who was a pupil of Aristotle, who was a pupil of Plato, who was a pupil of Socrates, who was a contemporary of Aristophanes: the line of descent is clear, but the attitude to philosophy in Athenian life was now very different from that suggested by Aristophanes' *The Clouds*. 'Schools' of philosophy were firmly established, and had introduced a wider curriculum into Athenian education. Furthermore, the great fifth-century tragedians had been established as 'classics': references especially to Euripides and his plays are common in what we have left of Menander and his contemporaries and they are references different in tone and in kind from the parodies of Aristophanes.

Socially, the theatre audience had changed. Poorer Athenians had been deprived of their vote, and possibly also of their theatre dole, and so both the political Assembly and the theatre audience was much more solidly middle class and educated. Their education had accustomed them to consider social and ethical problems, and stories involving such problems could be dramatized to produce both reflection and entertainment; and they would be more appreciative of an elegant and realistic portrayal of aspects of their own life than of what was in their eyes a rumbustious and rather primitive romp. Tragedy could not provide what they wanted, because all our evidence suggests that in the fourth century B.C., tragedy was already becoming more and more stylized, artificial and remote from the issues of real life. So the popular dramatic form of the time became one which, in content, tone and structure, shows descent not only from fifth-century comedy, but also from fifth-century tragedy. It became, in fact, what we call New Comedy.

The change was not, of course, as abrupt as our lack of evidence makes it appear. Our evidence for the productions of Greek Comedy in the years between 404 B.C., when Athens surrendered to Sparta, and 323 B.C., when Alexander the Great died, is, as so often in Greek drama, fragmentary, contradictory and hotly disputed. We have two Aristophanic plays produced in the first twelve years of the fourth century; we have fragmentary inscriptions of theatrical records for the period, which provide us with some names and dates of playwrights and their productions; we have a mass of references, ranging from the fourth century B.C. to the twelfth century A.D., which provide us with information which often we cannot check and which is sometimes contradictory; we have some contemporary works of arts which are clearly connected with the theatre; and we have a collection of fragmentary quotations, seldom more than twenty lines long and usually considerably shorter, which tell us little about the dramatic structure or dramatic treatment of the plays, but something of their subject-matter and style.

With all its deficiencies, this material tells us *something*. It tells us, for example, that Aristophanes was already writing a somewhat different type of comedy in the later years of his life. The fantasy, the earthy humour, the extravagant and imaginative language, the characteristic names – all these things are still there: in *Women in Assembly* Praxagora, a lady 'active in the market place', schemes to take over the government of Athens, and her husband has trouble with his constipation. But the Chorus no longer addresses the audience directly on public issues: that material now belongs to the actors. The manuscripts of these last plays sometimes indicate Choral Interlude when the stage is empty: and although some, if not all, of these indications are wrong, it is interesting that the copyist thought them

5

suitable insertions – no one tries to insert Choral Interludes in *The Acharnians* or *The Frogs. The God of Wealth*, Aristophanes' last extant play, is more concerned with ethical and domestic issues than with Athenian politics. For the first (but certainly not the last) time, a character called Chremes appears in a Greek comedy. And a slave character begins to play a more crucial role in the working out of a comic plot. The move towards New Comedy has already begun.

We know, too, some fifty names of comic playwrights who were producing in the years between 404 and 323 B.C., and nearly seven hundred titles of their plays. These titles range from *The Birth of Aphrodite* to *The Boeotian Girl*, from *The Doctor* to *Pot-Belly*, from *The Titans* to *The Stolen Girl*. From them, and from the fragments which survive, we can see a movement, uneven but steadying, from political comedy and fantastic setting to more private and social themes which, even if they have their own element of fantasy, will have to be treated more realistically. Burlesques of mythology are common, especially in the first half of the century. Such burlesque was not new in Comedy: it can be seen in action at the end of Aristophanes' *The Birds*, and several fifth-century titles indicate its presence. But in the comedy of the early fourth century, it is central. Were the tragic playwrights of the time perhaps so inadequate in their serious treatment of the stories as to suggest their extended use as comic material? Were the audience perhaps missing the satyr plays which traditionally provided such burlesque? (By the middle of the century at least, only one satyr play was being performed at each festival of the Great Dionysia.) Was it the obvious device of fantasy and distancing to employ, in a changing comic form, an element which provided a still recognizable pattern of action and motivation in the transition from 'the gods', who in fifth-century drama provided that pattern, to the human ethical standards and values which motivate Menander's characters and therefore the action of his plays? On our very inadequate evidence, we cannot be sure. But these plays somehow provide part of the bridge between comedy and tragedy which was to be important in the later New Comedy.

Other trends, too, can be observed. A good deal of the comedy and the dramatic action of these plays seems to concern people on the fringes of a citizen society: the organizing slave, the professional cook, the 'parasite' or hanger-on who makes his living, and especially his food, by buttering up his richer friends, the hetaira, or professional courtesan, who sometimes has a heart of gold, and the professional soldier. Such characters are as old as comedy: but their professional status and their central position in fourth-century comedy probably reflect changing attitudes in a changing society which was watching that comedy. With the possible exception of the soldier, they belong to private life: and even he is not fighting for Athens or for Greece, but has hired himself out in a private capacity, to make his fortune, and has returned to deal with private problems.

With these private problems New Comedy was increasingly concerned. The steadily growing corpus of Menander's work, the references to and fragments from his contemporaries' plays, and the Roman comedies of Plautus and Terence, which were based on the Greek New Comedy, show clearly that that comedy was concerned with an apparently very narrow range of material. A young man in love and the various vicissitudes of the affair; a girl lost, abandoned or stolen in childhood, who is eventually recognized and restored to family and status and so also to the possibility of marriage; an eccentric whose antics affect all those around him; a series of misunderstandings which cause chaos and confusion within a family; the repercussions of a returning soldier, or of what has been wrongly identified as his dead body; such themes, in a variety of patterns, form the basic material of the plays of Menander and his contemporaries. How narrow in fact is the range? And how important are the plays?

Of course the range is narrow compared with the swoop and sweep of Aristophanes. There are no Boeotians, Megarians, birds in heaven or landladies in hell here. But this is a comedy of manners, of human behaviour realistically presented, and manners can be adequately and entertainingly presented within quite a narrow compass, as the novels of Jane Austen and Barbara Pym admirably demonstrate. The issues are basic to human life and to human imagining, and they lie behind the comedies of Shakespeare as much as behind the romances from the house of Mills & Boon. Boeotians, Megarians and their like are not needed to make this sort of point. This is a different kind of drama, with a different dramatic technique and some different dramatic conventions. There are possibilities of variety even in the treatment of conventions; and a narrow range may produce a compensatory concentration. Menander's characters are much more naturalistic in presentation than are Aristophanes', and they are more subtly used to make their dramatic point. The total effect is much less funny – there are few belly-laughs in Menander. He produces, rather, an amused appreciation of what fools we mortals can sometimes be. He has been accused of escapism, of providing comfort for the middle classes in a world where they found life hard. Perhaps he did: but if so, it was surely a side-effect. The basis of Menander's world is real enough. Of course he concentrates on those aspects of it which will provide him with suitable material: that is what dramatists do. No one imagines that the real world behind French farce consisted *only* of people rushing in and out of bedroom doors: but such activities were no doubt part of it. In Menander's world, young men *did* sometimes become mercenary soldiers, unwanted babies *were* sometimes exposed and abandoned, pirates *did* sometimes steal children (Pompey's clearance of pirates from the Mediterranean was still three hundred years away), and respectable girls no doubt *were* sometimes raped or seduced during the relative freedom of the festivals which provided the only chance for young people of opposite sexes to meet before marriage: in which case, family complications *would* most certainly ensue. Such happenings were no doubt not as frequent in real life as in the plays, but they were recognizable. No doubt, too, lost children were not *found* as frequently in real life. But that pattern, which was at least possible in real life, goes back through tragedy (Euripides' *Ion*) to mythology, and so provides its own archetypal pattern for some of the stories.

Not all the stories are like that. In *Old Cantankerous* there is no rape or seduction, no lost or illegitimate children, not a recognition token in sight. But such incidents provide the normal pattern, presumably because they provide interest and excitement and opportunity for displaying human behaviour. And the whole approach has a universal quality that is easily transferable. The Old Comedy of Aristophanes has undoubtedly a universal appeal: but its form and approach, its humour and presentation, were rooted and grounded in its origins, and in the sovereign, democratic city-state of fifth-century Athens. When the origins became remote and the audience more sophisticated, when the sovereign city-state was no more, Old Comedy began to wither. It gradually lost its appeal for fourth-century Athenians, and it certainly did not attract the later and wider Graeco-Roman world. A comparison between Aristophanes and Menander has come down to us with the works of Plutarch from the second century A.D. Some of its points are illuminating:

Coarseness in words, vulgarity and ribaldry are present in Aristophanes, but not at all in Menander; obviously, for the uneducated, ordinary person is captivated by what the former says, but the educated man will be displeased.

Moreover, in [Aristophanes'] diction there are tragic, comic, pompous and prosaic elements, obscurity, vagueness, dignity and elevation, loquacity and sickening nonsense . . . But Menander's diction is so polished and its ingredients mingled into so consistent a whole that, although it is employed in connexion with many emotions and many types of character and adapts itself to persons of every kind, it nevertheless appears as one and preserves its uniformity in common and familiar words in general use.

Now Aristophanes is neither pleasing to the many nor endurable to the thoughtful, but his poetry is like a harlot who has passed her prime and then takes up the role of a wife, whose presumption the many cannot endure and whose licentiousness and malice the dignified abominate. But Menander, along with his charm, shows himself above all satisfying. He has made his poetry, of all the beautiful works Greece has produced, the most generally accepted subject in theatres, in discussions and at banquets, for readings, for instruction and for dramatic competitions . . . For what reason, in fact, is it truly worth while for an educated man to go to the theatre, except to enjoy Menander?[2]

This is an interesting and revealing view, and it reveals more of the writer and his age than of either of his subjects. There is a complete failure to understand the qualities of Aristophanes; and there is a linguistic and stylistic bias which completely ignores the fact that these men are dramatists, and remarkably able dramatists at that. No doubt pseudo-Plutarch and his contemporaries got the drama they deserved. But the comparison goes a long way to explain why the New Comedy was found to be more adaptable.

Menander's world, which looks narrower, was actually in many ways a wider one than Aristophanes'. Menander himself is the only notable New Comedy playwright who is also a native Athenian. Diphilus came from Sinope on the Black Sea, Philemon from Sicily and Apollodorus from the island of Euboea. Though he was an Athenian, Menander did not write only for the Athenian theatre: for he wrote something over one hundred plays, and even if he produced at both dramatic festivals for the thirty-two years of his working life (which is on the whole unlikely), that accounts for only sixty-four of them: and dramatists of his calibre wrote only for production, and not as a speculation. There were now theatres and dramatic festivals outside Athens and Attica; actors were highly professional, and beginning to be organized; they travelled all over the Greek world, and sometimes even acted as their country's ambassadors. Horizons had widened, there is a sense of being not only Athenian but part of a larger Greek world. The New Comedy plays, in form and content, were easily understood by non-Athenians, and could be adapted for their own purposes.

They were. This is in a very real sense the start of European

Comedy. By and through the Roman adaptations, it progressed to the *commedia dell'arte*, to Molière, and beyond. Here are some critical comments:

The reversals spring from the characterisation . . . The struggle between father and son is presented with rueful humour . . . The dialogue is replete with wit, yet as easy and natural as if there were none . . . The moral is obvious in the action . . . When the language takes a highly literary flow, the reason is often to be found in the self-importance of the speaker . . . He repeats certain words to fix a type in the minds of the audience . . . Plays that belong essentially to the society and stage of his own day, continue to give delight to audiences throughout the world.

These statements could all have been made about the plays of Menander. They are in fact a selection of critical comments on the plays of Richard Brinsley Sheridan.[3]

Eighteenth-century English comedy stands firmly in the tradition which Menander established. Five-act structure, action in one day (*The Rivals*) or, 'the mistakes of a night' (*She Stoops to Conquer*), contrast between town and country, love interest, masters and men, fathers and sons, fathers and daughters, husbands and wives, intrigue, misunderstanding, high and low comedy and the varied language that accompanies them (Tony Lumpkin in *She Stoops to Conquer* has distinct connections with the intriguing slave of ancient comedy), and comment on human behaviour and human society: it is all there, and it starts from Menander. New Comedy provides us with the first real dramatic use of invented material dealing with, more or less, ordinary people. It was therefore easily understood by other peoples. Its progress does not stop with the eighteenth century. T. S. Eliot's *The Confidential Clerk* is a comedy of manners which goes back for its inspiration beyond Menander to one of his sources. It is a modern reworking of the myth behind the *Ion* of Euripides, and it raises the same questions about human behaviour and human motivation as the original does. The *Ion* is, for us certainly, and probably for Menander also, the archetypal treatment of the lost-and-found-child story, and it contains, as do Menander's plays, both humour and serious undertones.

There are certainly things which put Menander in the tradition that stems from Aristophanes. There is, in both, wit and low comedy, the humour of family relationships, and the break of illusion (never with any certainty found in tragedy) which establishes a certain kind of rapport between actors and audience. Aristophanes' heroes, like Menander's, are middle-class Athenians, and like Menander's they eventually triumph over a series of obstacles: only the obstacles and the methods are different. Aristophanes' Lamachus lies behind Menander's Polemon and Thrasonides; embryonic 'clever' slaves appear in Aristophanes' *Frogs* and *God of Wealth*; food and cooking figure prominently in his *Acharnians* and *Women in Assembly*; characters who live or try to live by flattering others are found in his *Birds*, and apparently formed the Chorus of his rival Eupolis's *Flatterers*; and the ancient *Life of Aristophanes* tells us that in his *Kokalos* he brought in rape and recognition (of long-lost relatives). Menander is clearly a comic playwright in a continuing Athenian tradition – a truth quite simply demonstrated by the fact that he produced his plays *as* Comedies, and preserved in his *entr'actes* a vestige of the *komos*, the chorus of revellers that lies somewhere behind the dramatic form that we call comedy.

But there is another important strand in Menander's drama, which comes not from comedy but from tragedy, and in particular from the tragedies of Euripides. Plays like the *Ion*, *Helen* and *Iphigenia Among the Taurians*, the 'tragi-comedies' of Euripides, already show, before the end of the fifth century B.C., characteristics of attitude, structure and versification which Menander found useful. The prologue speech by a deity, for example (Hermes in the *Ion*, Pan in *Old Cantankerous*), which can tell the audience things they need to know, and which (most important) promises a happy ending, so that they can enjoy the theatrical thrills without being seriously concerned about the ultimate outcome; the light and elegant verse, the fast and witty dialogue; the implicit raised eyebrow which invites contemplation of motivation and behaviour; the series of misunderstandings, alarums and excursions, and escapes; the happy ending which is not without a wry twist – all these Euripides showed Menander. In the fourth century, our evidence suggests that serious dramatic thinking of any quality was no longer being done in the context of tragic production. But the plays of the great fifth-century tragedians, and especially of the 'modern' Euripides, provided pointers to a different and profitable treatment of the traditional material. Instead of 'modernizing' the mythical stories, Menander and his fellows secularized them. Euripides treated his mythical characters like contemporaries, Menander handles his contemporary characters with something of the universality of myth, and by his presentation of a universally recognizable human situation provides a kind of framework within which his successors could operate.

2. *Menander the Dramatist*

But Menander is not important simply for his successors. To the ancient world he was a poet 'second only to Homer', a 'mirror of life', a writer whose 'polished charm exercises a reforming influence and helps to raise moral standards', a writer 'of great invention, with a style adapted to any kind of circumstances, character and emotion' – a style which was recommended as a model for aspiring public speakers in Rome in the first century A.D.[4] He is all these things. But he is also a practical playwright of considerable skill, and his dramatic preoccupations and techniques are worth attention. *The Girl From Samos* illustrates many of them well. It presents two fathers, one mild and reasonable, the other choleric; the son of the first, in the absence abroad of both, has seduced the daughter of the second; there is a good-hearted courtesan, a slave in the know, and a cook. The ingredients are standard. But the play is far from the 'mixture as before'.

'Demeas' is usually the name of a father in New Comedy (other examples can be found in Menander's *The Man She Hated* and Terence's *The Brothers*), but he is not always mild and reasonable: far from it in Terence's play, which is based on a lost play by Menander. In *The Brothers*, Demeas is the choleric father, and the adoptive father in that play (Micio) is a very different character from our Demeas. Demeas in *The Girl From Samos* has no 'philosophy of education', and has his moments of quick temper and ill-considered action, as when he ejects Chrysis from his house. But his temper springs not from a choleric nature, but at least partly from a guilty desire to remove blame from his adopted son. Both father and son tread warily in the adoptive relationship, and that is what causes much of the trouble. The fact that the relationship *is* adoptive provides not only an interesting variation on a basic theme, but interesting possibilities of dramatic action and dramatic comment, as father and son have to work their own way out of the situation. Standard procedures do not necessarily apply here.

Nikeratos, the neighbour, is not only choleric, he is foolish with it. His staccato conversation in Act One mirrors his butterfly brain; he is slow on the uptake, and over-violent in reaction in Act Four. But these characteristics are necessary to move the action as Menander wants it to move. Nikeratos must not learn the truth before Demeas does; and his ejection of Chrysis helps to secure her safety and to move the action to its desired climax.

'Moschion', to judge from the parts played by characters of that name in *The Rape of the Locks*, *The Sikyonian*, *The Harpist* and the play of *Title Unknown*, is usually a young and somewhat irresponsible man, who either fails to get his girl or incurs considerable difficulty in doing so. The Moschion of *The Girl From Samos* is no exception, but he is also different. He is adopted and (perhaps because of his attitude to this) he is weak, unable to face responsibility, willing to involve others in his difficulties, and anxious always to shift the blame from himself. His actions (and inactions) cause the initial situation and the initial complications, and in the final act produce sheer but plausible farce. He is the first character we see, because he speaks the Prologue which, although it tells us facts we have to know, tells us more about the self-centred, irresponsible (and so potentially dangerous) young man who delivers it.

Chrysis, the girl from Samos who gives the play its name, and whose expulsion by Demeas in the central scene was chosen by the Mytilenean mosaicist[5] to represent the play, is not a common courtesan. She has a stable and affectionate relationship with Demeas (she could not, as a non-Athenian, hope for marriage with him); she is good-natured and loyal, she risks real hardship and danger, because an 'unprotected' alien woman would find life hard in fourth-century Athens, and Nikeratos in a temper might well inflict physical injury upon her. She has to be what she is, to be what Menander wants her to be, the catalyst of the action. Her good nature and frustrated maternal instinct lead her originally to help Moschion; Demeas's affection for her as well as for Moschion makes his reaction particularly violent; her need for shelter causes her to accept Nikeratos's offer and so introduces his as yet unknown grandchild into his house; and her protection of the baby precipitates the crisis and the resolution.

Parmenon, the slave who knows all, contributes to the plot mainly by his absence. Menander likes sometimes to confound the conventions of his comedy, and here his slave does not manipulate or organize, but timidly and prudently removes himself (and his information) from possible involvement. But his rare appearances are dramatically significant. In Act One, his attitude highlights Moschion's weakness and indecisiveness; in Act Two, his 'shopping slave' role provides comic bustle and comic tone; in Act Three, his scenes with the cook and Demeas lower the tension after Demeas's monologue, and complicate the action by allowing Demeas to associate the baby with Moschion and Chrysis; and his final appearance in Act Five with Moschion gives him the traditional slave role in knockabout farce, but also helps to underline the folly of his young master.

The cook fulfils his traditional role of providing low comedy, but he provides it at significant points of the play. With Parmenon in Act Three, he provides comic reassurance after Demeas's potentially tragic monologue-cum-messenger speech, and he does the same thing later in the Act, after Demeas's second monologue. Here, too, he points the irrationality of Demeas's behaviour and of his treatment of Chrysis.

Menander's dramatic style, like his literary style, is economical. Characters reveal themselves and others, provide information and entertainment, and advance the action. That action results from what the characters are in their peculiar circumstances. And what they are is often complicated and contradictory, just like real people. Menander uses character to create misunderstanding, and misunderstanding to create comedy. He does not present 'character studies' in our sense of the words; his interest in character is ethical rather than psychological, but his people are shrewdly observed, and plausible. His presentation of the quirks of human nature is thoughtful as well as entertaining. The comment on human behaviour is not overt, but it is certainly there.

He puts the five-act structure to good dramatic use. New characters enter or a new situation emerges before each break, so that our interest is held. The fathers come home, so double trouble is likely (Act One); a marriage is being arranged – too early in the play, there must be further complications to come (Act Two); the baby is introduced into Nikeratos's house, that could be dangerous (Act Three); all appears to be settled, so what is yet to come? (Act Four); and what comes in Act Five is the release of farce, a farce which has wry undertones. Within this structure, he uses variety of tone (misunderstanding, pathos and low comedy), of presentation (monologue and dialogue), and of metre (the whole of Act Four, which is the emotional climax of the play, is in the emotionally heightened 'recitative' long metre). He also employs parallelism of scene and structure, to underline effects: Chrysis is forcibly ejected from both stage houses (Acts Three and Four), Demeas's monologues bracket a passage of comic dialogue in Act Three, and both fathers declaim like tragic heroes (Acts Three and Four), but with very different effect.

Vivid details add realism to the text: Chrysis's confidence that she can handle Demeas; her attitude to the child; Moschion's daydreaming and his attitude to legitimacy; Demeas's story of the baby, the nurse and the servant-girl; all these are memorable, and they all contribute to our understanding of the characters, and therefore of the action. Menander gets a lot into nine hundred lines of text. We are still in process of recovering at least part of the text of his plays. It does not seem likely that future discoveries will be to his dramatic disadvantage.

3. *The Rediscovery of Menander*

The continuing discovery of sizeable sections of the text of Menander is one of the most exciting contributions made by twentieth-century scholars. Until the early years of this century, he was known only from the unanimous praise of ancient critics, from aphorisms quoted by later writers,[6] from words cited by grammarians to illustrate a grammatical or linguistic usage, from short passages quoted by later authors to illustrate their own points, and from a very few papyrus fragments. Then the publication in 1907 of the *Cairo Codex*, part of a papyrus book of the fifth century A.D., gave us quite large sections of three plays (*The Girl From Samos, The Rape of the Locks* and *The Arbitration*), some hundred lines of *The Hero*, and sixty-four lines of a play whose title is still unknown. It was now possible to make some reasonable judgements about Menander's dramatic style and stagecraft. There, more or less, things rested for half a century, until in the late 1950s the Bodmer papyrus, from the third century A.D., provided us with one virtually complete play (*Old Cantankerous*), along with its production notice; it also contained more pieces of *The Girl From Samos*, and about half of *The Shield*, and these were published in 1969. Since then, other papyrus fragments have been identified, among them parts of *The Man She Hated, The Double Deceiver* and *The Sikyonian(s)* – it is still not certain whether the last-named play referred to more than one native of Sikyon. What is certain is the fascinating story of its rediscovery. In 1906, a piece of papyrus containing some hundred and fifteen lines of this play was found in Egypt, serving as part of the cartonage of a mummy case, and was published by a French scholar. Nearly sixty years later, two other French scholars found large sections of the missing parts of the play, which had been used in the making of two further papier mâché mummy cases, by then in Paris. All three sections of papyrus, from three separate mummy cases, proved not only to be from the same play, but from the same copy of it. That copy had been made in the third century B.C., a century at the start of which Menander was still alive and writing. Together they supply us with about five hundred lines of the play. (Note to museum curators: there are still

some three hundred lines missing. Please check your mummy
cases . . .)

Papyrus texts are not easy to read. They offer handwriting of
variable quality; they do not leave gaps between words; they indicate
a change of speaker only by a colon, occasionally adding a stroke
drawn under the start of the line where the change takes place, but
seldom indicating the new speaker's name; they are often carelessly
copied and casually corrected; they contain no stage directions. But in
spite of such difficulties, the general authenticity of Menander's
Greek and Menander's stagecraft is unmistakable, and we are grateful
to have it. We are not without hope of having more, from the same
kind of source.

4. *Menander's Theatre*

The theatre for which Menander wrote his dramas seems at first sight
very unsuitable to the production of domestic comedy. It was large,
holding perhaps 17,000 spectators, it was open to the skies, it had no
curtain or lighting, and it had a standard set which normally offered a
city street with two or three houses opening on to it. The actors wore
everyday clothes, but they also wore masks which covered the whole
head. A certain exaggeration and distortion of expression was therefore inevitable, and for some characters (slaves, and others likely to
be butts of low comedy) distortion seems to have been sometimes
exaggerated into the grotesque. The mask fixed the expression for
the duration of the performance: no subtle nuances could therefore be
suggested by a suddenly raised eyebrow. This did not really matter,
as the raised eyebrow would not in any case have been visible: the
nearest spectators were sixty-six feet from the actors, on the other
side of the circular dancing floor on which the Chorus performed.
Nuances had to be conveyed by words, voice and gesture, by attitude
of head and body, and by bodily movement. Such 'body language' is
perhaps more natural to a Mediterranean people than it is to us: but it
is not a technique wholly unfamiliar to modern actors, and it is one
which can be easily appreciated by a modern audience. The actors
who wore these masks (male actors, probably three in number, who
shared all parts between them) occupied an acting area over sixty feet
wide, which was raised above the level of the orchestra or dancing
floor, probably by four or five feet. It was backed by a stage building,
which had three doors and wings which projected on to and defined
the outer limits of the stage.

All this sounds very limiting to a dramatist, and perhaps it was. But all dramatists work within the conventions of their own theatres, and Menander might have been equally puzzled by the National Theatre or the Barbican, or by the proscenium stage which provides a three-sided room sometimes poised above a row of potted plants and the heads of a (musical) orchestra. Samuel Beckett and others can produce effective drama in a setting more limited and with actors even fewer than Menander's. Conventions do not limit a real dramatist, and Menander was certainly that. Furthermore, his was community drama in the real sense, performed on a national holiday and as part of a national festival, and the daylight and the admirable acoustics made communication between actors and audience easy. Menander's actors' delivery may have been more formal than we are accustomed to, but these actors also constantly break the dramatic illusion to involve the audience in the action. That, too, was part of the convention of the Greek comic theatre. The 'naturalism' and 'realism' of Menander's drama lie not in the set or the acting style of the fourth-century theatre, but in the text which presents people, their relationships and their behaviour, and that is easily transferable to another theatre and to its conventions.

Menander's plays present a comedy whose interest is not simply historical or antiquarian. They provide us with a genuine dramatic experience.

FURTHER READING

W. G. Arnott, *Menander, Plautus, Terence* (*Greece & Rome, New Surveys in the Classics* no. 9, 1975).

W. G. Arnott, *Menander* (Loeb Classical Library, vol. I, 1979).

David Bain, *Actors and Audience* (Oxford, 1977).

D. M. Bain, *Menander, Samia* (Aris & Phillips, 1983).

S. M. Goldberg, *The Making of Menander's Comedy* (Athlone, 1980).

A. W. Gomme and F. H. Sandbach, *Menander, A Commentary* (Oxford, 1973).

E. W. Handley, 'Comedy' in *The Cambridge History of Classical Literature*, vol. I (Cambridge, 1985), pp. 355–425 and 779–83.

E. W. Handley, *The Dyskolos of Menander* (Methuen, 1965).

R. L. Hunter, *The New Comedy of Greece and Rome* (Cambridge, 1985).

F. H. Sandbach, *The Comic Theatre of Greece and Rome* (Chatto & Windus, 1977).

All these books also contain useful bibliographies.

Old Cantankerous

[Dyskolos
or
The Misanthrope]

Introductory Note to *Old Cantankerous*

The play, about a 'loner' at odds with the world, and the effects of his attitude on himself and other people, was first produced at the dramatic festival held in Athens in January, 316 B.C.,[1] when Menander was about twenty-six years old: it won the first prize. It is our first extant Comedy of Manners, and it was produced early in Menander's writing career. His dramatic mastery is already evident in the economy and delicacy with which characters and situations are presented.

The setting is rural and romantic. The shrine is real (it is still there), but its proximity to the two houses is dictated by dramatic necessity. Pan as Prologue sets the scene and explains the necessary background. He is never seen again, but his influence on the play is persistent: his shrine is visibly central, there are constant references to it and to him in the text, and the interest of the god adds both romance and irony to the action.

Synopsis[2]

A cantankerous man, Knemon, married a widow, who had one son from her previous marriage. They had a daughter, but his wife soon left him because of his behaviour, and he continued to live like a hermit on his farm. Sostratos fell violently in love with the girl and came to ask for her hand. The cantankerous man refused. Sostratos won over her brother, who did not know what to say. Then Knemon fell into a well, and was quickly rescued by Sostratos. He made up the quarrel with his wife, and agreed to give the girl to Sostratos as his legal wife. Then, quite reformed, he gave Sostratos's sister to Gorgias, his wife's son.

Production Notice[3]

Produced at the Lenaia in the archonship of Demogenes,[4] it won first prize. The principal actor was Aristodemos of Skarphe.[5] An alternative title is *The Misanthrope*.

CHARACTERS

PAN, *the god of country life*
SOSTRATOS, *a young man about town*
CHAIREAS, *his friend*
PYRRHIAS, *his servant*
KNEMON, *a cantankerous old farmer*
A GIRL, *his daughter*
GORGIAS, *his step-son*
DAOS, *Gorgias's servant*
SIMICHE, *Knemon's servant*
KALLIPIDES, *Sostratos's father*
GETAS, *his servant*
SIKON, *a cook*

Sostratos's MOTHER *and*
MYRRHINE, *Knemon's estranged wife*
also appear

ACT ONE

SCENE: *a village in Attica, about fourteen miles from Athens. In the centre of the stage is the shrine of Pan and the Nymphs, with statues at its entrance. On the audience's left of this is Knemon's house, on the right that of Gorgias. A statue of Apollo of the Ways stands by Knemon's door.*

[*Enter* PAN *from shrine.*]

PAN [*addresses audience*]: Imagine, please, that the scene is set in Attica, in fact at Phyle, and that the shrine I'm coming from is the one belonging to that village (Phylaeans are able to farm this stony ground). It's a holy place, and a very famous one. This farm here on my right is where Knemon lives: he's a real hermit of a man, who snarls at everyone and hates company – 'company' isn't the word: he's getting on now, and he's never addressed a civil word to anyone in his life! He's never volunteered a polite greeting to   10 anyone except myself (I'm the god Pan): and that's only because he lives beside me, and can't help passing my door.[6] And I'm quite sure that, as soon as he does, he promptly regrets it.

Still, in spite of being such a hermit, he did get married, to a widow whose former husband had just died, leaving her with a small son. Well, he quarrelled with his wife, every day and most of the night too – a miserable life. A baby daughter was born, and that just made things worse. Finally, when things got so bad that there   20 was no hope of change, and life was hard and bitter, his wife left him and went back to her son, the one from her former marriage. He owns this small-holding here, next door, and there he's now struggling to support his mother, himself and one loyal family servant. The boy's growing up now, and shows sense beyond his years: experience matures a man.

The old man lives alone with his daughter, and an old servant   30 woman. He's always working, fetching his own wood and doing his own digging – and hating absolutely everyone, from his neighbours here and his wife, right down to the suburbs of Athens. The girl has turned out as you'd expect from her upbringing, innocent and good. She's careful in her service to the Nymphs who share my shrine, and so we think it proper to take some care of her,

23

40 too. There's a young man. His father's well-off, farms a valuable property here. The son's fashionable and lives in town, but he came out hunting with a sporting friend, and happened to come here. I've cast a spell on him, and he's fallen madly in love.

There, that's the outline. Details you'll see in due course, if you like – and please do like. Ah! I think I see our lover coming with his friend; they're busily discussing this very topic.

[*Exit* PAN *into shrine. Enter* CHAIREAS *and* SOSTRATOS *right.*]

50 CHAIREAS: *What?* You saw a girl here, a girl from a respectable home, putting garlands on the Nymphs next door, and you fell in love at first sight, Sostratos?

SOSTRATOS: At first sight.

CHAIREAS: That was quick! Or was that your idea when you came out, to fall for a girl?

SOSTRATOS: You think it's funny. But I'm suffering, Chaireas.

CHAIREAS: I believe you.

SOSTRATOS: That's why I've brought you in on it. For I reckon you're a good friend, and a practical man, too.

CHAIREAS: In such matters, Sostratos, my line is this. A friend asks me for help – he's in love with a call-girl. I go straight into action,
60 grab her, carry her off, get drunk, burn the door down, am deaf to all reason. Before even asking her name, the thing to do is to *get* her. Delay increases passion dangerously, but quick action produces quick relief.

But if a friend is talking about marriage and a 'nice' girl, then I take a different line. I check on family, finance and character. For now I'm leaving my friend a permanent record of my professional efficiency.

SOSTRATOS: Great. [*Aside*] But not at all what I want.

CHAIREAS: And now we must hear all about the problem.

70 SOSTRATOS: As soon as it was light, I sent Pyrrhias my huntsman out.

CHAIREAS: What for?

SOSTRATOS: To speak to the girl's father, or whoever is head of the family.

CHAIREAS: Heavens, you can't mean it!

SOSTRATOS: Yes, it was a mistake. It's not really done to leave a job like that to a servant. But when you're in love, it's not too easy to remember propriety. He's been away for ages, too, I can't think what's keeping him. My instructions were to report straight back
80 home to me, when he'd found how things stood out there.

[*Enter* PYRRHIAS, *running as if pursued.*]

24

PYRRHIAS: Out of the way, look out, everyone scatter! There's a maniac after me, a real maniac.

SOSTRATOS: What on earth, boy –?

PYRRHIAS: Run!

SOSTRATOS: What *is* it?

PYRRHIAS: He's pelting me with lumps of earth, and stones. Oh, it's terrible.

SOSTRATOS: Pelting you? Where the devil are you going?

PYRRHIAS [*stopping and looking round*]: He's not after me any more, perhaps?

SOSTRATOS: He certainly isn't.

PYRRHIAS: Oh, I thought he was.

SOSTRATOS: What on earth are you talking about?

PYRRHIAS: Let's get out of here, please.

SOSTRATOS: Where to?

PYRRHIAS: Away from this door here, as far as possible. He's a real son of pain, a man possessed, a lunatic, living here in this house, the man you sent me to see – oh, it's terrible! I've banged my toes *90* and pretty well broken the lot.

SOSTRATOS: And your errand?

PYRRHIAS: What? He beat me up! This way [*moving towards exit, right*].

SOSTRATOS: This chap's off his head.

PYRRHIAS: It's true, sir, I swear it, on my life. For goodness' sake, keep your eyes open. I can hardly talk, I'm so out of breath.

Well, I knocked at the house door, and asked to see the owner. A miserable old crone answered the door, and from the very spot where I stand speaking to you now, she pointed him out. He was *100* trailing around on that hill there, collecting wild pears – or a real load of trouble for his back.

CHAIREAS: He's in a proper tizz. [*To* PYRRHIAS] So, my friend . . .?

PYRRHIAS: Well, I stepped on to his land and made my way towards him. I was still quite a way off, but I wanted to show some courtesy and tact, so I called to him and said, 'I've come to see you, sir, on a business matter. I want to talk to you about something that's to your advantage.' But 'You horrible heathen,' he promptly replied, 'trespassing on *my* land! What's the idea?' And he picks up a lump of earth and lets fly with it, right in my *110* face.

CHAIREAS: The hell he did.

PYRRHIAS: And while I had my eyes shut, muttering 'Well, God damn you', he picks up a stick and sets about me, saying 'Business is it – what business is there between you and me? Don't you know where the public highway is?' And he was shouting at the top of his voice.

CHAIREAS: From what you say, the farmer's a raving lunatic.

PYRRHIAS: To finish my story: I took to my heels, and he ran after me for the better part of two miles, round the hill first, then down here to this wood. And he was slinging clods and stones at me, even his *pears* when he'd nothing else left. He's a proper violent piece of work, a real old heathen. For goodness' sake, move off!

SOSTRATOS: Chicken!

PYRRHIAS: You don't realize the danger. He'll eat us alive.

CHAIREAS [*edging away*]: He seems to be a bit upset at the moment. Put off your visit to him, Sostratos, that's my advice. I assure you that in any sort of business, finding the psychological moment is the secret of success.

PYRRHIAS: Yes, do show some sense.

CHAIREAS: A poor farmer's always a bit touchy – not just this one, but nearly all of them. Tomorrow morning early, I'll go and see him on my own, now that I know where he lives. For the moment, you go home and stay there. It'll be all right. [*Exit* CHAIREAS, *hurriedly, right.*]

PYRRHIAS: Yes, let's do that.

SOSTRATOS: He was delighted to find an excuse. It was quite clear from the start that he didn't want to come with me, and that he didn't approve at all of my notion of marriage. [*To* PYRRHIAS] But as for you, you devil, God rot you entirely, you sinner.

PYRRHIAS: Why, what have *I* done, sir?

SOSTRATOS: Some damage to property, obviously.

PYRRHIAS: I swear I never touched a thing.

SOSTRATOS: And a man beat you although you were doing no wrong?

PYRRHIAS: Yes, and [*looking to the left*] here he comes. [*Calling to* KNEMON] I'm just off, sir. [*To* SOSTRATOS] You talk to him. [*Exit* PYRRHIAS, *right.*]

SOSTRATOS: Oh, I couldn't. I never convince anyone when I talk. [*Looks to left*] How can one describe a man like this? He doesn't look at all amiable to me, by God he doesn't. And he means business. I'll just move a bit away from the door: that's better. He's actually yelling at the top of his voice, though he's all on his own. I don't think he's right in the head. To tell the truth, I'm afraid of him, I really am.

[*Enter* KNEMON, *left.*]

26

KNEMON: Well, wasn't Perseus the lucky one, twice over, too. First, he could fly, so he never had to meet any of those who walk the earth: and then he had this marvellous device with which he used to turn anyone who annoyed him into stone. I wish I had it now [*looking at audience*]. There'd be no shortage of stone statues all round here.

Life is becoming intolerable, by God it is. People are actually   160
walking on to my land now, and *talking* to me. [*Ironically*] Of course, I'm used to hanging about on the public highway – sure I am! When I don't even work this part of my land any longer, I've abandoned it because of the traffic. But now they're following me up to the tops, hordes of them. Heavens, here's another one, standing right beside the door.

SOSTRATOS [*aside*]: I wonder if he'll hit me?

KNEMON: Privacy – you can't find it anywhere, not even if you want   170
to hang yourself.

SOSTRATOS [*addressing him*]: Am I offending you, sir? I'm waiting here for someone, I arranged to meet him.

KNEMON: What did I tell you? Do you and your friends think this is a public walk-way? or Piccadilly Circus?[7] Sure, make a date to meet at my door, if you want to see someone. Feel free, put up a bench if you want, build yourselves a club-house. What I suffer! Sheer impertinence, that's the whole trouble, in my opinion. [*Exit* KNEMON *into his house.*]

SOSTRATOS: And in *my* opinion, this is going to need a special effort. It'll stretch us to the limit, that's quite clear. Should I go and fetch   180
Getas, my father's man? Yes, I'll do that. He's a real ball of fire, and he's *very* experienced. He'll settle this crabby old chap in no time, see if he doesn't. I don't want any delay, for a good deal can happen in one day. Oh, there's the door, someone's coming out.

[*Enter Knemon's daughter, from Knemon's house, carrying a large jug.*]

GIRL [*not seeing Sostratos*]: Oh, dear! What a catastrophe! It's dreadful! What'll I do now? Nurse was drawing water, and she's dropped   190
the bucket down the well.

SOSTRATOS [*aside*]: God Almighty and all the hosts of heaven, what incomparable beauty!

GIRL: And when Daddy was going out, he told me to have hot water ready.

SOSTRATOS [*to audience*]: Ladies and Gentlemen, what a vision!

GIRL: If he finds out, he'll make mincemeat of her, poor soul. But no time for useless talk! Dearest Nymphs, you must supply our water. But if there's a service going on inside, I don't want to disturb them —

SOSTRATOS [*coming forward*]: If you give the jug to me, I'll fill it and
200   bring it straight back to you.

GIRL: Oh, yes, *please*. And do hurry.

SOSTRATOS [*aside*]: Country girl she may be, but she has pretty manners. Great God, what heavenly power can save me now? [*Goes into shrine.*]

GIRL: Oh! What was that noise? Is Daddy coming? I'll catch it if he finds me out here. [*She moves towards her own door.*]

    [*Enter* DAOS, *from Gorgias's house.*]

DAOS [*talking back over shoulder*]: I've spent a lot of time working for you here, while master's digging all on his own. I've got to go and help him. Damn you, Poverty, why do we have so much of you?
210   Why do you sit inside all the time? Are you never going to leave us?

SOSTRATOS [*emerging from shrine*]: Here's your jug.

GIRL: Over here, please.

DAOS: Now, what does *he* want?

SOSTRATOS [*handing over jug*]: Goodbye, and look after your father. [*Girl goes into house.*] Oh, it's agony! [*Pulling himself together*] Oh, stop whining, Sostratos, it'll be all right.

DAOS [*aside*]: *What*'ll be all right?

SOSTRATOS [*still talking to himself*]: No need to panic. Do what you were going to do just now, go and fetch Getas and lay the whole problem clearly before him. [*Exit* SOSTRATOS, *right.*]

DAOS: What the devil's going on here? I don't like this at all. A young man doing a girl a service, that's not right. It's your fault,
220   Knemon, damn you. An innocent girl, and you leave her all alone, in a lonely place, with no proper protection. Perhaps this chap knows this, and has slipped in quietly, thinking it's his luck. Well, I'd better tell her brother about this, right away, so that we can look after her. I think I'll go and do that now — I see a carnival
230   crowd coming this way: they're a bit drunk, and it's no moment for me to tangle with them.

    [*Exit* DAOS, *left.*]

FIRST CHORAL INTERLUDE

ACT TWO

[*Enter* GORGIAS *and* DAOS, *left.*]

GORGIAS: Do you really mean to tell me that you behaved so casually and irresponsibly?

DAOS: What do you mean?

GORGIAS: For heaven's sake, Daos, you should have confronted the chap, whoever he was, the moment he approached the girl, and warned him never to let anyone see him doing that again. Instead, you stood back as if it had nothing to do with you. It really isn't possible to deny the blood tie. I'm still responsible for my sister. 240 Her father wants nothing to do with us, but that's no reason for us to imitate his disagreeable attitude. If she gets into trouble, the disgrace affects me too. For other people have no idea who is to blame, they simply see the result. Come on.

DAOS: But Gorgias, sir, I'm terrified of the old man. If he catches me near his door, he'll string me up on the spot.

GORGIAS: Yes, he's a bit difficult. If you tangle with him, there's no 250 way you can force him to reform, and you can't change his attitude by good advice. Against force – well, he's got the law on his side; and he's naturally resistant to persuasion!

DAOS: Just a minute. Our walk hasn't been wasted. Here comes that chap back again. I told you so!

GORGIAS: The one with the smart city cloak? That the one you mean?

DAOS: Yes, indeed.

GORGIAS: A right rogue, too, from the look in his eye.

[*Enter* SOSTRATOS, *right, not seeing the others.*]

SOSTRATOS: Getas wasn't at home when I called. My mother's planning to sacrifice to some god or other – no idea which – she 260 does this every day, trailing round the whole district, making offerings, and she'd sent Getas out to hire a cook, locally. Well, I've waved goodbye to the religious bit, and come back to business here. I've decided to cut out all this traipsing about, and do my own talking for myself. I'll knock on the door: that'll stop any further debate.

GORGIAS [*coming forward*]: Young sir, may I give you a word of quite serious advice?

SOSTRATOS [*startled, but amiable*]: Yes, of course. What is it? 270

29

GORGIAS [*earnestly*]: In my view, all men, be they rich or poor, eventually reach a point where their luck stops or changes. The successful man continues to prosper and flourish only as long as he can accept his good fortune without harming others. But, come the point where his prosperity entices him to commit a crime, then, in my opinion, he takes a turn for the worse. While the
280   needy, provided that in their necessity they keep clear of crime, and accept their poverty like honest men, come in due course into credit, and can expect their shares in life to improve. Let me put it this way: if you're well-endowed with worldly goods, don't rely on them too much, and don't despise us because we're poor. Let everyone see that you deserve your prosperity to last.

SOSTRATOS: You think that at the moment I'm stepping a bit out of line?

GORGIAS: I think you've set your heart on doing something quite
290   disgraceful. Your idea is to seduce an innocent girl – a respectable man's daughter, too – or you're watching your chance to do something that deserves the death-sentence, several times over.

SOSTRATOS: Help!

GORGIAS: It's not fair that you, with time on your hands, should plague us who have none. And let me tell you, when a poor man's wronged, he becomes a very difficult customer. To start with, he gets a lot of sympathy: and then he takes his bad treatment not just as an injury, but as a personal insult.

SOSTRATOS: Young man, please let me speak for a moment too.

300   DAOS [*to* GORGIAS]: That's fair, sir, it really is.

SOSTRATOS: *You're* pontificating without knowing the facts. I saw a girl here, and I've fallen in love with her. If that's the 'crime' you're talking about, then perhaps I'm guilty. There's nothing more to say, except that I'm not here after *her* – it's her father I want to see. I'm a free man, I have a reasonable income, I'm ready to marry her without a dowry, and I swear always to love and cherish her. If I've
310   come here with any criminal purpose, or with any idea of plotting mischief against you, may Pan here, sir, and the Nymphs strike me dead right here, beside the house. And let me tell *you*, if that's your idea of me, I don't like it at all!

GORGIAS: Well, if I spoke a bit strongly, forget it now. You've convinced me completely, and I'm on your side. I'm an interested party. I'm the girl's half-brother, my friend, and that's why I can speak like this.

320   SOSTRATOS: Then you can certainly help with the next move.

GORGIAS: How?

SOSTRATOS: I can see you're a good-natured chap –

GORGIAS: I don't want to fob you off with empty excuses: but face facts. The girl's father is an oddity – no one like him, past or present.

SOSTRATOS: Oh, the chap with the temper! I think I know him.

GORGIAS: He's trouble: and more than trouble. His property here is really a very decent one,[8] but he persists in farming it all by himself. He won't have any help – no farm servant, no locally hired   *330* labour, no neighbour to lend a hand; just himself alone. His chief pleasure is never to set eyes on another human being. Mostly he works with his daughter beside him – she's the only one he talks to, never an easy word to anyone else. And he says he'll only let her marry when he finds a husband of his own kidney.

SOSTRATOS [*gloomily*]: That means never.

GORGIAS: So don't put yourself to any trouble, my friend. It'll be useless. Leave us to cope with this. We're family, it's our job.   *340*

SOSTRATOS: For heaven's sake, have you never been in love?

GORGIAS: I can't be, my friend.

SOSTRATOS: Why? What's to stop you?

GORGIAS: Simple arithmetic. I count up my troubles. There's no time at all for anything else.

SOSTRATOS: Yes, I can see you *haven't* been in love. What you say on the subject certainly suggests lack of experience. You tell me to give up. But that's no longer in my hands, it's in God's.

GORGIAS: Well, you're doing us no harm, but *you're* suffering to no good purpose.

SOSTRATOS: Not if I get the girl.

GORGIAS: You won't get her. But you can come with me and ask.   *350* He works the field next to mine.

SOSTRATOS: How'll we do it?

GORGIAS: I'll bring up the subject of the girl's marriage. It's something I'd be glad to see settled. He'll promptly find fault with everyone, and fulminate against the way they live. And if he sees you looking elegant and idle, he won't stand the sight of you.

SOSTRATOS: Is he there now?

GORGIAS: No, but he'll soon be going out. This is the way he always goes.

SOSTRATOS [*eagerly*]: Taking the girl with him, you mean?

GORGIAS: Maybe. Maybe not.   *360*

SOSTRATOS: Lead on, then! I'm ready.

GORGIAS: What a suggestion!

31

SOSTRATOS: Please, be my friend.

GORGIAS: How?

SOSTRATOS: I'll tell you how. Let's go ahead to the place you mean.

GORGIAS: Then what? Are you going to stand there, in your smart cloak, while we work away?

SOSTRATOS: Why not?

GORGIAS: Because he'll throw his sods at you right away, and call you a lazy devil. You'll have to do some digging along with us. If he sees that he might, just might, be prepared to listen even to you, if he thought you were a poor farmer.

370 SOSTRATOS: I'll do anything you say. Lead on.

GORGIAS: Why inflict pain on yourself?

DAOS [*aside*]: What *I* want is for us to get as much as possible done today – and for *him* to get lumbago and stop coming here and bothering us.

SOSTRATOS: Give me a mattock, then.

DAOS: Here, take mine and get on with it. While you do that, I'll be building up the wall. That's got to be done too.

SOSTRATOS: Give it here. You've saved my life.

DAOS [*to* GORGIAS]: I'm off, sir. You two come on after me [*Exit* DAOS, *left*.]

SOSTRATOS: Well, here we go. I must either win the girl and live, or die in the attempt.

380 GORGIAS: If you really mean it, good luck!

SOSTRATOS: Heavens, man, you think you're putting me off, but everything you say is making me twice as enthusiastic for the job. If the girl hasn't grown up among a pack of women and so knows nothing of 'life's miseries', has had no frightening stories from aunt or nurse, but has been pretty properly brought up by a fierce father who's naturally against all vice – then surely it's bliss to win her? [*He lifts the mattock and staggers*] Help! This must weigh

390 a couple of hundredweight. It'll do for me before I've done with it. Still, best foot forward, now that I've started on the job. [SOSTRATOS *and* GORGIAS *go off left.*]

[*Enter* SIKON *the cook, right, dragging a sheep.*]

SIKON: This sheep's a real beauty. Oh, the Hell with it. If I lift it up and carry it on my shoulders, it catches the young shoots of fig trees in its mouth and gobbles up the leaves, struggling and straining away from me. But if it's put on the ground, it refuses to move. Here's a paradox: I'm the cook, but I'm the one being turned into mincemeat hauling this creature along the road. Thank

32

God! Here's the Nymphs' shrine where we're to sacrifice. Good   *400*
day, Pan. [*Shouts*] Hey, Getas! Hurry up!

[*Enter* GETAS, *right, staggering under a load of rugs, pots, pans and batterie de cuisine.*]

GETAS: A four-donkey load, that's what these blasted women tied up for me to carry.

SIKON: Looks like lots of company expected. What a fantastic number of rugs you've got there.

GETAS: Where shall I –

SIKON: Pile them here.

GETAS [*dropping the lot*]: There! If the next dream is about Pan of Paiania,⁹ off we'll go on a twenty-mile trot, to sacrifice to *him*. I know.

SIKON [*sharply*]: Dream? Whose dream?

GETAS: Don't snap at me, my friend.

SIKON: But, Getas, tell me who had the dream.   *410*

GETAS: Mistress.

SIKON: And what on earth *was* the dream?

GETAS: You'll be the death of me. She thought that Pan –

SIKON: You mean *this* Pan?

GETAS: This very one.

SIKON: What was he doing?

GETAS: He'd got young master, Sostratos –

SIKON: He's quite a lad!

GETAS: And he was putting fetters on him.

SIKON: Help!

GETAS: Then he was giving him a leather jacket and a mattock, and telling him to dig on the land next door there.

SIKON: How peculiar.

GETAS: Well, that's why we're sacrificing, to make sure this frightful dream has a happy ending.

SIKON: I see. Now, pick up all this stuff again and take it inside. Let's get the couches properly arranged, and everything organized. I   *420*
want nothing to hold up the sacrifice once they arrive. Good luck to it! And take that scowl off your face, you old misery. I'll feed you up properly today.

GETAS: I've always been a great admirer of you and of your art, [*aside*] but I don't trust you an inch! [*Exeunt* SIKON *and* GETAS *into the shrine.*]

SECOND CHORAL INTERLUDE

33

ACT THREE

[*Enter* KNEMON *from his house, speaking back over his shoulder.*]

KNEMON: Lock the door, woman, and don't open it for *anyone*, until I get back. It'll be quite dark by then, I expect. [*He moves off towards left.*]

[*Enter Sostratos'* MOTHER *and party, right.*]

430 MOTHER: Do get a move on, Plangon.[10] We should have *finished* the sacrifice by now.

KNEMON: What the devil's all this about? Oh, Hell! Hordes of people . . .

MOTHER: Parthenis, pipe Pan's tune. One shouldn't, they say, approach this god in silence.

[*Enter* GETAS, *from shrine.*]

GETAS: So you finally got here.

KNEMON: Oh, God, how disgusting.

GETAS: We've been hanging around waiting for you for ages.

MOTHER: Is everything ready?

GETAS: Of course. The sheep at any rate can't await your convenience. It's pretty well dead already, poor thing.

440 MOTHER [*to attendants*]: Come on, inside! Get baskets, water, offerings ready.

GETAS [*to* KNEMON]: And what are *you* gaping at, hophead?

[*Exeunt* MOTHER, GETAS *and party into shrine.*]

KNEMON: Damn and blast them! They're stopping me from working – I can't leave this house unprotected. I tell you, Nymphs next door are a perpetual nuisance. I think I'll knock the house down, and build another one somewhere else. And look at the way they sacrifice, the devils. They bring hampers and bottles of wine, not for the gods' benefit – oh, no – for their own. Piety extends as far as

450 the incense and the cake: that's all put on the fire, so the god can have *that*. They allow the gods the tail-end, too, and the gall-bladder – they're not edible. But everything else they polish off themselves. [*Knocks at his door*] Woman! Open the door, quick. I suppose I'll just have to. work indoors today. [*The door opens and* KNEMON *goes in.*]

[*Enter* GETAS *from shrine, talking back over his shoulder.*]

GETAS: You've forgotten the *pot*, you tell me? You're all dopey from

34

a hangover! What're we going to do now? Have to bother the god's
neighbours, I suppose. [*He knocks at Knemon's door*] Door! Honestly, I can't imagine a more useless set of girls anywhere. Door!   460
Nothing in their heads but sex. Door, *please!* And then lies, if
anyone catches them at it. Do–or! What the devil's wrong here?
DOOR! Not a soul at home. Uh-uh, I think someone's coming
now, running like mad.

KNEMON [*opening door*]: Why are you plastered to my door, you
   miserable trash? Tell me that!

GETAS: No need to bite my nose off.

KNEMON: I'll do that, by God I will, and eat you up alive, too.

GETAS: Oh, please don't.

KNEMON: Is there any contract, you godless rubbish, between you
   and me?

GETAS: Contract? No. But I haven't come to demand payment of a   470
   debt, or to serve a summons. I only want to borrow a pot.

KNEMON: A *pot?*

GETAS: A pot.

KNEMON: Damn you, do you think I'm a sacrificer of bulls, like you
   lot?

GETAS: I shouldn't expect you to sacrifice as much as a snail. And a
   very good day to you, sir. [*Turns away*] The women told me to
   knock at the door and ask. Well, I've done that. No pot. I'll go back
   and tell them. This chap's a real old viper. [*He goes into the shrine.*]   480

KNEMON: Man–eating tigers, that's what they are: blithely knock as
   if they knew us. If I catch anyone near our door, and don't make an
   example of him for all the neighbourhood to see, you [*to audience*]
   may take me for a real old Johnny Raw. This chap, whoever he
   was, was lucky to get away. [*He goes back into his house.*]

   [*Enter* SIKON *from shrine, talking back over his shoulder.*]

SIKON: Damn you! Insulted you, did he? Perhaps your request was
   made without delicacy. Some people have no idea how to do a
   thing like this. *I've* found the art of it. I cater for thousands in   490
   Athens, *and* I bother their neighbours and borrow pots from them
   all. You need a soft approach when you want a favour. An older
   chap answers the door: I promptly address him as 'Father' or
   'Dad'. If it's an old woman, then 'Ma'. If it's a middle-aged
   woman, I call her 'Madam'. If a youngish servant, then 'My dear
   chap'. You all deserve to be strung up. Such ignorance! 'Door,
   door!' indeed. Now, *my* line is 'Come on, Dad, you're just the man
   I want!' [*He knocks at the door.*]

KNEMON [*opening the door*]: You back again?

SIKON: Goodness, what's this?

500 KNEMON: You're annoying me on purpose, I think. Haven't I told you not to come near my door? [*Shouts*] Woman, bring my strap. [*She does so, and he beats* SIKON.]

SIKON: Oh no, let me go.

KNEMON: Let you *go*?

SIKON: Yes, sir, *please*. [*He breaks free and runs away from* KNEMON.]

KNEMON: Come back here.

SIKON: God send you –

KNEMON: *Still* talking?

SIKON: I only came to borrow a cook-pan.

KNEMON: I haven't got one – no cook-pan, no chopper, no salt, no vinegar, nothing. I've simply told everyone in the neighbourhood to keep away from me.

SIKON: You didn't tell me.

KNEMON: Well, I'm telling you now.

510 SIKON: Yes, worse luck. [*Wheedling*] Couldn't you tell me, please, where a man could go and get a pan?

KNEMON: Still nattering away? Don't say I didn't warn you!

SIKON: A very good day to you.

KNEMON: I don't want a good day from any of you.

SIKON: Bad day, then.

KNEMON [*going into house*]: This is intolerable!

SIKON [*rubbing his shoulders*]: He's given me a pretty pounding. 'There are ways and ways of asking a favour' – and a fat lot of difference it makes here! [*Ponders*] Try another house? But if they're so quick to start a punch-up here, that makes it difficult. Perhaps better *roast* the meat? Yes, I think so. And I do have a

520 casserole dish. Be blowed to the locals! I'll use what I've got. [*Goes into the shrine.*]

[*Enter* SOSTRATOS, *left, limping badly.*]

SOSTRATOS: Anyone who's short of trouble should come to Phyle for the hunting. Oh, I'm sore! The small of my back, all my back, my neck, my whole body! [*Addresses audience*] You see, I went hard at it at once, quite the young enthusiast, swinging the mattock right up then driving it down deep, working like a navvy. I went hard at it, a short, sharp burst. Then I kept turning round, to see

530 when the old man might be coming, with the girl. And that was precisely when I began to rub my lumbar muscles – furtively at first, but as all this went on for hours and hours, I started to straighten up, and I went stiff as a plank. Not a soul arrived on the scene. The sun was baking hot, and when Gorgias looked over,

he'd see me working away like a well-beam, struggling up then slumping straight down again, absolutely rigid. 'I don't think he'll come now, my friend,' he said. And I promptly replied 'So what do we do now? Look for him tomorrow and call it a day now?' (For Daos had arrived to take over the digging.)

Well, that's how the first assault fared. I've come back here, I honestly can't tell you why, but something draws me spontaneously to the place.

[*Enter* GETAS *from shrine, talking back over his shoulder and rubbing his eyes.*]

GETAS: What the devil? Do you think I've got thirty pairs of hands, man? I get the charcoal glowing for you, fetch, carry, clean, cut up the offal, make the meal-cakes, bring round 'this here', see to 'that there'[11] – all the time quite blind with the smoke. Oh, I'm having a marvellous holiday!

SOSTRATOS: Hey, Getas!

GETAS: Who wants me now?

SOSTRATOS: I do.

GETAS: And who are you?

SOSTRATOS: Open your eyes.

GETAS: Oh, I see. It's young master.

SOSTRATOS: What are you all doing here?

GETAS: Why, we've just finished the sacrifice, and now we're getting lunch ready.

SOSTRATOS: Mother here?

GETAS: Ages ago.

SOSTRATOS: And Father?

GETAS: We expect him any minute. Do come in.

SOSTRATOS: Yes, when I've done a little errand. In a way, the sacrifice here is quite convenient. I'll go just as I am and invite the young man here, and his servant, to join us. For if they share in the sacrifice, they'll be more inclined to support my wedding plans in the future.

GETAS: Oh? You're going off to invite people to lunch? As far as I'm concerned, they can come in their thousands. I realized a long time ago that not a bite would come my way. Fat chance. Bring the whole world, do. You've sacrificed a *fine* sheep, a *real* joy to behold. These are all very fine ladies, but would they share anything with me? Not on your life: not as much as a pinch of cooking salt.

SOSTRATOS: It'll be all right today, Getas – I'll play the prophet on that myself, Pan, though I also pray as I always do when I pass you

– and I'll be generous. [*He goes off, left.*]
[*Enter* SIMICHE *from Knemon's house.*]

SIMICHE: Oh calamity, calamity, calamity!

GETAS: Oh, Hell! Here's the old man's woman.

SIMICHE: What's to become of me? I wanted to get the bucket out of the well, if I could, by myself, without telling master; so I tied the mattock to a poor rotten old piece of rope, and it promptly broke on me.

GETAS [*aside*]: Oh, great!

SIMICHE: Oh, dear! Now I've dropped the mattock into the well too, as well as the bucket.

GETAS [*aside*]: Then all that's left is to throw yourself in after them.

SIMICHE: Unfortunately, he wanted to shift some dung that was lying in the yard, and he's been running round for ages looking for the mattock, and yelling – oh, there's the door: here he comes.

GETAS: Run, run, poor woman, he'll kill you. No, better stand up to him.

KNEMON [*rushing out of his house*]: Where's the culprit?

SIMICHE: I didn't mean to do it, sir, it slipped out of my hand.

KNEMON: Inside, you.

SIMICHE: Oh, what are you going to do?

KNEMON: Let *you* down, on a rope.

SIMICHE: Oh, please don't!

KNEMON: On this very same rope too, I assure you.

GETAS [*aside*]: Just the job, if it's really rotten.

SIMICHE: I'll get Daos, shall I, from next door?

KNEMON: Get Daos, you infidel, when you've ruined me? Don't you hear me? Inside, you, at the double. [*She goes in.*] Oh dear, oh dear, I'm all alone now, not a soul to help. *I'll* go down the well, nothing else for it.

GETAS: We could give you a rope and grapple.

KNEMON: Damn you to all eternity, if you speak a word to me. [*Goes in.*]

GETAS: And I'd deserve it, too. He's gone rushing in again. Poor man, what a life he leads. That's your genuine Attic farmer. He struggles with stony soil that grows thyme and sage, getting a good deal of pain and no profit. Oh, here comes young master with his guests. Local farm-labourers they are. How peculiar. Why is he bringing them here now, and how did he get to know them?

SOSTRATOS [*entering left with* GORGIAS *and* DAOS]: I simply won't take no for an answer. We have masses of food. Surely to goodness no one refuses an invitation to lunch after a friend has been sacrificing? For your friend I've been, I assure you, for ages before we met. Here, Daos, take these tools inside, and then come and join us.

GORGIAS: Don't under any circumstances leave my mother alone in the house, Daos. See that she has all she needs. I won't be long. [SOSTRATOS, GORGIAS *and* GETAS *go into the shrine, and* DAOS *into Gorgias's house.*]

THIRD CHORAL INTERLUDE

ACT FOUR

[*Enter* SIMICHE, *from Knemon's house.*]

620   SIMICHE: Help! Oh, dear. Help!

SIKON [*entering from shrine*]: Dammit! In the name of all the powers of heaven, let us get on with our drink-offering. You insult us, you hit us – the hell with you! What an extraordinary establishment!

SIMICHE: Master's down the well.

SIKON: How come?

SIMICHE: He was going down to get the mattock and bucket, and he slipped at the top, and he's fallen in.

SIKON: Not Old Cantankerous here? *He's* got what he deserved, all right! My dear good woman, it's up to you now.

630   SIMICHE: How?

SIKON: Take a heavy basin, or a rock, or something like that, and heave it down on top of him.

SIMICHE: Oh, *please* go down.

SIKON: Good God! Me? To struggle with a dog in the well, like the man in the story?[12] Not on your life!

SIMICHE: Oh, where on earth is Gorgias?

GORGIAS [*entering from shrine*]: Who, me? What's the matter, Simiche?

SIMICHE: I tell you again, Master's down the well.

GORGIAS [*calling*]: Sostratos, here a minute! [SOSTRATOS *enters from shrine.*] Simiche, lead the way, inside, quick. [*They go into Knemon's house.*]

SIKON: There *is* a God, there really is! You wouldn't lend a cook-pan

640   to worshippers, you miserly old heathen. Now that you've fallen in, drink the well dry, and then you won't have a drop of water to offer anyone either. Now the Nymphs have given me my revenge – quite right too. No one does down a cook and gets off scot-free. There's something sacrosanct about our profession (but you can treat a *waiter* any way you like). [*There is a cry from inside.*] He's not *dead*, is he? 'Daddy, oh darling Daddy' a girl's weeping and wailing.

Several lines of the text are damaged here, but from the words that survive, it is clear that Sikon is envisaging the rescue operation, which will produce Knemon . . .

. . . soaked to the skin and shivering. Lovely! I'd love to see it, by
God I would. [*Shouts into the shrine*] Pour an offering to help them, 660
ladies. Pray that the old man's rescue may be – bungled, so that he's
damaged, crippled. That would make him a much less aggravating
neighbour to the god here, and to all who come to worship him. It
matters to me, too, if I'm ever hired for the job. [*Goes into shrine.*]
[*Enter* SOSTRATOS, *from Knemon's house.*]

SOSTRATOS [*addressing audience*]: My friends, by all the gods of
heaven I swear, I have never in my whole life seen a man so
conveniently half-drowned. That episode was a delight! As soon as
we got there, Gorgias jumped straight down into the well, and the 670
girl and I did nothing in particular up top. Well, what *could* we do?
Except that she was tearing her hair, crying and pounding away at
her breast, and I was standing there like a nanny – I really was, and
a fine fool I looked – pleading with her to stop it, worshipping at
her shrine and feasting my eyes on a perfect picture. For the victim
down below I cared less than nothing, except for trying all the time
to haul him up – that did inconvenience me a bit! And I tell you, I 680
very nearly did for him. For as I gazed into the girl's eyes, I let the
rope go, two or three times. But Gorgias was a veritable Atlas: he
kept a grip on him and eventually, with considerable difficulty, got
him up.

When he was safely out, I came out, and here I am. I couldn't
control myself any longer – I very nearly went up to the girl and
kissed her. That's how madly in love I am. I'm preparing the
ground – but the door's opening. God in heaven, look at that! 690

[KNEMON *is wheeled out on a couch,* GORGIAS *and the* GIRL *with
him.*]

GORGIAS: Can I do anything for you, sir? You only have to ask.

KNEMON: Oh, I'm in a very bad way.

GORGIAS: Cheer up!

KNEMON: Don't worry, Knemon will never trouble any of you
again, ever.

GORGIAS: Look, this is the kind of thing that happens when you live
like a hermit. You came very close to death just now. A man of
your age should end his days with someone to look after him.

KNEMON: I know I'm in a bad way, Gorgias. Ask your mother to
come, tell her it's urgent. We only learn from bitter experience, it 700
seems. Little daughter, please help me to sit up.

SOSTRATOS [*viewing process*]: Lucky fellow!

KNEMON [*to* SOSTRATOS]: Why are you hanging about there, you
miserable man?

Several lines are missing here, but it is clear that Gorgias has fetched Myrrhine, and that Knemon has begun his great speech.

710 KNEMON: . . . and not one of you could change my views on that, make up your minds to it. One mistake I did perhaps make, in thinking that I could be completely self-sufficient, and would never need anyone's assistance. Now that I've seen how sudden and unexpected death can be, I realize I was stupid to take that line. You always need to have – and to have handy – someone to help you. When I saw how people lived, calculating everything for
720 profit, I swear I grew cynical, and I never even imagined that any man would ever do a disinterested kindness to another.

I was wrong. By his noble efforts Gorgias, all by himself, has managed to demonstrate that. I never let him come near my door, never did him the slightest service, never said 'good morning' or gave him a kind word. And yet he's saved my life. Another man might (with some justification) have said 'You don't let me come near you; *I'm* keeping well away. You've never done anything for my family: I'm doing nothing for you now.' [*To* GORGIAS, *who is looking embarrassed*] What's the matter, boy? Whether I die now
730 (which seems only too likely, I'm not at all well), or whether I live, I'm adopting you as my son, and anything I have, consider it all your own. My daughter here I entrust to your care. Find her a husband. Even if I make a complete recovery, I won't be able to do that, for I'll never find anyone I approve of. *If* I live, leave me to live my own life, but take over and manage everything else.

You've got some sense, thank God, and you're your sister's natural protector. Divide my property, give half for her dowry, and use the other half to provide for her mother and myself. [*To his*
740 *daughter*] Lay me down again, my dear. I don't think a man should ever say more than is strictly necessary, so I'll add only this, my child: I want to tell you a little about myself and my ways. If everyone was like me, there'd be no law-suits or dragging one another off to gaol, and no wars: everyone would be satisfied with a moderate competence. But you may like things better as they are. Then live that way. The cantankerous and bad-tempered old man won't stop you.

GORGIAS: I accept all that. But, with your assistance, we must find a husband for the girl without delay, if you agree.

750 KNEMON: Look, I've told you my intentions. Leave me alone, for goodness' sake.

GORGIAS: Someone wants a word with you –

KNEMON: For God's sake, NO!

GORGIAS: . . . to ask for your daughter's hand in marriage.

KNEMON: I've no further concern with that.

GORGIAS: But it's the man who helped to rescue you.

KNEMON: Who?

GORGIAS: He's here. Come on, Sostratos.

KNEMON: He's certainly been in the sun. A farmer, is he?

GORGIAS: Yes, and a good one, Father. He's not soft, not the kind that strolls idly round all day.

In two badly damaged lines, Knemon probably gives his consent to the marriage.

KNEMON: Wheel me in. You see to him. And look after your sister. [*He is wheeled into his house.*]

GORGIAS: You'd better consult your family about this, Sostratos.   760

SOSTRATOS: My father will make no difficulties.

GORGIAS [*formally*]: Then I betroth her to you, Sostratos, giving her to you in the sight of heaven, as is right and proper. You've been frank and straightforward in approaching the business, without any deceit in your courtship. And you were ready to do anything to win the girl. You've lived soft, but you took a mattock and dug the land, you were willing to *work*. A man really proves his true worth when, although he's well-off, he's ready to treat a poor man as his equal. A man like that will bear any change of fortune with a good grace. You've given adequate proof of your character. Just   770 stay that way!

SOSTRATOS: In fact, I hope to improve. But self-praise is a bit boring. Oh, good, here's my father.

GORGIAS: Is Kallipides your father?

SOSTRATOS: Indeed he is.

GORGIAS: A very rich man – and he deserves it, he's a very good farmer.

[*Enter* KALLIPIDES, *right.*]

KALLIPIDES: Perhaps I'm too late. The others may have devoured the sheep and gone back to the farm long ago.

GORGIAS: Goodness, he seems to be starving. Shall we break the news to him now?

SOSTRATOS: No, let him eat first. He'll be in a better mood then.

KALLIPIDES: Well, Sostratos? Lunch over?

SOSTRATOS: Yes, but we've kept some for you. Go on in.

KALLIPIDES: That's just what I'm doing [*Goes into shrine.*]   780

43

GORGIAS: Now's your chance. Go in, and you can talk to your father on your own, if you want to.

SOSTRATOS: You'll wait inside, won't you?

GORGIAS: I won't set foot outside the house.

SOSTRATOS: Then I'll fetch you shortly.

[SOSTRATOS *goes into the shrine, and* GORGIAS, MYRRHINE *and the* GIRL *go into Knemon's house.*]

FOURTH CHORAL INTERLUDE

ACT FIVE

[*Enter* SOSTRATOS *and* KALLIPIDES, *from shrine.*]

SOSTRATOS: You're not doing all that I wanted, Father. I expected better of you.

KALLIPIDES: But I've given my consent! I'm quite willing for you to marry the girl you love – in fact, I say you must.

SOSTRATOS: That's not the way it looks to me.

KALLIPIDES: For heaven's sake! I don't need to be told that a young man's marriage is more stable if it's love that prompts him into it.   790

SOSTRATOS: So, *I* can marry the young man's sister and reckon that he's no disgrace to our family. Then how can you refuse to let him marry *my* sister?

KALLIPIDES: That's no good. I've no desire to acquire *two* beggars-in-law at one go. One's quite enough for us.

SOSTRATOS: You're talking about money, a very unstable substance. If you're sure it will stay with you for ever, then be careful never to share what you have with anyone. But when you're not   800
the absolute owner, when you hold everything on a lease from Fortune, then don't grudge a man a share of it, Father. For Fortune may take it all from you and bestow it on another, perhaps less deserving, person. That's why I tell you, Father, that while you have control of it, you should use it generously, help everyone, and by your actions enrich as many people as possible. Such generosity never dies, and if ever *you* have a fall, it will ensure the same generosity for you in turn. A real friend is much better   810
value than secret wealth, kept buried somewhere.

KALLIPIDES: You know me, Sostratos. The money I've made I shan't bury with me – what's the point? It's yours. You've found a friend and want to keep him. Go ahead, and good luck to you. No need to preach at me. Off with you! Hand it over, share it. You've quite convinced me, and I'm perfectly happy about it.

SOSTRATOS: Perfectly?

KALLIPIDES: Absolutely. Don't worry about it.

SOSTRATOS: Then I'll call Gorgias.   820

GORGIAS [*entering from Knemon's house*]: I heard all your conversation, right from the beginning, from the doorway on my way out.

45

Well, now: I accept you as a good friend, Sostratos, and I'm remarkably fond of you. But I don't want to take on anything that's beyond me, and I assure you that, even if I wanted to, I couldn't do it.

SOSTRATOS: I don't understand.

GORGIAS: My sister I give you to be your wife. But for me to marry *your* sister – thank you, but –

SOSTRATOS: You're *refusing*?

830 GORGIAS: I'd get no pleasure from living a soft life on the proceeds of other people's hard work. I prefer what I've earned myself.

SOSTRATOS: Nonsense, Gorgias! You're saying you're not worthy of the match.

GORGIAS: I reckon that *personally* I'm a worthy match for her. But it's not right to accept a fortune when one has so little.

The next few lines are badly damaged and what follows is at best an approximation of the sense.

KALLIPIDES: That's an honourable answer. But you're a bit inconsistent.

GORGIAS: How?

KALLIPIDES: You're a poor man – and you want to give the impression of liking it. You've seen me convinced. Please agree.

840 GORGIAS: That settles it! I'd be doubly deficient, in mind as well as in means, to refuse the one man who offers me a solution to my troubles.

SOSTRATOS: Then it only remains to formalize the engagement.

KALLIPIDES: I now betroth my daughter to you, young man, for the procreation of legitimate children, and I give you with her a dowry of £30,000.

GORGIAS: And I have £10,000 for the other girl.

KALLIPIDES: *Do* you? Don't overstretch yourself.

GORGIAS: Well, I have the farm.

KALLIPIDES: Keep it for yourself, Gorgias. Now, go and bring your mother and sister here, to join our womenfolk.

GORGIAS: I'll do that.

850 SOSTRATOS: We'll all stay here tonight for a party, and have the weddings tomorrow. And bring the old man with you, Gorgias. Perhaps he'll get better treatment here with us.

GORGIAS: He won't want to come, Sostratos.

SOSTRATOS: Persuade him.

GORGIAS: I'll try. [*He goes into Knemon's house.*]

SOSTRATOS: We must have a fine drinks party now, Dad, and the women must make a night of it too.

KALLIPIDES: Don't you believe it! *They'll* do the drinking, and we'll certainly do the night work. I'll go and organize everything properly for you. [*He goes into the shrine.*]

SOSTRATOS: Do that. [*To audience*] A sensible man should never   860
completely despair about anything. There's nothing that can't be achieved by concentration and hard work. I'm a living example of this truth! In one single day I've achieved a marriage that no one would ever have thought possible.

[*Enter* GORGIAS *with his* MOTHER *and the* GIRL, *from Knemon's house.*]

GORGIAS: Come on now, hurry up.

SOSTRATOS: This way, ladies. [*Calling*] Mother, here are your guests. [*To* GORGIAS] Knemon not here yet?

GORGIAS: *Knemon?* Why, he begged me to bring the old servant woman too, so that he could be absolutely on his own.

SOSTRATOS: He's a hopeless case.

GORGIAS: That's how he is.

SOSTRATOS: Well, forget him. Let's go in.   870

GORGIAS: Sostratos, I'm shy with women in the same –

SOSTRATOS: Nonsense! In with you! Remember, we're all *family* now.

[*They go into the shrine, and* SIMICHE *enters from Knemon's house, talking over her shoulder.*]

SIMICHE: I'll go too, by God I will. You can lie there all on your own. You're a real misery. They wanted to take you to the shrine, but you wouldn't go. Something awful will happen to you, you mark my words, something much worse than you're suffering now.

GETAS [*entering from shrine*]: I'll go and have a look. [*A flautist*[13] *starts playing*] Hey, what do you mean by fluting at me, you blasted   880
nuisance? I'm not ready for you yet, I'm ordered out here to visit the sick. Stop that! [*The music stops.*]

SIMICHE: One of your lot can go and sit with him. *I'm* sending my young lady off to her wedding, and I want a word with her. I want to talk to her, and say goodbye.

GETAS: Quite right. In you go. I'll look after *him* while you're away. [SIMICHE *goes into the shrine.*] I've been plotting for ages for a chance like this, but I had to work at it. And I may not be able to do it yet. [*Calls*] Hey, cook! Sikon! Out here to me, and hurry up. [*Rubbing hands in glee*] Boy oh boy, I think we have some real fun here.

[*Enter* SIKON *from shrine.*]

890 SIKON [*slightly drunk, and pompous*]: You want me?

GETAS: Yes, I do. Do you want to get your own back for your recent – er – experience?

SIKON: My recent *experience*? Bugger you, don't start that.

GETAS: The old terror's asleep, all by himself.

SIKON: And how is he?

GETAS: Not too bad.

SIKON: He couldn't get up and hit us?

GETAS: He couldn't even get *up*, I reckon.

SIKON: Oh, boy. I'll go in and ask the loan of something. He'll do his nut!

GETAS [*suddenly inspired*]: Look, suppose we haul him out first, put him here, and *then* knock at the door and make our 'requests', really infuriate him? That'll be fun, I tell you.

900 SIKON: But what about Gorgias? I'm a bit scared he might catch us and wallop us.

GETAS: There's a great din inside at the party. No one will hear a thing. It is positively our duty to civilize this chap. For we're related to him, now that the families are connected, and if he's always going to be like this, it'll be a job to put up with him, I tell you.

SIKON: Just take care that no one sees you bringing him out here.

GETAS: You go, then.

SIKON: Right. Hang on a minute, don't slope off and leave me to it.

[SIKON *goes into Knemon's house, and emerges carrying* KNEMON.]

GETAS: No noise, for heaven's sake.

SIKON: I'm not *making* a noise, for earth's sake.

GETAS: Over to the right.

SIKON: There.

GETAS: Put him here. Now for the crunch.

910 SIKON: Right. I'll go first. Now [*to flautist*] you watch the beat. [*He knocks rhythmically at Knemon's door*] Door! Do-or! Door, please! Door! DOOR!

KNEMON [*wakening*]: Oh, this is murder.

SIKON [*still knocking*]: Door, please! Door! Do-or! Door! DOOR!

KNEMON: Oh, this is murder.

SIKON [*turning round*]: Who's this? You from this house?

KNEMON: Of course I am. What do you want?

SIKON: Cook-pans and a basin, please.

KNEMON: Help me up, someone!

SIKON: You have them, you really have. And I'd like seven wine-

tables and twelve dinner-tables. Hey, boys! Tell the staff inside.
I'm in a hurry.

KNEMON: I haven't any of these things.

SIKON: Haven't *any*?

KNEMON: I've told you so a thousand times.

SIKON: I'm off, then. [*Moves across stage.*]

KNEMON: Oh, dear, how did I get here? Who put me down in front   *920*
of the house? [*To* GETAS] You be off, too!

GETAS: Oh, sure. [*Knocks at door*] Boy! Boyo! Maids! Men! Porter!

KNEMON: You're mad, fellow. You'll knock the door down.

GETAS: Nine rugs, please.

KNEMON: Impossible!

GETAS: And an oriental hanging, brocaded, a hundred feet long.

KNEMON: I wish I had – my strap. Woman! Simiche! Damn and blast
the lot of you. [SIKON *comes forward*] What do *you* want?

SIKON: A mixing bowl, a big bronze one.

KNEMON: Oh, help me up, someone!

GETAS: You've got the hanging, you know you have, Pa, Pappy.   *930*

KNEMON: I haven't the bowl, either. Oh, I'll murder that Simiche.

SIKON: Sit down and shut up. You hate company, you loathe the
ladies, you refuse to join the party. You'll have to put up with all
this, there's no one here to help you. Grind your teeth there, and
listen to my tale.[14] When your wife and daughter arrived, first
there were embraces and kisses. They were having a pleasant time,
and a little way off, I was getting the drinks ready for the men.   *940*
They – are you listening? Don't go to sleep!

GETAS: No, indeed.

KNEMON [*groaning*]: Oh, oh!

SIKON: Don't you want to be involved? Listen to the rest of the
story. The libation was ready, and a rug was spread out on the
ground. I was busy with the tables, that was my job – are you
listening? I'm a cook, as it happens. Remember?

GETAS: He's weakening.

SIKON [*becoming more and more extravagant in language and gesture*]: Someone else was decanting a venerable old vintage into a
dimpled jar, mixing it with the Naiads' rill, and pledging the men
sitting round, while another pledged the ladies (though *that* was
like pouring water into sand – get me?). And one of the girls, her   *950*
young face's bloom shaded, began to dance. She was a bit tipsy,
actually, but she danced quite modestly, diffidently and a bit
nervously. Then another joined hands with her, and danced
too.

49

GETAS: Poor old man, you have plumbed the depths of human misery. [*Suddenly*] Dance! On to your feet! We'll help you.

KNEMON: What do you want *now*, you pests?

GETAS: Just try. On to your feet, we'll help you. Oh, you *are* a clumsy clot.

KNEMON: No, *please*.

GETAS: Shall we take you to the party, then?

KNEMON: Oh, what shall I do?

GETAS: Dance!

KNEMON: Take me in, then. Perhaps it'll be better to put up with that.

GETAS: Now you're showing some sense. Hooray, we've won! [*Calls*] Hey, Donax! [*Servant comes out*] You too, Sikon, pick him up and take him inside. [*To* KNEMON] And you be careful. If ever we find you making a nuisance of yourself again, we won't treat you so tenderly then, I can tell you. [*Calls*] Hey, bring us garlands and a torch. [*They are brought out, and he distributes them*] Take that one. There! [*All go into the shrine except* GETAS, *who addresses the audience*] You've enjoyed our victory over the old man, now please applaud us, young and old. And may laughter-loving Victory, daughter of a noble line, smile upon us all our days.

[*Exit* GETAS, *into shrine.*]

960

The Girl From Samos

[Samia
or
The Marriage Connection]

Introductory Note to *The Girl From Samos*

The play has been variously dated between 315 B.C. and 309 B.C. None of the evidence is conclusive, but the assured handling of character, situation and dialogue suggests a date later rather than earlier in the range. This is the work of a more confident and experienced Menander than the playwright of *Old Cantankerous*. See Introduction, pp. 12–14.

CHARACTERS

MOSCHION, *a young Athenian gentleman*
DEMEAS, *his adoptive father*
PARMENON, *their servant*
CHRYSIS, *a Samian girl, Demeas's mistress*
NIKERATOS, *Demeas's neighbour*
A COOK

ACT ONE

SCENE: *a street in Athens: There are two houses, that of Demeas on the audience's left, that of Nikeratos on the right. Between them is an altar and image of Apollo.*

The text of Acts One and Two is badly mutilated, but from what does remain, and from the rest of the play, it is possible to make reasonable deductions about the content of the missing portions. The Prologue is spoken by Moschion, the junior lead. This play has no need of a divine Prologue, because Moschion can tell us all the necessary facts. Some ten or eleven lines are missing from the start of his speech: it is likely that in them he explained that he had been adopted by Demeas, an elderly bachelor.

MOSCHION [*addressing audience*]: . . . Oh, what's the point of moaning? It hurts, because I *did* do wrong. Telling the story will be painful, I reckon, but it will make more sense to you if I explain in some detail what my father's like. Right from the time when I was a very small boy, I had everything I wanted; I remember it well, but I won't dwell on it now. He was kind to me when I was too young to appreciate it. I was treated just like every other boy of 10 good family,[1] 'one of the crowd', as the saying goes, though I certainly wasn't born with a silver spoon in my mouth (we're all alone, so I can tell you that). I made my mark when I backed a dramatic production and gave generous contributions to charity. I had horses and hounds, too – at father's expense. I was a dashing officer in the Brigade, sufficiently in funds to give a bit of help to a friend in need. Thanks to my father, I was a civilized human being. And I gave him a civilized return: I behaved myself.

   Then – I'll tell you all about us at one go, I've nothing else to do – 20 then Father fell for a girl from Samos. Well, it could happen to anyone. He tried to keep it quiet, being a bit embarrassed. But I found out, for all his precautions, and I reckoned that if he didn't establish himself as the girl's protector, he'd have trouble with younger rivals for her favours. He felt a bit awkward about doing this (probably because of me), but I persuaded him to take her into the house.

Some twenty or so lines are missing here, in which Moschion probably explained that Chrysis was now in residence in Demeas's house, that she had been pregnant and under instructions from Demeas to get rid of the child, that Demeas and his neighbour Nikeratos were abroad on business, and that Nikeratos had a daughter, Plangon.

. . . Well, this girl's mother became friendly with Father's girl, and she was often in their house, and they'd visit us, too. One day, I came home from our farm, and happened to find them all here in our house, with some other ladies, to celebrate the festival of Adonis.[2] The proceedings, as you can imagine, were producing a good deal of fun, and I joined them as a sort of spectator. In any case, the noise they were making would be keeping me awake, for they were taking their tray 'gardens' up to the roof, and dancing, and making a real night of it, all over the place.

I hesitate to tell you the rest of the story. Perhaps I'm ashamed, where shame is no help, but I'm still ashamed. [*Pause*] The girl got pregnant. Now I've told you that, you know what went before, too. I didn't deny that I was responsible, but went without being asked to the girl's mother, and promised to marry her daughter as soon as my father came home. I gave my word I would. The baby was born a few days ago, and I formally acknowledged it as mine. Then, by a lucky chance Chrysis – that's the girl from Samos – had her baby too.

About twenty-five lines are missing, which must have explained that Chrysis' baby had died, and that she had taken Plangon's to nurse in its place. Moschion left the stage, probably left, to the harbour, and Chrysis entered from the house, possibly carrying the baby. Her opening lines are lost – they may have been to or about the baby – and then the text continues.

CHRYSIS: Here they come, hurrying home. I'll just wait and hear what they're talking about.

    [*Enter* MOSCHION *and* PARMENON, *left.*]

MOSCHION: You actually *saw* my father with your own eyes, Parmenon?

PARMENON: How often do I have to tell you? Yes, I did.

MOSCHION: And our neighbour, too?

PARMENON: Yes, they're both back.

MOSCHION: I'm very glad.

PARMENON: Now, you've got to brace yourself, and raise the question of your marriage right away.

MOSCHION: How can I? I've lost my nerve now that the crunch has come.

PARMENON: What do you mean?

MOSCHION: It's too embarrassing to face my father.

PARMENON [*his voice rising*]: And the girl you seduced, and her mother? What about *them*? Man, you're shaking like a leaf.

CHRYSIS [*coming forward*]: For goodness' sake, what's all the shouting about?

PARMENON: Oh, Chrysis is here, too. [*To* CHRYSIS] You really   *70* want to know why I'm shouting? That's a laugh. I want the wedding *now*, I want this chap here to stop wailing at this door here. I want him to remember that he gave his word. Ceremonial offerings, garlands, pounding sesame for the wedding cake – that's what I want to be helping with. Don't you think I've got good reason to shout?

MOSCHION: I'll do everything that's required. No need to go *on* about it.

CHRYSIS: I'm sure you will.

MOSCHION: What about the baby? Do we let Chrysis here go on nursing it and saying it's her own?

CHRYSIS: Why ever not?

MOSCHION: Father will be furious.

CHRYSIS: He'll cool down again. For he's in love too, my dear,   *80* desperately in love, just as much as you. And that brings even the angriest man to terms pretty fast. And I'd put up with anything, myself, before I'd let a wet-nurse bring up Baby here in some slum.

Some twenty-three lines are missing, during which Chrysis and Parmenon clearly went into the house, leaving Moschion soliloquizing on stage. Only fragments of the end of his speech remain.

MOSCHION: . . . most miserable man in the world. I'd better hang   *90* myself right away. A man conducting his own case needs to win favour.[3] I haven't enough experience of cases like this. I'll go and practise in some quiet place. This is a tricky case I've got on my hands. [*He goes off, right.*]

    [*Enter* DEMEAS *and* NIKERATOS, *left, with luggage and servants.*]

DEMEAS: You must notice the change of scene already, the difference between here and that horrible place.

NIKERATOS: Oh, yes. Black Sea, thick old men, fish by the boat-load, a life to make you sick: the city of Byzantium, everything gall and wormwood. God! But here is pure benefit for the poor.   *100*

DEMEAS: Dear Athens! I wish you all the blessings you deserve, so that we who love our city may be prosperous and happy. [*To servants*] Inside with the luggage, boys. You there, why are you standing goggling at me like a paralytic? [*The servants take the luggage inside.*]

NIKERATOS: What I found most extraordinary about that place, Demeas, was that sometimes you couldn't see the sun for weeks on end. It looked as if a thick fog was hiding it.

110 DEMEAS: Well, there was nothing very marvellous to see there, so the natives get only the bare minimum of light.

NIKERATOS: How right you are.

DEMEAS: Well, let's leave that for others to worry about. Apropos of the business we were discussing, what do you mean to do?

NIKERATOS: You mean your son's marriage?

DEMEAS: Yes, of course.

NIKERATOS: I haven't changed my mind. Let's name a day and get on with it. And good luck to it.

DEMEAS: That's your considered opinion?

NIKERATOS: It certainly is.

DEMEAS: Mine, too. And I got there first!

NIKERATOS: Call for me as soon as you come out.

DEMEAS: There are a few points . . .

About fourteen lines are missing from the end of the act. Demeas and Nikeratos obviously went into their respective houses, and one of them must have indicated the arrival of a band of revellers.

[FIRST CHORAL INTERLUDE]

ACT TWO

[*Enter* MOSCHION, *right, and* DEMEAS, *from his house. Neither sees the other.*]

The beginning of Moschion's speech is mutilated, but the general sense is clear.

MOSCHION: Well, I haven't done any of the rehearsing I intended. 120
When I got outside the city on my own, I started imagining the
wedding service, planning the guest-list for the reception, seeing
myself escorting the ladies to the ritual bath, cutting and handing
round the wedding-cake, humming the wedding-hymn – behaving
like an utter fool. When I'd had enough – help! Here's my father.
He must have heard what I was saying. Glad to see you, Father.

DEMEAS: Glad to see you, son.

MOSCHION: You look a bit – er – grim.

DEMEAS: I do. I thought I had a mistress, but I seem to have acquired 130
a wife.

MOSCHION: A wife? What do you mean? I don't understand.

DEMEAS: I seem to have become – quite without my knowledge and
consent – the father of a son. Well, she can take him and get out of
the house – to the Devil, for all I care.

MOSCHION: Oh, *no!*

DEMEAS: Why not? Do you expect me to bring up a bastard in my
house, to humour someone else? That's not my line at all.

MOSCHION: For Heaven's sake! What's legitimacy or illegitimacy?
We're all human, aren't we?

DEMEAS: You must be joking.

MOSCHION: By God I'm not, I'm perfectly serious. I don't think
birth means anything. If you look at the thing properly, a good 140
man's legitimate, a bad man's both a bastard and a slave.

*Some twenty lines are missing or mutilated, but it is clear that in the course of
them Moschion persuaded his father to keep the child, and Demeas raised the
question of his son's marriage, and found him willing.*

MOSCHION: I'm longing to get married . . . and I want to be
obedient, Father, not just to seem so.

DEMEAS: Good boy! . . . If our neighbours here agree, you shall
marry her at once. 150

59

MOSCHION: I hope you'll ask no questions, but accept that I'm serious, and help me?

DEMEAS: Accept that you're serious? Ask no questions? I understand, Moschion. Now I'll run over to my neighbour here, and tell him to start getting ready for the wedding. All that you want from our household will be waiting for you.

MOSCHION: I'll go in now, sprinkle myself with holy water, pour a libation, put incense on the fire – and then I'll fetch the girl.

160 DEMEAS: No, not yet, until I'm sure we have her father's consent.

MOSCHION: He won't say no. But it wouldn't be the thing for me to go in with you, and get in the way of the preparations. [*He goes off, left.*]

DEMEAS: Coincidence must really be a divinity. She looks after many of the things we cannot see. I had no idea that Moschion had fallen in love!

About twenty-seven lines are missing, and the next twenty-five are badly damaged. But enough survives to make it clear that Nikeratos came out of his house, and Demeas persuaded him that the wedding should take place that day.

DEMEAS: Parmenon! Hey, Parmenon! [*Enter* PARMENON *from the*
190 *house*] Go and get garlands, an animal for sacrifice, sesame seeds for the cake. Buy up the market, and come back here.

PARMENON: You leave it to me, sir.

DEMEAS: And hurry up. Do it now. And bring a cook, too.

PARMENON: A cook too. After I've bought the rest?

DEMEAS: Yes.

PARMENON: I'll get some money and be off at the double. [*He goes into the house.*]

DEMEAS: You not on your way to market yet, Nikeratos?

NIKERATOS: I must just go in and tell my wife to get the house ready. Then I'll be right on Parmenon's heels. [*He goes into his own house.*]

PARMENON [*reappearing with basket, and talking back over his shoulder*]: I haven't a clue what it's all about, except these are my orders, and I'm off to market *now*.

200 DEMEAS: Nikeratos will have a job persuading his wife, and we mustn't waste time on explanations. [*Seeing* PARMENON] You still here? Run, man, run!

About ten lines are missing from the end of the Act, during which Parmenon obviously left for the market, right, Demeas went into his house, and the Chorus entered.

[SECOND CHORAL INTERLUDE]

ACT THREE

[*Enter* DEMEAS, *from his house.*]
DEMEAS: In the midst of a fair voyage, a storm can suddenly appear
from nowhere. Such a storm has often shattered and capsized those
who a moment ago were running nicely before the wind. That's
what's happened to me now. Five minutes ago, I was organizing   210
the wedding, attending to the religious obligations, with everything going according to plan. [*He moves down stage and addresses
audience*] I'm coming down-stage to you, now, as the victim
of a knock-out blow. It's incredible! Tell me if I'm sane or
mad. Am I getting the facts all wrong and bringing disaster on
myself?

The minute I went in, full of enthusiasm to get the wedding
organized, I gave the servants a straightforward account of every-   220
thing, told them to make all the necessary preparations – clean,
bake, arrange the ritual basket.[4] Things were going quite well, but
the speed at which things were happening naturally produced a
certain amount of confusion. The baby had been dumped out of
the way on a couch, and it was howling. The women servants were
all shouting at once – 'Flour, please! Water, please! Oil, please!
Charcoal, here!' I was passing some of these, lending a hand, and I
happened to go into the pantry. I was inspecting and selecting   230
more supplies, and didn't come out immediately. Well, while I
was in there, a woman came downstairs into the room next to the
pantry – it's where the weaving's done, in fact, and you have to go
through it to go upstairs or into the pantry. This woman was
Moschion's old nurse, getting on now. She was once my slave, but
I set her free. She saw the baby crying and no one taking a bit of
notice of it. She didn't know I was inside, but thought she could   240
speak safely, so she went up to the baby, with all the usual
baby-talk like 'Who's a little love, then?' and 'Precious treasure!
Where's Mummy?' She cuddled it, and walked it up and down,
and when it stopped crying, she murmured to herself, 'Dear me,
it seems only yesterday that I was cuddling and nursing Moschion,
just like this, and now that his son here has been born . . .'   250

Four or five lines are lost or damaged.

61

. . . Then a servant-girl came running in, and the Nurse said, 'Give the baby his bath. What do you all think you're doing? His father's wedding day, and you're neglecting the little one.' The girl immediately hissed 'Don't *shout*. Master's at home.' 'No! Where is he?' 'In the pantry!' And then, raising her voice, 'Mistress is asking for you, Nurse' and, quietly, 'Quick! He hasn't heard a word. We're in luck.' The Nurse said, 'My tongue will be the death of me', and off she went, I don't know where.

I came walking out quite calmly just as I did here a moment ago, as if I hadn't heard or understood a word. In the outer room I saw my Samian, all by herself, with the baby in her arms, breast-feeding it. So *she*'s obviously the baby's mother. But the father, whether it's mine or – Ladies and Gentlemen, I can't bring myself to say it or even to think it. I'm simply telling you what I heard. I'm not angry – not yet. I know the boy, of course I do, and he's always been a good boy, and behaved very properly to me. But then again, when I remember that the woman was once Moschion's nurse, and that she didn't know I could hear what she was saying; and when I look at Chrysis, who adores the baby and has insisted on keeping it against my wishes – well, I'm absolutely fit to be tied.

Oh, good! Here's Parmenon back from the market. I must let him take his party into the house.

[*Enter* PARMENON, *right, with provisions and* COOK.]

PARMENON: For God's sake, Cook! I can't imagine why you bother to carry knives around with you. You're quite capable of slicing through everything with your tongue.

COOK [*loftily*]: You don't understand. You're not a professional.

PARMENON: No?

COOK: Not in my view, I assure you. I'm only asking about the number of covers you mean to set, the number of ladies coming, the time of the meal, whether I need an extra waiter, if your dinner-service is big enough, if the kitchen's under cover, if everything I need is available –

PARMENON: In case you haven't noticed, mate, you're making a very fine mincemeat of me, a real professional job.

COOK: Go and boil your head.

PARMENON: The same to you, and make a right job of it. Inside, all of you!

[COOK *and entourage go into Demeas's house.*]

DEMEAS: Parmenon!

PARMENON: Someone want me?

DEMEAS: Yes, I do.

PARMENON: Oh, hello, sir.

DEMEAS: Deliver your basket, and come back here.

PARMENON: Sure. [*Swaggers into house.*]

DEMEAS: I'm sure that no business like this would get past *him*. He's got a finger in every pie. Ah, there's the door, he's coming out. *300*

[*Enter* PARMENON *from the house, speaking back over his shoulder.*]

PARMENON: Chrysis, see that the cook gets everything he wants, and for God's sake keep the old crone away from the wine-bottles! [*To* DEMEAS] At your service, sir!

DEMEAS [*grimly*]: *My* service, indeed. Over here, you, away from the door. A bit farther.

PARMENON: There!

DEMEAS: Now you listen to me, Parmenon. I don't *want* to beat you, I really don't. I have my reasons.

PARMENON: Beat me? Whatever for?

DEMEAS: You're part of a conspiracy to keep something from me, so I've discovered.

PARMENON: *Me?* I swear by angels and archangels and all the hosts *310*
of heaven –

DEMEAS: Stop! No swearing. I'm not guessing. I *know*.

PARMENON: God strike me down –

DEMEAS: Look me straight in the face, man.

PARMENON: There. I'm looking.

DEMEAS: The baby – whose is it?

PARMENON: Well –

DEMEAS: Whose baby is it? I want an answer.

PARMENON: Chrysis'.

DEMEAS: And who's the father?

PARMENON: You are, according to her.

DEMEAS: That's done it. You're trying to cheat me.

PARMENON: Me, sir?

DEMEAS: I tell you, I know the whole story, every last detail. I've found out that it's *Moschion*'s child, that you're in the plot, and that Chrysis is nursing it now for his sake.

PARMENON: Who says?

DEMEAS: Everyone. Answer me – is this true? *320*

PARMENON: Yes, sir, it's true, but we didn't want it to get out –

DEMEAS [*outraged*]: Not get *out*? [*Shouts*] Bring me a horsewhip, someone, to deal with this snake-in-the-grass.

PARMENON: Oh, please, NO.

DEMEAS: I'll *brand* you, so help me.

PARMENON: Brand *me*?

63

DEMEAS: This very minute.

PARMENON: I've had it. [*He runs off, right.*]

DEMEAS: Hey, where are you going? I've a rod in pickle for you. Grab him, someone! [*Raising hands to heaven*] O citadel of Cecrops' land, O vault of heaven on high, O – why the noisy imprecation, Demeas? Why all the shouting, you fool? Control yourself, stiffen the upper lip.

It's not *Moschion* who's done you wrong. [*To audience*] That may seem a remarkable statement, Ladies and Gentlemen, but it's true.
330 For if he'd done this from malice aforethought, or in the grip of the passion of love, or from dislike of me, he'd still be brazening it out and marshalling his forces against me. As it is, he's cleared himself completely, in my judgement, by his enthusiastic agreement to this marriage, when it was proposed to him. It wasn't love, as I thought then, that prompted his enthusiasm, but a desire to get away somehow from the house, and from that Helen of mine. *She*'s the one to blame for what's happened. She caught him, I imagine, when he'd had a spot too much to drink, when he wasn't quite in control of himself. Yes, that's obviously what happened.
340 Strong wine and young blood can work a lot of mischief, when a man finds at his side someone who has used these things to set a trap for him. I *cannot* believe that a boy who's always been well-behaved and considerate to others could treat me like this: not if he's ten times adopted and not my natural son. It's not his origins I care about, it's his character. But that – creature – she's a trollop. She's poison. She'll have to go.

350 Now, Demeas, be a man. Forget how you've missed her, stop loving her, cover up what's happened as far as you can for your son's sake, and throw the fair Samian out on her ear. The hell with her. You've got an excuse – she kept the child. No need to give any other reason. Bite on the bullet, stiff upper lip, honour of the family!

[*Enter* COOK *from house.*]

COOK: Is he here, by the front door? [*Shouts*] Hey, Parmenon! Damn the fellow, he's run out on me, didn't lift a finger to help me.

DEMEAS [*rushing into house*]: Out of the way! Back, you!

360 COOK: Well! What's up? A maniac with a grey beard ran into the house. What on earth's the matter? Oh, well, it's nothing to do with me. I tell you, he's loopy, he must be. Well, he was shouting his head off. A fine thing if he shatters all my crockery that's been set out. Oh, there's the door. Damn and blast Parmenon for bringing me here. I'll just step a bit out of the way. [*He moves away as* DEMEAS *pushes* CHRYSIS *with the baby out of the house.*]

DEMEAS: Are you deaf? Get out!

CHRYSIS: But – where to?

DEMEAS: To hell. This minute.

CHRYSIS: Poor me.

DEMEAS: Yes, poor you. Very affecting, your tears. *I'll* stop your   *370*
    game, I assure you.

CHRYSIS: What game?

DEMEAS [*remembering he wants to keep the scandal secret*]: Never mind.
    You've got the child and the old crone. Now go to hell.

CHRYSIS: Is it because I kept the baby?

DEMEAS: Yes, and because . . .

CHRYSIS: Because what?

DEMEAS: Just because of that.

COOK [*aside*]: Oh, that's what the trouble is. Now I see.

DEMEAS: You didn't know how to behave properly when you were
    well off.

CHRYSIS: I don't understand.

DEMEAS: You came here to me, Chrysis, in a cotton frock – do you
    understand *that*? – a simple cotton frock.

CHRYSIS: Well?

DEMEAS: I was everything to you then, when you were poor.

CHRYSIS: Aren't you now?   *380*

DEMEAS: Don't speak to me. You have all your belongings. I'll give
    you some servants too. Now, get out!

COOK [*aside*]: Here's a fine frenzy. I'd better go over. [*Approaches*]
    Look here, sir –

DEMEAS: Why are *you* shoving your oar in?

COOK: No need to bite my nose off.

DEMEAS [*ignoring him*]: Another girl will be happy with what I have
    to offer, Chrysis – yes, and give thanks to heaven for it.

COOK: What *does* he mean?

DEMEAS: You've got a son, you have all you want.

COOK [*aside*]: Not biting yet. [*To* DEMEAS] Still, sir –

DEMEAS: I'll smash your head in, fellow, if you say a word to me.

COOK: With some justice, too. There, I'm off inside now. [*He goes
    into house.*]

DEMEAS [*to* CHRYSIS]: A fine figure *you* make! Once you're on the   *390*
    town, you'll very quickly find your true value. Other girls,
    Chrysis, not at all in your style, run off to dinner parties for a
    pound or two, and swallow strong drink until they die: or they

starve, if they're not prepared to do this and do it smartly. You'll learn the hard way, like everyone else. And you'll realize what a stupid mistake you've made. [CHRYSIS *moves towards him*] Stay where you are! [*He goes into the house.*]

CHRYSIS: What shall I do? What's to become of me?

[*Enter* NIKERATOS, *right, with a sheep.*]

NIKERATOS: This sheep, once it's sacrificed, will satisfy the ritual
400   demands of all the inhabitants of heaven. It's got blood, an adequate gall-bladder, super bones and an enlarged spleen – all the things that the Olympians want. I'll chop up the skin, and send it to my friends as a tasty bit: it's all that'll be left for me. [*Sees* CHRYSIS] Heavens! What's this? Chrysis in tears in front of the house? Yes, it is. Whatever's the matter?

CHRYSIS: Your fine friend has thrown me out, that's all.

NIKERATOS: Heavens! Demeas?

CHRYSIS: Yes.

NIKERATOS: But why?

CHRYSIS: Because of the baby.

410   NIKERATOS: Yes, I did hear from my womenfolk that you'd kept a child and were nursing it. Sheer lunacy! But Demeas is an easy-going chap. He wasn't angry at first, was he? Only later on? Quite recently?

CHRYSIS: Yes. He'd told me to get the house ready for the wedding, and then, when I was up to my eyes in it, he burst in like a maniac, and he's locked me out of the house.

NIKERATOS: He's out of his mind. The Black Sea isn't a healthy place. You come along and see my wife. Cheer up. It'll be all right.
420   He'll come to his senses when he thinks over what he's doing. [*He escorts* CHRYSIS *into his house.*]

THIRD CHORAL INTERLUDE

ACT FOUR

[*Enter* NIKERATOS, *from his house, speaking back over his shoulder.*]

NIKERATOS: You'll be the death of me with your nagging, woman.
I'm *on my way now* to tackle him. [*Shuts the door*] I'd have given a
good deal – by God I would – for this not to have happened. Right
in the middle of the wedding preparations, something very unlucky has happened. A woman, thrown out of house and home,
has crossed our threshold with a child in her arms; there have been
tears, and the women are all upset and disorganized. Demeas really
is a clot. By God, I'll see that he pays for it.

 [*Enter* MOSCHION, *left, not seeing* NIKERATOS.]

MOSCHION: Will the sun *never* set? All I can say is, Night has
forgotten her job. Will it be always afternoon? I'll go and have a
bath – my third. There's nothing else to do.   *430*

NIKERATOS: Glad to see you, Moschion.

MOSCHION [*eagerly*]: Are we starting the wedding now? Parmenon
told me when I ran into him in the market just now. Can I fetch
your daughter now?

NIKERATOS: You don't know what's been going on here!

MOSCHION: No, what?

NIKERATOS: You may well ask. Something very unpleasant indeed.

MOSCHION: Heavens, what is it? I've heard nothing.

NIKERATOS: My dear boy, your father has just thrown Chrysis out
of the house.

MOSCHION: You can't mean it.

NIKERATOS: True, I assure you.

MOSCHION: But what for?

NIKERATOS: Because of the baby.

MOSCHION: Then where is she now?

NIKERATOS: In our house.

MOSCHION: What a terrible thing. Quite extraordinary.

NIKERATOS: You think so? Then . . . [*They go on speaking quietly
together.*]

 [*Enter* DEMEAS *from his house, speaking back over his shoulder.*]

DEMEAS: If I get my hands on a stick, I'll knock tears out of you all *440*
right. Stop this nonsense! Get on and help the cook. [*Sarcastically*]
There's really something to cry about, I must say; our house has

67

lost a really valuable treasure. Her behaviour makes that quite clear. [*He bows to the altar*] Grant us, Lord, successfully to effect this marriage we are about to celebrate. For [*turning to audience*] celebrate it I shall, Ladies and Gentlemen, and swallow my rage. [*Turns back to altar*] Guard me, O Lord, from self-betrayal, and constrain me to sing the marriage-hymn. [*Gloomily*] I'll not be in very good voice, in my present mood, but what of it? Who cares what happens now?[5]

450

NIKERATOS: Go on, Moschion, you tackle him first.

MOSCHION: All right. [*Moves forward*] Father, why are you behaving like this?

DEMEAS: Like what, Moschion?

MOSCHION: Need you ask? Why has Chrysis gone and left us? Tell me that.

DEMEAS [*aside*]: Someone's organizing a diplomatic approach to me. Oh, dear. [*To* MOSCHION] It's none of your business, it's mine and mine alone. Such nonsense! [*Aside*] This is dreadful. *He's* part of the plot against me too.

MOSCHION: Beg your pardon?

DEMEAS [*aside*]: He must be: otherwise, why come and speak for her? He should surely have been *pleased* at what's happened.

MOSCHION: What do you imagine your friends will say when they hear about this?

DEMEAS: I imagine my friends will – you leave my friends to me, Moschion.

460

MOSCHION: I'd be failing in my duty if I let you do this.

DEMEAS: You'll try to stop me?

MOSCHION: Yes, I will.

DEMEAS: This beats all! This is more scandalous than the previous scandals.

MOSCHION: It's never right to let anger rip.

NIKERATOS [*approaching*]: He's right, Demeas.

MOSCHION: Nikeratos, you go and tell Chrysis to come back here at once.

DEMEAS: Let it be, Moschion, let it be. For the third time I tell you, I know everything.

MOSCHION: Everything? What do you mean?

DEMEAS: Don't bandy words with me!

MOSCHION: But I've got to, Father.

DEMEAS: *Got* to? Am I not to be master in my own house?

MOSCHION: Then grant it to me as a favour.

DEMEAS: A favour? I suppose you're asking me to quit my house and

leave you two together? Let me get on with your wedding 470
arrangements. You will, if you've any sense.

MOSCHION: Well, of course I will. But I want Chrysis to be one of
the guests.

DEMEAS: You want *Chrysis* . . . ?

MOSCHION: I insist upon it – mainly for your sake.

DEMEAS [*aside*]: Now it's obvious. Now it's clear. I call heaven to
witness that Someone has joined my enemies and is plotting
against me. I'll burst a blood-vessel, I really will.

MOSCHION: What are you talking about?

DEMEAS: You really want me to tell you?

MOSCHION: Of course I do.

DEMEAS [*moving away*]: Come here.

MOSCHION [*following*]: Tell me.

DEMEAS: Oh, I'll tell you. The child is yours. I know, I was told by
Parmenon, who's in your confidence. So stop playing games with
me.

MOSCHION: But – what harm is *Chrysis* doing you if the child is
mine?

DEMEAS: Who is to blame, then? Tell me that.

MOSCHION: But – how is *she* at fault?

DEMEAS: I don't believe it! Have you two *no* conscience? 480

MOSCHION: What's all the shouting about?

DEMEAS: Shouting, is it, you scum? What a question. Listen:
you take the blame on yourself, right? And you dare to look
me in the face and ask this? Have you turned against me
completely?

MOSCHION: Me? Against you? How?

DEMEAS: *How?* Need you ask?

MOSCHION: But, Father, what I did isn't such a terrible crime. I'm
sure thousands of men have done it before.

DEMEAS: God in Heaven, what a nerve! In the face of this audience I
ask you, who is the baby's mother? Tell Nikeratos, if you don't
think it 'such a terrible crime'.

MOSCHION [*aside*]: It'll certainly turn into one, if I tell *him*. He'll be 490
furious when he finds out.

NIKERATOS [*suddenly joining in*]: You wicked monster! I'm beginning to have a suspicion of what's been going on. Absolutely
outrageous!

MOSCHION [*misunderstanding*]: That's me done for now.

DEMEAS: Now do you see, Nikeratos?

NIKERATOS: I certainly do. [*In tragic vein*] O deed most dread! O

Tereus, Oedipus, Thyestes! O all the incestuous loves of legend! You've put them all in the shade.

MOSCHION [*bewildered*]: Me?

NIKERATOS: How could you have the effrontery, the audacity, to behave like this? Demeas, now you should assume Amyntor's rage, and blind your son.[6]

500 DEMEAS [*to* MOSCHION]: It's your fault that he's got to know about this.

NIKERATOS: Is nothing sacred? No one inviolate? And *you*'re the man to whom I'm to give my daughter in marriage? I'd rather – touch wood and *absit omen* – I'd rather marry her to our local Lothario. And we all know how unfortunate that would be.

DEMEAS [*to* MOSCHION]: You did me great wrong, but I tried to keep it quiet.

NIKERATOS: You're a coward and a slave, Demeas. If it were my bed he'd defiled, he'd certainly never again be abusing anyone else's. Nor would his partner. The trollop I'd be selling promptly next day. Simultaneously and publicly, I'd disinherit my son. There 510 wouldn't be an empty seat in barber's shop or public gardens – the whole world would be there from first light, talking about me and saying, 'Nikeratos is a *man*, prosecuting for murder, and quite right too.'

MOSCHION: *Murder?* What murder?

NIKERATOS: Murder's what I call it, when anyone acts against authority and behaves like this.

MOSCHION: My throat's dry. I'm petrified with fright.

NIKERATOS: And to crown it all, I've welcomed to my hearth and home the girl responsible for these horrors.

DEMEAS: Throw her out, Nikeratos, do. Consider yourself wronged when I am, as a true friend should.

NIKERATOS: I'll explode with rage at the sight of her. [*To* MOSCHION] You dare look me in the face, you barbarous savage? Out of my way! [*He rushes into his house.*]

520 MOSCHION: Father, for God's sake, *listen*.

DEMEAS: Not a word!

MOSCHION: Not even if nothing you suspect is true? I'm just beginning to understand what's going on.

DEMEAS: What do you mean, 'nothing'?

MOSCHION: Chrysis isn't the mother of the baby she's nursing. She's doing me a favour by saying it's hers.

DEMEAS: *What?*

MOSCHION: It's true.

DEMEAS: Why is she doing you this 'favour'?

MOSCHION: I don't want to tell you, but if you know the truth, I'll be cleared of the more serious charge, and admit to the minor one.

DEMEAS: You'll be the death of me, if you don't get on and tell me.

MOSCHION: The baby's mother is Nikeratos's daughter. I'm the father. I was trying to keep it from you.

DEMEAS: What are you saying?

MOSCHION: The simple truth.

DEMEAS: Be careful. No trying to pull wool over my eyes. 530

MOSCHION: You can check the facts. What good would it do me to lie?

DEMEAS: No good at all. There's the door – [NIKERATOS *staggers out of his house.*]

NIKERATOS: O misery, misery me! What a sight I have seen! I'm rushing out in a frenzy, pierced to the heart with pain unlooked-for.

DEMEAS: What on earth is he going to tell us?

NIKERATOS: My daughter – my own daughter – I found her just now *breast-feeding the baby.*

DEMEAS [*To* MOSCHION]: Then your story's true.

MOSCHION: You listening, Father?

DEMEAS: You've done me no wrong, Moschion. But I've wronged you by suspecting what I did.

NIKERATOS: You're the man I want, Demeas.

MOSCHION: I'm off!

DEMEAS: Don't be afraid.

MOSCHION: It's death just to look at him. [*He runs off, left.*]

DEMEAS: What on earth is wrong?

NIKERATOS: Breast-feeding the baby in the house – that's how I've 540 just found my daughter.

DEMEAS: Perhaps she was just pretending.

NIKERATOS: It was no pretence. When she saw me, she fainted.

DEMEAS: Perhaps she thought –

NIKERATOS: You'll be the death of me with your perhapses.

DEMEAS [*aside*]: This is my fault.

NIKERATOS: Beg your pardon?

DEMEAS: I find your story quite incredible.

NIKERATOS: I tell you, I *saw* it.

DEMEAS: You're drivelling.

NIKERATOS: It's not just a fairy-tale. But I'll go back and – [*He turns back towards house.*]

DEMEAS: Just a minute, my friend. I have an idea. [NIKERATOS *goes in.*]

He's gone. That's torn it. This is the end. Once he finds out the truth, he'll be in a real rage, bawling his head off. He's a rough customer, insensitive, blunt as they come. To think that I – I – had such suspicions! I'm as good as a murderer, I deserve to die, I really do. [*Shouts are heard from Nikeratos's house*] Heavens, what a noise! This is it. He's yelling for fire, threatening to burn the baby. I'll have to watch my grandson roasting. There's the door again. The man's a whirlwind, a positive tornado.

NIKERATOS [*rushing out*]: Demeas, Chrysis is plotting against me, and doing the most terrible things.

DEMEAS: Oh?

NIKERATOS: She's persuaded my wife and daughter to admit nothing, and she's grabbed the baby and refuses to give it up. Don't be surprised if I kill her with my bare hands.

DEMEAS: *Her?* Your wife?

NIKERATOS: Yes, she's in the plot too.

DEMEAS: Don't do it, Nikeratos.

NIKERATOS: I just wanted to warn you. [*He rushes back in.*]

DEMEAS: He's raving mad. Gone rushing back inside again. How shall we deal with this crisis? I don't ever remember being in such a mess. Best tell him frankly what has happened. God! There's the door *again*.

[*Enter* CHRYSIS, *running, from Nikeratos's house, carrying the baby.*]

CHRYSIS: Help! What'll I do? Where can I be safe? He'll take my baby.

DEMEAS: This way, Chrysis.

CHRYSIS: Who's that?

DEMEAS: Inside my house – run! [*She runs towards him, as* NIKERATOS *rushes out.*]

NIKERATOS: Hey you! Where are you going?

DEMEAS: Lord, I'll be fighting a duel, I think, before the day's over. [*He stands in Nikeratos's way*] What do you want? Who are you chasing?

NIKERATOS: Out of my way, Demeas. Just let me get my hands on the baby, and the women'll talk.

DEMEAS: Never!

NIKERATOS: You'll fight me?

DEMEAS: I will. [*To* CHRYSIS] Quick! For God's sake, get inside.

NIKERATOS: Then I'll fight *you*.

DEMEAS: Run, Chrysis, he's stronger than I am. [*She runs into Demeas's house.*]

NIKERATOS: You started this. I call witnesses to that.

DEMEAS: And *you*'re chasing a free woman, and trying to hit her.

NIKERATOS: Blackmailer!

DEMEAS: Blackmailer yourself.

NIKERATOS: Bring out my baby.

DEMEAS: That's a laugh. It's *mine*.

NIKERATOS: It is not.

DEMEAS: Yes, it is.

NIKERATOS [*shouting*]: Good people all –

DEMEAS: Go on, bawl your head off.

NIKERATOS: I'll go and murder my wife. Nothing else for it. 580

DEMEAS: That's just as bad. I won't let you. Hey, stop! Where are you going?

NIKERATOS: Don't you lay a finger on me.

DEMEAS: Control yourself.

NIKERATOS: You're doing me down, Demeas, that's quite clear. You know all about it.

DEMEAS: Then ask your questions of me, and don't upset your wife.

NIKERATOS: Your son's hocussed me, hasn't he?

DEMEAS: Rubbish. He'll still take the girl, it's not like that at all. [*He takes Nikeratos's arm*] Take a turn here with me.

NIKERATOS: Take a *turn*?

DEMEAS: Yes. Get a grip on yourself. Tell me, Nikeratos, have you never heard actors in tragedies telling how Zeus once turned into a 590 stream of gold, flowed through a roof and seduced a girl who'd been locked up?

NIKERATOS: So what?

DEMEAS: Perhaps we should be prepared for anything? Think! Does any part of your roof leak?

NIKERATOS: Most of it does. But what's that got to do with it?

DEMEAS: Sometimes Zeus is in a shower of gold, sometimes a shower of rain. Do you understand? This is *his* doing. How quickly we've found the solution!

NIKERATOS: You're having me on.

DEMEAS: Heavens, no! Wouldn't dream of it. You're surely just as good as Danaë's father. If Zeus honoured her, then perhaps your daughter –

NIKERATOS: Oh, dear, Moschion has made a cake of me.

DEMEAS: Don't worry, he'll marry her. But what happened was 600 divinely inspired, you can be sure of that. I can name you thousands walking the streets of this city today, who are children of gods. And you think your case exceptional! To start with

73

[*pointing*] there's Chairephon[7] – there he is – always dining out and never paying his share. Don't you think *he*'s divine?

NIKERATOS: I suppose so. There's no point in hair-splitting.

DEMEAS: Very wise, Nikeratos. Then there's Androcles[8] – so many years in this world, but he hops and skips his way into everything, a real busybody. His hair's black, but even if it were white, he wouldn't die, not even if someone were to cut his throat. He's divine, isn't he? But seriously, pray that this marriage turns out well. Burn your incense, make your offerings. My son will come any minute to fetch his bride.

NIKERATOS: I suppose I must accept this.

DEMEAS: Wise man!

NIKERATOS: But if I'd caught him then –

DEMEAS: Let it be. Remember your blood-pressure. Go and get things ready in the house.

NIKERATOS: All right.

DEMEAS: And I'll do the same in here.

NIKERATOS: You do that.

DEMEAS: You're a smart chap. [NIKERATOS *goes in*] And thank God I've discovered that my suspicions were quite unfounded. [*He goes into his own house.*]

FOURTH CHORAL INTERLUDE

ACT FIVE

[*Enter* MOSCHION, *left*.]

MOSCHION [*addressing audience*]: Just now, when I was cleared of the charge quite wrongly laid against me, I was pleased, and thought myself quite lucky. But now that I've had time to collect my wits and think over what happened, I'm furious, absolutely livid, that my father could have thought me capable of such behaviour. If it weren't for the problem about the girl, if there weren't so many obstacles – like my sworn word, my love for her, our long relationship (things that leave me no freedom of choice) – he certainly wouldn't make such a charge against me again, not to my face. No, I'd have been off from the city, out of his way, away to the Foreign Legion[9] to spend my life as a serving soldier there. But no such heroics now, I won't do it, for *your* sake, Plangon darling. It's impossible, forbidden by Love, the master of my will. 630

Still, that's no reason why I should ignore the insult, or take it lying down. I'd like to scare him, even if it's only an act, by *saying* that I'm off abroad. He'll be more careful in future not to treat me so unfairly, if he sees me taking this insult seriously. Ah, here's Parmenon. Just the man I want, and just when I want him. 640

PARMENON [*entering right, and not seeing* MOSCHION]: God Almighty! What a fool I've been, beneath contempt, really. I'd done nothing wrong, but I panicked and ran away from Master. What had I done to justify that? Let's look at the case dispassionately and in detail:

Item: Young master seduced a respectable girl: Parmenon's presumably not to blame for that!

Item: She got pregnant: no fault of Parmenon's.

Item: The baby was brought to our house: Moschion brought him, not I. 650

Item: One of our household said she was the mother: Parmenon had nothing to do with that. So why run away, you lily-livered ass? It's ludicrous.

Item: Master threatened to brand me. Now you've got it. It makes not a scrap of difference whether that punishment is deserved or not, in either case it's not very pretty.

MOSCHION: Hey!

PARMENON: Good evening to you.

MOSCHION: Stop this nonsense, and go inside. Hurry up.

PARMENON: What for?

MOSCHION: Bring me a military cloak, and a sword.

PARMENON: A sword? For *you*?

660 MOSCHION: And do it now.

PARMENON: But what for?

MOSCHION: Go and do what I tell you, and keep quiet about it.

PARMENON: Why, what's up?

MOSCHION: If I get my hands on a whip –

PARMENON: No, no, I'm on my way.

MOSCHION: Then hurry up about it. [PARMENON *goes in*] Father'll come out now. Of course, he'll beg me to stay, and for some time he'll beg in vain. That's vital. Then, when I think fit, I'll let myself be persuaded. All that's needed is a bit of plausible acting – which, Heaven knows, I'm not very good at. Uh-uh. Here we go. That's the door, someone's coming out.

670 PARMENON [*entering from house*]: You're quite out of date, I find, on what's going on here. Your information's inaccurate and your intelligence service poor. You're getting into a tizz and driving yourself to despair, *quite* unnecessarily.

MOSCHION: Where's the cloak and the sword?

PARMENON: You see, your wedding's under way. [*Raptly*] Wine a-mixing, incense a-burning, sacrifice ready, offerings alight with the Fire-god's flame!

MOSCHION: Parmenon, *where's the cloak and the sword*?

PARMENON: You're the one they're waiting for, for ages now. Why not fetch the bride right away? You're in luck, you've nothing to fear. Cheer up. [*In alarm, as* MOSCHION *advances*] What are you after?

MOSCHION [*slapping* PARMENON's *face*]: Read me a lecture, would you, you outrageous oaf?

PARMENON: Oh, what are you doing, Moschion?

MOSCHION: Go inside this minute, and bring out what I told you to bring.

PARMENON: You've split my lip.

MOSCHION: Still talking back?

680 PARMENON: I'm going. A fine reward I've won, I must say.

MOSCHION: Get on with it.

PARMENON: They really are celebrating your wedding.

MOSCHION: The same old story still? Tell me something new. [PARMENON *goes in*] *Now* he'll come out. [*Pause*] Ladies and Gentlemen, suppose he doesn't beg me to stay, but loses his temper and lets me go? That's something I left out of my calculations just now. What do I do then? Perhaps he won't do it – but suppose he does? Anything's possible in this life. A fine fool I'll look if I have to do a U-turn.

[*Enter* PARMENON *from the house, with cloak and sword.*]

PARMENON: There! Here's your cloak and sword. They're all yours.

MOSCHION: Give them here. [*Casually*] Anyone in the house see you?

PARMENON: No one.

MOSCHION: No one *at all*?

PARMENON: No.

MOSCHION: Oh, blast you!

PARMENON: On your way. You're talking twaddle.

DEMEAS [*entering from house*]: Where is he then? Tell me that. [*Sees* MOSCHION] Good heavens! What's this?   690

PARMENON [*To* MOSCHION]: Quick march! Now!

DEMEAS: What's the fancy dress for? What's wrong? Going on your travels, Moschion? Enlighten me.

PARMENON: As you see, he's already on the road and on the march. And now I must say goodbye to the household too. I'll do that now. [*He goes in.*]

DEMEAS: Moschion, I love you for your anger, and I'm not surprised[10] that you're hurt at being unfairly accused. But consider the target for your bitter anger. I'm your *father*. I took you when you were a little boy, and I brought you up. If your journey through life has been a pleasant one, I'm the man who made   700 provision for it. So, it was your duty to put up with anything I did, even if it hurt you, and to bear with me as a good son should.

My charges against you were unjustified, I was wrong, I made a mistake, I was out of my mind. All right. But ponder this point. At the cost of hurting others, I still looked carefully after your interests. I tried to keep my suspicion to myself, and did not publish it for the entertainment of our enemies. But now you want to make my mistake public, calling witnesses to testify to my stupidity. That's not fair, Moschion. Don't brood on the one day   710 when I came a cropper, and ignore all the others that went before.

There's a lot more I could say, but I'll let it go there. You know very well that sons get no credit for reluctant obedience. Give in gladly, that's the way to do it.

[*Enter* NIKERATOS *from his house, talking back over his shoulder.*]

NIKERATOS: Stop nagging me. Everything's *been* done – baths, ritual, wedding ceremony, the lot. The bridegroom, if he ever does come, can take his bride away. [*Sees the others*] Heavens! What's going on here?

DEMEAS: I've no idea, I assure you.

NIKERATOS: Well, you *should* know. A soldier's cloak! I believe he means to be off.

DEMEAS: That's what he says.

NIKERATOS: Oh, *does* he? Then he's got to be stopped. He's a seducer, caught in the act, admitting his guilt. I'll arrest you on the spot, boy.

MOSCHION [*drawing his sword*]: Yes, arrest me, do.

NIKERATOS: You never take me seriously. Put up your sword at once.

720   DEMEAS: For heaven's sake, Moschion, put it up and don't aggravate him.

MOSCHION [*sheathing sword*]: There! Let it go. Your entreaties have succeeded, your appeals to me.

NIKERATOS: *Appeals?* You come here!

MOSCHION: You'll arrest me, perhaps?

DEMEAS: Stop this nonsense! Bring the bride out here.

NIKERATOS: You're sure?

DEMEAS: Quite sure. [NIKERATOS *goes into his house.*]

MOSCHION: If you'd done this right away, Father, you wouldn't have had to bother with your recent sermon.

NIKERATOS [*returning with his daughter*]: After you, dear. [*Members of the two households assemble*] In the face of witnesses, I give you, Moschion, this woman to be your wife, for the procreation of legitimate children. And as dowry I give her all my possessions when I die (which God forbid! May I live for ever).

MOSCHION: I take her, to have, to hold and to cherish.

DEMEAS: All that remains is to fetch the ritual water. Chrysis, send out
730   the women, the water-carrier and the musician. And someone bring us out a torch and garlands, so that we can form a proper procession.

MOSCHION [*as these things are brought out*]: Here he comes.

DEMEAS: Moschion, put on your garland, and deck yourself like a bridegroom.

MOSCHION: There!

DEMEAS [*to audience*]: Pretty boys, young men, old men, ladies and gentlemen, all together now – please clap loudly. Dionysus loves applause, and it shows you liked our play. And may Victory, immortal patron of the finest festivals, grant her perpetual favour to this company.

[*All leave, right, in procession.*]

The Arbitration

[Epitrepontes]

Introductory Note to *The Arbitration*

The play is seriously damaged. Only half the text is intact, the rest being either lost or badly damaged. But what remains looks masterly. Character, and the motivation that comes from it, creates the dramatic action, which in turn further illuminates character. Pamphile exposes the child to save her marriage, Charisios leaves home rather than return Pamphile and her dowry to her father, Smikrines is more concerned for his dowry than his daughter, Daos (unsuccessfully) attempts a lucrative fiddle, Syros acts in defence of the child, Onesimos delays acting because of personal considerations, Habrotonon is both good-natured and (quite reasonably) concerned for her own prospects; and the result is a satisfactory solution in which only Daos and Smikrines remain unsatisfied. There is economy in the plotting: Syros conveniently introducing the child and the ring where they can be recognized, Habrotonon conveniently able to identify the child's mother; and there is irony in the action: Smikrines solemnly and unwittingly deciding his grandson's future, Charisios discovered to have condemned the action for which he was responsible. The plotting is tight, dramatic suspense is sustained, there are some excellent scenes, and the varieties and vagaries of human nature are well observed and presented. As often in Menander, there is consideration of the consequences of human behaviour, as well as appreciation of its entertainment value.

81

CHARACTERS

CHARISIOS, *a young Athenian gentleman*
CHAIRESTRATOS, *his friend and neighbour*
ONESIMOS, *his servant*
PAMPHILE, *his wife*
SMIKRINES, *his wife's father*
HABROTONON, *a guitar-girl*[1]
SYROS, *a charcoal-burner, servant of Chairestratos*
DAOS, *a shepherd*
KARION, *a cook*

The Prologue was probably spoken by a deity. SYROS's wife appears, but does not speak, nor does SOPHRONE, Pamphile's old nurse.

ACT ONE

SCENE: *a street in a suburb of Athens. The house on the audience's left belongs to Charisios, that on the right to Chairestratos.*

Most of Act One is mutilated or destroyed. But it is fairly certain, from the surviving fragments and from the rest of the text, that the play opened with a dialogue between Karion and Onesimos, which told the audience that Charisios, outraged at his wife's producing a child after five months of marriage, had moved next door, and was drowning his sorrows with wine and women. What Onesimos could not tell the audience was that the child was actually Charisios' own, the result of rape at a festival, and that after being exposed it had been rescued, and was now with a servant of Chairestratos's. This information, vital to an appreciation of the play's action, must have been conveyed by a divinity, in a delayed Prologue.

[KARION *and* ONESIMOS *are on stage.*]

KARION: Hey, Onesimos, is it really true that it's your young master who's the present protector of Habrotonon, the guitar-girl? And him not long married! Do tell.

ONESIMOS: Yes, it's quite true . . . (*Material missing.*)

KARION: I like you, Onesimos. You're nosey too! . . . It's my favourite thing, knowing everything . . . (*Material missing.*)

Why aren't you getting lunch? He's been sitting at table for ages, and he's creating . . . (*Material missing.*)

If this happens, then I've really been overdoing the seasoning . . . (*Material missing.*)

When a lazy man's in good health, he's actually far worse off than when he's running a temperature. He eats twice as much, but still gets nothing done.

Act One ends with a conversation between Smikrines and Chairestratos. At first, Smikrines is soliloquizing, Chairestratos eavesdropping.

SMIKRINES: And he's drinking very expensive wine! That's what staggers me. It's not the drinking that bothers me: what I find

130   almost incredible is that a man can bring himself to drink wine costing £5 a bottle!²

CHAIRESTRATOS [*aside*]: Just what I expected. He'll barge in and break up the party.

SMIKRINES: But that's none of my business. Damn him! He got a large dowry with my daughter, but he thinks nothing of deserting her. He's sleeping out, and he's paying £20 a day to a pimp.

CHAIRESTRATOS [*aside*]: He's got the sum right. His information service is quite reliable.

SMIKRINES: That's enough to keep a man for a month, and for ten days more.

140   CHAIRESTRATOS [*aside*]: His arithmetic's good. Fifty pence a day, enough to give a starving man a bowl of porridge – or it used to be.

HABROTONON [*entering from Chairestratos's house*]: Charisios is waiting for you, Chairestratos. Who's that, darling?

CHAIRESTRATOS: The bride's father.

HABROTONON: Why does he look like a miserable old schoolmaster?

Some verses are missing, and the rest of the act is damaged. The general sense is clear, but allocation of lines to speakers is not, nor is the interpretation of details.

HABROTONON: Bless you, don't speak like that.

160   SMIKRINES: You go to hell! You'll pay for this, and pay dearly. I'm going in now, and when I know how my daughter's fixed, I'll work out how I'm going to launch my attack on Charisios. [*He goes into Charisios' house.*]

HABROTONON: We'd better warn Charisios that he's here, hadn't we?

CHAIRESTRATOS: Yes, we had. What a nuisance he is, turns a house upside down.

HABROTONON: I wish he'd do the same to lots of houses.

CHAIRESTRATOS: Lots?

HABROTONON: Well, one. The one next door.

CHAIRESTRATOS: You mean mine?

HABROTONON: I mean just that. Let's go and join Charisios.

CHAIRESTRATOS: Yes, there's a bunch of young drunks coming this
170   way, and it's no moment to tangle with them. [*They go into Chairestratos's house.*]

FIRST CHORAL INTERLUDE

ACT TWO

The first thirty-four lines of the act are lost. There are traces of a monologue, perhaps by Onesimos, and Smikrines must have emerged from his visit to his daughter, because he is on stage for the scene which follows the monologue. Perhaps he had an altercation with Onesimos, who has clearly left the stage when the text resumes. This is the arbitration scene which gives the play its name.

[*Enter* DAOS *and* SYROS, *and* SYROS's *wife carrying a baby.* DAOS *carries a little bag. The men are arguing.*]

SYROS: You're trying to get out of doing the decent thing.

DAOS: And *you're* trying to blackmail me. You'll come to a bad end. You've no right to keep what's not yours.

SYROS: What we need is someone to arbitrate.

DAOS: Right! Let's do that.   220

SYROS: But who will act for us?

DAOS: Anyone'll do me. My claim is just. I can't imagine what made me offer to cut you in.

SYROS [*catching sight of* SMIKRINES]: Will you accept him as arbitrator?

DAOS: Sure. What luck!

SYROS [*approaching* SMIKRINES]: I wonder, sir, if you could spare us a moment?

SMIKRINES: Yes? What for?

SYROS: We're at loggerheads about something.

SMIKRINES: And where do I come in?

SYROS: We're looking for someone impartial to hear the case. If it's not inconveniencing you, will you please settle our dispute?

SMIKRINES: Damn your eyes! Traipsing about in overalls, presenting legal cases!

SYROS: All the same . . . It won't take long, and it's not a difficult   230
case. Do us a favour, sir. Please don't turn up your nose. Whenever there's an issue, justice ought to prevail, everywhere, and it's everyone's business to see that it does. It's an obligation that touches all.

DAOS [*aside*]: A right tub-thumper I've tangled with. Why on earth did I ever offer him a deal?

85

SMIKRINES: Tell me now, will you both accept my decision?

BOTH: We will.

SMIKRINES: Then I'll hear your case. No reason why not. [*To* DAOS]
You haven't said a word. You start.

240 DAOS: I'll start a little way back, not just with my dealings with him,
so that you can get the story absolutely clear.

Well, sir, about a month ago I was herding my sheep on the
common near here, not a soul in sight, and there I found a little
new-born baby. It had been abandoned, and it had a necklace, and
some other trinkets like that.

SYROS: They're what the quarrel's about.

DAOS: He's not letting me tell my story.

SMIKRINES [*To* SYROS]: If you interrupt, I'll wallop you with my
stick.

SYROS [*apologetically*]: And serve me right too.

SMIKRINES [*To* DAOS]: Go on.

250 DAOS: Right. Well, I picked up the child and took it home, with its
trinkets; thought I'd bring it up. Seemed a good idea *then*. But
night brought second thoughts, as it usually does; and I began to
wonder, 'Why should *I* be embarking on the bothersome business
of bringing up a child? And the expense – where would *I* get the
money? Why should *I* have the worry?' That's roughly where I'd
got to.

Next morning, back to my shepherding. *He* came along to the
same spot to burn some stumps – he's a charcoal-burner, I've
known him for years – and we started talking. He saw that I was a
260 bit down-in-the-mouth, and 'Something on your mind, Daos?'
he says, 'Anything wrong?' 'I'm an interfering fool,' I say, and I
tell him the whole story, how I found the baby and took it home.
And before I'd even finished the story, he promptly began pleading (with a 'Bless you, Daos' at every turn), 'Give me the child, if
ever you hope for fortune and freedom. I've got a wife,' he says,
'and her baby died.' That's his wife there, with the baby in her
arms. [*Turning to* SYROS] You admit you were pleading, [*ironically*]
my dear friend Syros?

270 SYROS: I do.

DAOS: He took up the whole day, persistently trying to persuade me.
And finally I agreed, I handed over the baby, and off he went,
calling down countless blessings on my head, and trying to kiss my
hands. [*To* SYROS] You admit this?

SYROS: I do.

DAOS: I never saw him again. Then, suddenly, today he turns up

with his wife, and demands the trinkets put out with the child
(trashy bits and pieces they are, not worth anything), and claims
that I'm doing him down because I don't hand them over, but
claim them for myself. But I maintain that he ought to be grateful   *280*
that he got what he asked for. No need to put me in the dock for
not giving him the lot. If we'd been walking together, and made
the discovery together, sharing the lucky find, he'd have had half
and I'd have had half. But I found it on my own. [*To* SYROS] You
weren't there at all, and you think you can claim the lot, while I get
nothing?

   Final point: I gave you something that was *mine*. If you like it,
keep it. If not, if you've changed your mind, hand it back. No need   *290*
to feel ill done by, or deprived. You've no right to claim the lot,
part by gift and part by force. [*To* SMIKRINES] My case rests.

SYROS: Has he finished?

SMIKRINES: Are you deaf? Of course he's finished.

SYROS: Thank you. My turn now. He did find the child on his own,
and his account is quite correct. That is what happened, sir, and I
do not dispute it. I got the child from him by begging and
pleading, quite true. A shepherd that he talked to, one of his mates,   *300*
told me that he'd found some jewellery along with the baby. It's
that jewellery, sir, that the baby's here to claim, in person. [*To his
wife*] Give me the child, dear. [*Takes the baby and holds it up*] This
child claims his necklace and his tokens of recognition, Daos. He
points out that they were put there for his adornment, not to keep
you in food. And I associate myself with his claim, for I'm his legal
guardian: your gift made me that. [*He hands the baby back to his
wife.*]

   [*To* SMIKRINES] Now sir, in my view, the point you have to
decide is this: should the trinkets, gold or whatever they are, be
kept for the baby until he grows up, because that's why his   *310*
mother, whoever she was, gave them to him? Or should the thief
keep them, just because he was the first to find something that
doesn't belong to him? [*To* DAOS] Why, you may ask, didn't I ask
for them when I took the child? Because I did not then have the
right to speak on his behalf. Even now, I am asking absolutely
nothing for myself. You talk about 'sharing the lucky find'. But
there is no question of a 'find' when damage to a person is
involved. That's not a 'find', it's plain theft. [*To* SMIKRINES] A
further point, sir. This child may come from a noble family, and   *320*
may one day look far beyond the life of the working folk who
reared him. He may rise to his own level, find the spirit for some

gentlemanly exploit – lion-hunting, army service or athletic prowess. You've been to the theatre, I'm sure, and know all the stories, how heroes like Neleus and Pelias[3] were found by an old goatherd, dressed just like me, and when he realized that they were of a class superior to his own, he would tell them the story of how he'd found them and taken them home. He'd give them a bag of tokens, from which they'd discover the true story of their birth. And men who had lived till then as goatherds, would turn into princes. Now, if Daos had taken these tokens and sold them to put a few pounds in his pocket, these noble princes would have remained undiscovered all their lives. It's really not fair that I should feed and clothe the child, sir, while Daos takes his only hope of rescue and makes it vanish into thin air. Tokens saved one man from marrying his sister, they helped another to find and save his mother, another lot saved a brother.[4] Nature, sir, makes human life precarious: we must make provision to protect it, carefully calculating all possible means of doing so.

'Hand the baby back,' he says, 'if you don't want it.' And he thinks this is a powerful argument! But there is no justice in that. [*To* DAOS] You should return this child his property. Are you trying to get your hands on him too, to make your next attempt at crime safer, now that a lucky chance has rescued some of his things? [*To* SMIKRINES] My case rests, sir. Pass judgement as you think right.

SMIKRINES: That's not difficult. All the articles exposed with the child are the child's property. That's my judgement.

DAOS: Fair enough. But who gets the child?

SMIKRINES: Certainly not you, who are trying to defraud him, but his helper and champion against your attempted depredations.

SYROS: God bless you, sir!

DAOS: That's a terrible verdict, by God it is. I found everything, I'm stripped of everything. He found nothing, he gets the lot. Must I really hand them over?

SMIKRINES: That's my verdict.

DAOS: It's a terrible verdict, be damned if it isn't.

SYROS: Hand them over. Quick, now!

DAOS: God, what I suffer.

SYROS: Open your bag and show them. That's where you've got them. [*As* SMIKRINES *moves away, right*] Wait a minute, sir, till he hands them over.

DAOS: Why did I ever accept *him* as an arbitrator?

SMIKRINES: Hand them over. You're a convicted criminal.

DAOS [*doing so*]: It's scandalous, that's what it is.

SMIKRINES [*to* SYROS]: Is everything there?

SYROS: Yes, I think so. Unless he swallowed something when I was making my case and he was losing.

DAOS [*brooding*]: I wouldn't have believed it possible.

SYROS: Well, goodbye, sir. I wish all judges were like you. *370*
[SMIKRINES *goes off, right.*]

DAOS: It's not fair. There's never *been* a more scandalous verdict.

SYROS: You deserved it, you twister.

DAOS: Twister yourself. Mind you keep them safe for him. I warn you, I'll be watching you day and night.

SYROS: On your way and be damned to you. [DAOS *goes off, left.*]

SYROS [*to his wife*]: Take these trinkets in to young master Chairestratos here. We'll stay tonight, and get back to work tomorrow, after we've paid our dues.[5] But first, let's go over them one by one. *380*
Got a box? [*Wife shakes her head.*] Then put them in your pocket.
[*Enter* ONESIMOS *from Chairestratos's house. He does not see* SYROS, *and is unnoticed by him.*]

ONESIMOS [*looking up the street*]: This cook's infernally late. Not a sign of him. By this time yesterday they were sitting over their port.

SYROS: This looks like a cock, a tough one too. Here. This one's set with stones. And here's an axe.

ONESIMOS: What's going on here? [*He approaches.*]

SYROS: Here's a ring, gold-plated but iron underneath. The stone's engraved with a bull or a goat, I can't tell which. There are some letters engraved, 'Made by Kleostratos'. *390*

ONESIMOS: Here, let me see that.

SYROS: There. And who are you?

ONESIMOS: It is!

SYROS: Is what?

ONESIMOS: The ring.

SYROS: *What* is it? I don't know what you're talking about.

ONESIMOS: It's my master Charisios' ring.

SYROS: You're raving.

ONESIMOS: The one he lost.

SYROS: Give it back here, you ruffian.

ONESIMOS: Give back *our* property to please *you*? Where did you get it?

SYROS: Angels and ministers of grace defend us! It's a terrible job, looking after an orphan child's property. Everyone you meet immediately wants to grab it. Hand back the ring, I say.

400 ONESIMOS: You must be joking. That's my master's ring, I swear it.

SYROS: Give in to this fellow? I'd rather die. That settles it, I'll sue the lot of them, one after the other. It's Baby's property, not mine. [*To his wife*] Here's a necklace, you take it, and a piece of crimson cloth. Take them inside. [*Wife, with child, goes into Chairestratos's house.*] Now [*to* ONESIMOS] What have you got to say?

ONESIMOS: I'm saying this ring belongs to Charisios. He lost it once when he was drunk, he told me.

SYROS: My master's Chairestratos. You keep that ring safe – or, give it to me, and I'll look after it.

ONESIMOS: I'd rather keep it myself.

410 SYROS: Makes no difference to me. We're both bound for the same house, I believe.

ONESIMOS: They've got company now, and it's perhaps not the best moment to tell him about this. I'll do it tomorrow.

SYROS: I'll wait. Tomorrow I'm quite ready to put my case to any judge you like. [ONESIMOS *goes into Chairestratos's house.*] Well, I didn't come so badly out of that either. Looks like I've got to devote all my energies to the practice of law. It's the only way to preserve property nowadays. [*Goes into Chairestratos's house.*]

SECOND CHORAL INTERLUDE

ACT THREE

[*Enter* ONESIMOS, *from Chairestratos's house.*]

ONESIMOS: Half a dozen times I've embarked on the business of
going to my master and showing him the ring: and half a dozen. *420*
times I've got very close to it, been right on the brink of it – and
then I funk it. I'm sorry now I ever told him anything.[6] He keeps
on saying, 'God damn that blasted tell-tale.' I'm afraid he'll make it
up with his wife, and then get rid of the tell-tale, who knows too
much for comfort. Best not stir in another ingredient to the
mixture we've already got: the present stew's quite bad enough.
[*Broods.*]

   [*Enter* HABROTONON, *from Chairestratos's house, speaking back
over her shoulder. They do not see one another.*]

HABROTONON: Let me go, please! Leave me alone! [*Shuts door.*] Oh, *430*
dear! I think I've made a fool of myself. How was I to know? I
expected a spot of loving, but the man positively hates me: it's
uncanny. He won't even let me sit beside him at table, but keeps
me at a distance.

ONESIMOS: Well, should I give it back to the fellow I took it from
just now? No, that's stupid.

HABROTONON: I'm sorry for him. Why is he wasting all this
money? For anything *he*'s done, I could qualify at this very
moment to join the Vestal Virgins![7] It's very sad. I've been sitting
around for three days now, my virtue still 'pure and undefiled'. *440*

ONESIMOS: In God's name, how could I? Just tell me, how could
I . . . ?

   [*Enter* SYROS, *from Chairestratos's house.*]

SYROS: Where is he? Where's the chap I've been chasing round the
house? [*He sees* ONESIMOS.] See here, friend, either give me back
the ring, or show it to the man you're going to show it to. Let's get
the business settled, I've got work to do elsewhere.

ONESIMOS: Well, it's like this, mate. This is my master's ring, I
know it is, it belongs to Charisios. But I'm a bit reluctant to show it
to him. See, if I take it to him, I'm as good as making him the father
of the child it was left with.

SYROS: How do you make that out, dim-wit? *450*

ONESIMOS: He lost it last year at the Tauropolia[8] – you know, the

all-night festival that women attend. It's a fair guess that a girl got raped, and had this baby and – obviously – exposed it. If we could find the girl and produce the ring, that would be proof. But without her evidence, we'll only produce suspicion and chaos.

SYROS: That's *your* problem. But if this is a try-on, in the hope that I'll give you a little something in return for the ring – forget it.
460   Going shares isn't my line, not at all.

ONESIMOS: And it's not what I want, either.

SYROS: That's that, then. I'm off to town now, but I'll be right back, to see what's the next move in this game. [*He goes off, right.*]

HABROTONON [*coming forward*]: Onesimos, the baby the woman's nursing now in the house – was it the charcoal-burner who found it?

ONESIMOS: Yes, so he says.

HABROTONON: Poor lamb, it's a pretty little thing.

ONESIMOS: This ring was with it, and it's my master's ring.

HABROTONON: Oh, poor thing. Then, if he really is your master's son, can you stand by and watch him being brought up as a slave?
470   That would be a capital crime.

ONESIMOS: As I was saying, no one knows who the mother is.

HABROTONON: He lost the ring, you say, at the Tauropolia?

ONESIMOS: Yes, he was drunk and disorderly, so I was told by the boy who was attending him.

HABROTONON: I suppose he came across the woman when they were celebrating and unprotected. [*Thoughtfully*] You know, something very like that actually happened. I saw it.

ONESIMOS: *You* saw it?

HABROTONON: Yes, last year, at the very same festival. I was playing for some young ladies, and this girl was dancing with them. I was still a virgin myself then.

ONESIMOS: Oh yeah?

HABROTONON: Take my oath on it.

480   ONESIMOS: This girl – do you know who she was?

HABROTONON: No, but I might find out. She was a friend of the ladies who engaged me.

ONESIMOS: Did you hear her father's name?

HABROTONON: No. But I'd know her if I saw her. She was very pretty; rich, too, they said.

ONESIMOS: Perhaps she's the one.

HABROTONON: I don't know. But she was with us, then she wandered off, then suddenly ran up on her own, crying and tearing her

hair. And her silky wrap, very thin and pretty, was quite ruined, all *490*
torn to pieces.

ONESIMOS: And did she have this ring?

HABROTONON: She may have done. But she didn't show it to me.
I'll tell no lies.

ONESIMOS: I wonder what I do now?

HABROTONON: Well, it's your business. But if you'll show some
sense and listen to me, you'll go to your master and tell him the
whole story. If the mother's a girl of good family, why shouldn't
he know what's happened?

ONESIMOS: First let's find out who she *is*, Habrotonon. Help me
with this now, do.

HABROTONON: Oh no, I couldn't, not until I know the name of her
attacker. I'm scared of telling a tale to the ladies I mentioned, and *500*
putting them on the wrong track. After all, another man in his set
could have accepted the ring from him as security, and then lost it;
perhaps he was gambling, and put it in to guarantee his contribution to the jackpot; or he may have been under pressure in some
deal, and handed it over. Thousands of things like that happen
every day, when men get drinking. Until I know the guilty man's
name, I'm not going to start a search for the girl, or breathe one
word of anything like this.

ONESIMOS: Fair enough. So what does a man do? *510*

HABROTONON: Onesimos, I've just had an idea. See what you
think. I'll pretend this happened to *me*, and I'll go in to Charisios,
wearing the ring.

ONESIMOS: Go on. I'm beginning to see . . .

HABROTONON: When he sees me wearing it, he'll ask me where I
got it, and I'll say, 'At the Tauropolia, when I was still a virgin.'
And I'll tell the girl's story as my own – I know most of it, anyway.

ONESIMOS: Clever girl!

HABROTONON: If he's the man responsible, he'll rush right in and *520*
give himself away. He's a bit tipsy now, and he'll blurt out the
whole story before I even ask. I'll go along with everything he
says, and avoid any mistakes by letting *him* mention details first.

ONESIMOS: Super!

HABROTONON: I'll side-step any slips by flattery, and the usual
platitudes. 'Ooh, you were a brute! In such a hurry, too!'

ONESIMOS: Great!

HABROTONON: 'You threw me down so roughly', I'll say, 'and tore
my poor dress to pieces.' And before I do all this, I'll go in and cry *530*
over the baby and kiss it and ask the woman where she got it.

93

ONESIMOS: You're a genius!

HABROTONON: And to crown it all, I'll say, 'So you've got yourself a baby son', and show him the child that's just been found.

ONESIMOS: You're a minx, Habrotonon, and a clever one.

HABROTONON: Then, if the verdict's 'proven' and he is clearly the child's father, we'll have plenty of time to look for the girl.

540 ONESIMOS: One point you haven't mentioned – you'll get your freedom. If he thinks you're the baby's mother, he'll buy your freedom at once, won't he?

HABROTONON: I don't know. But it would be nice if he did.

ONESIMOS: Of course you know! And do I get anything out of this, Habrotonon?

HABROTONON: Oh, *yes*. You get my eternal gratitude for all my blessings.

ONESIMOS: And suppose you then abandon the search for the girl, drop the whole business and welsh on me, what then?

HABROTONON: Heavens, why on earth would I do that? Do I look like a girl dying to have a family? Just give me my freedom, that's all the reward I want.

ONESIMOS: Then I hope you get it.

HABROTONON: You like my idea?

550 ONESIMOS: I like it very much. If you try to double-cross me, I'll fight you then: I'll have plenty of ammunition. For the moment, let's see how it all goes.

HABROTONON: Agreed, then?

ONESIMOS: Agreed.

HABROTONON: Then give me the ring. Quick!

ONESIMOS: Here you are.

HABROTONON: Sweet Persuasion be my friend! May the words I speak do the trick. [*She goes into Chairestratos's house.*]

ONESIMOS: That's one smart little girl! No sooner sees that the love-game's no road to freedom, but only to heartache, then off 560 she goes on the other track. But me, I'll stay a slave for ever, drivelling and paralytic, quite incapable of a scheme like this. Still, if she pulls it off, perhaps something'll come my way too. Well, it would be only fair . . . You fool, Onesimos, expecting gratitude from a woman. I only hope I take no stick.

My mistress is in a dangerous position now. For if a girl is found who is both a citizen's daughter and mother of this child, Charisios 570 will promptly desert Pamphile and marry *her* . . . Today, too, I think I've side-stepped quite neatly: this brew was none of *my* stirring. No more meddling, thank you. If anyone finds that I've

been interfering or speaking out of turn, I give him full authority to
cut out my – molars. Who's this coming? Oh, it's Smikrines, back
again from the city, all set to make more mischief. Perhaps
someone's told him the truth. I'd rather keep out of his way. Better   580
go before he sees me. [*He goes into the house as* SMIKRINES *enters,
right.*]

*The next fifty lines are badly damaged, but what does survive suggests that
Smikrines had a monologue in which he complained that Charisios'
behaviour was now a public scandal. Then Karion probably burst out of
Chairestratos's house, complaining of the turmoil caused by Habrotonon's
scheme, and both accepted the story as true. Then Chairestratos may have
appeared, complaining that Habrotonon was giving herself airs.*

SMIKRINES: Perhaps you think I'm meddling, interfering in another
man's business? But I've every right to take my daughter home,
and that's what I'll do. My mind's pretty well made up. I call you   660
all to witness . . . Hates this *dolce vita*, does he? Drinking with
some man, having some girl at night, tomorrow some other
outrage. And he's connected by marriage to *our* family! . . . He'll   690
pay for being so high and mighty, ruining his life in a brothel with
the fine lady he's adding to his household. That's how he'll live,
thinking we don't notice. He'll be taking another one soon and
setting up a harem. I see it all.[9]

*The end of the act, perhaps another ten lines, is lost. Then would have
followed the choral interlude.*

[THIRD CHORAL INTERLUDE]

ACT FOUR

[*Enter* SMIKRINES *and* PAMPHILE, *in conversation, from Charisios'* *house.*]

The opening of the conversation may have been lost.

PAMPHILE: But if, in your attempt to rescue me, you can't *persuade* me to do this, you would no longer be my father, but my master.

SMIKRINES: Does it need argument or persuasion? Isn't it *obvious*, Pamphile? It speaks for itself. But if I must argue, I'm ready, and
720   I'll put three points to you. There's no hope of saving the marriage for either of you.

Some thirty lines are lost or mutilated, but the words which survive suggest that Smikrines argued that Charisios would go his own sweet way, that Pamphile would not be able to compete with the mistress's arts, and that Charisios could not afford to keep up two establishments.

750   Just think what it would cost! Double expenses for all the women's festivals! Financial ruin, you mark my words. He's done for, everyone knows that, and you must consider your own position. He says he's 'got to go down to the harbour': once there, he'll stay. You'll be upset, putting off dinner, waiting for him, while he's drinking with *her.*

There follows a large gap in the text, perhaps about ninety lines. Smikrines obviously went on arguing, and the following fragment probably comes from his speech.

It's difficult, Pamphile, for a lady to fight a tart. *She* fights unfairly, knows more tricks, has no shame, coaxes him more.

Pamphile clearly refused to go with her father and, to judge from Onesimos's speech later, made a good and dignified case for herself. This part of the conversation was overheard by Charisios. Smikrines then left without her, and she probably spoke again, possibly about her grief at having to abandon her baby. The next short fragment comes from that speech.

PAMPHILE: I was absolutely burnt out with weeping.

96

[PAMPHILE *is still on stage when* HABROTONON *enters from Chairestratos's house, carrying the baby.*]

HABROTONON: I'll just take him outside. Poor dear, he's been crying for ages. *I* don't know what's wrong with him.

PAMPHILE [*not seeing her*]: God pity me, I'm so unhappy!

HABROTONON [*to baby*]: Poor darling, when will you see your mother?

PAMPHILE: I'll go in.

HABROTONON [*seeing and recognizing her*]: Just a minute, please, madam.

PAMPHILE: Are you addressing me?

HABROTONON: Yes, I am. Turn and face me.

PAMPHILE: Do you know me, madam?

HABROTONON: It's the girl I saw. Hello, darling.   860

PAMPHILE: And who are *you*?

HABROTONON: Give me your hand! Tell me, sweetheart, did you go to watch the Tauropolia last year?

PAMPHILE: Madam, where did you get the baby you're carrying? Tell me!

HABROTONON: Recognize something it's wearing, love? [PAMPHILE *starts back.*] No need to be afraid of me, madam.

PAMPHILE: Is this not your own child?

HABROTONON: I pretended it was, not to do down his real mother, but to give me time to find her. And found her I have! You're the girl I saw before.

PAMPHILE: But who's the father?   870

HABROTONON: Charisios.

PAMPHILE: Are you sure, my dear?

HABROTONON: Quite sure. But – aren't you his wife, from next door.

PAMPHILE [*happily*]: Oh, *yes!*

HABROTONON: Dear madam, some power above has looked with pity on you both. Oh, there's the neighbour's door, someone's coming out. Take me into your house, and I'll tell you the whole story, from beginning to end.

[*They go into Charisios' house, as* ONESIMOS *emerges from Chairestratos's house.*]

ONESIMOS: He's mad, I swear it, quite loopy, really raving, absolutely crazy! My master, I mean, Charisios. He's fallen into   880 black depression, or something very like it. There's no other explanation.

You see, he was crouched down inside the door here for ages,

97

listening to his wife's father discussing the whole business with her, apparently, and I can't *tell* you, Ladies and Gentlemen, how he kept changing colour. 'Sweetheart,' he cried, 'what wonderful words!' And he punched himself hard on the head. Then a minute
890 later, 'What a wife I've got, and what a mess I've made of things!' Finally, when he'd heard everything, he went back into the house, where there was moaning, tearing of hair, lunatic raving without end. 'I'm a criminal,' he kept saying. '*I* behave like this and father a bastard child. But I didn't feel or show a scrap of mercy to the girl who was the victim of a similar outrage. I'm a heartless brute.' He
900 reproaches himself savagely, eyes blood-shot, all worked up. I'm terrified, my mouth dry with fear. In this state, if he sets eyes on me, who told him about his wife, he might kill me. That's why I've stepped quietly out here. But where to turn? What to do? I'm finished, done for. Oh, there's the door, he's coming out. O God, save me if you can! [*He rushes into Charisios' house as* CHARISIOS *emerges from Chairestratos's.*]

CHARISIOS: 'An upright man' – that was me – careful of my
910 'honour', a judge of 'right' and 'wrong', my own life '*pure et sans reproche*'. Well, some Power above has well and truly turned the tables on me, and quite right too. I've finally shown that I'm human. 'You miserable worm' (says the Power) 'with your peacock airs and pretentious talk, you "don't tolerate" a girl's bad luck that's no fault of hers. I'll show you that you've come the same sort of cropper yourself. And then, she'll treat you tenderly, while you insult her. And so you'll be obviously unfortunate – and a clumsy, heartless brute into the bargain.' [*Sarcastically, to himself*] Just like your sentiments, wasn't it, what she said to her father just
920 now. 'I'm his wife,' she said, 'his life's partner. Accidents happen, and it's not for a wife to run away when they do.' But *you* [*to himself*] you're on such a pedestal . . .

Charisios develops this theme through several damaged lines, then continues.

Her father will press her hard. But what's her father to me? I'll be quite blunt. 'Look here, Smikrines,' I'll say, 'stop making
930 trouble. My wife's not leaving me. Why are you upsetting Pamphile and putting pressure on her? Why do you keep coming here?'

[*Enter* ONESIMOS, *from Charisios' house, followed by* HABROTONON.]
ONESIMOS: I'm in a really terrible mess. For God's sake, girl, don't desert me.

98

CHARISIOS: Hey! Have you been standing there listening to me, you sinner?

ONESIMOS: Oh, *no*, sir, I've just this minute come out.

The next fifteen lines are badly damaged. Habrotonon joins in the conversation, and Charisios discovers that the baby is not hers.

CHARISIOS: Are you telling me, Onesimos, that you two were   950
having me on?

ONESIMOS: The woman tempted me, I swear she did.

HABROTONON: No need to squabble, darling. The baby belongs to your lawful wedded wife, no one else.

CHARISIOS: I wish it did.

HABROTONON: I take my oath on it.

CHARISIOS: What tale is this?

HABROTONON: No tale. It's the truth.

CHARISIOS: The baby's *Pamphile*'s? But it's mine too!

HABROTONON: Yes, yours too.

CHARISIOS: *Really* Pamphile's? Habrotonon, don't keep me in suspense . . .

The last twenty lines of the act are missing or mutilated. Charisios must have been convinced of the truth, and gone in to Pamphile, and Onesimos and Habrotonon must have left the stage.

[FOURTH CHORAL INTERLUDE]

ACT FIVE

The beginning of the act is lost. What is left, suggests that it may have opened with a monologue by Chairestratos, who is unaware of the truth just discovered by Charisios, and who has fallen in love with Habrotonon.

CHAIRESTRATOS [*brooding*]: Contrariwise, Chairestratos, you have to consider the inevitable consequence. How do you propose to continue to be Charisios' loyal friend? She's not a common tart,
985   who's available to anyone. It's serious, she's had a child, she's no slave. [*Pause*] Oh, stop it! Forget her. Let her first have a tête-à-tête with her 'dearest, sweetest Charisios' . . .[10]

Some seventy lines are missing here, during which Charisios and Onesimos may have emerged and enlightened Chairestratos. Two lines remain from the end of the scene, spoken by CHARISIOS.

1060   . . . self-control. *He* would never have kept his hands off her, I'm quite sure. But I shall. [*The stage is left empty.*]
     [*Enter* SMIKRINES, *right, with* SOPHRONE, *Pamphile's old nurse.*]
SMIKRINES: Damn me if I don't box your ears, Sophrone. You're preaching at me too, are you? In too much of a hurry, am I, to take my daughter away? You sinful old hag! Am I to stand by while her precious husband devours *my* dowry-money, and do no more than talk about what is mine? Is that your advice? Surely it's better to strike quickly. One word more and you'll be sorry. Is *Sophrone* to
1070   be my judge? You persuade Pamphile to come, when you see her. If you don't, Sophrone, so help me God, on the way home – did you see that pond we passed? I'll hold you down in it *all night*. I'll *murder* you. I'll teach you to argue with *me*.
     The door's locked. Better knock. Hey, boys! Door! Open up. Are you deaf?
ONESIMOS [*opening door*]: Who is it? Oh, it's Smikrines, old Grumpy, come to fetch his dowry and his daughter.
SMIKRINES: Yes, it is, damn you.
1080 ONESIMOS: Quite right too. A smart man, one with all his marbles, doesn't waste time. And embezzlement of a dowry is *so* remarkable an occurrence!
SMIKRINES: God in heaven –

100

ONESIMOS: Do you really think God has so little to do, Smikrines, that he can dole out good and bad every day to every individual?

SMIKRINES: I don't understand.

ONESIMOS: I'll explain – in words of one syllable. There are, in round numbers, a thousand cities, right? And thirty thousand inhabitants in each. Does God bless or punish every one of them individually? 1090

SMIKRINES: Of course not. That would make His life a burden.

ONESIMOS: Then does God not care for us, you'll ask. Oh, yes, He does. He's put a guardian in each one of us, namely his character. That stands guard inside us, ruining us if we abuse it, rewarding someone else. *That*'s our God, responsible for success and failure in each one of us. Keep on its right side, behave properly, and you'll be happy.

SMIKRINES: And is *my* character doing something stupid now, you 1100 scum?

ONESIMOS: It's grinding you to powder.

SMIKRINES: Damn your impudence!

ONESIMOS: Smikrines, do you really think it's right for a man to take his daughter from her husband?

SMIKRINES: No one's suggesting that it's right. But at the moment it's unavoidable.

ONESIMOS [*to* SOPHRONE]: You see? Wrong's 'unavoidable', according to *his* logical processes. Character, nothing but character is proving his ruin. [*To* SMIKRINES] And now, when you're already on the road to ruin, pure chance has saved you, and you arrive to find all those problems smoothed away and resolved. But I warn you, Smikrines, don't let me catch you rushing your fences 1110 again. Drop all your complaints – and go and greet your grandson.

SMIKRINES: My *grandson*, scum of the earth?

ONESIMOS: You were thick too, though you thought you were so clever. That was no way to look after a marriageable daughter. That's how we manage to produce five-month babies. It's a miracle!

SMIKRINES: I don't know what you're talking about.

ONESIMOS: But I think old Sophrone does. [*To* SOPHRONE] Last year at the festival, my master took the girl away from the dancing 1120 – get me? Yes, and now they've recognized one another, and all is sweetness and light.

SMIKRINES [*to* SOPHRONE]: What's all this, you old sinner?

ONESIMOS: 'Nature willed, and Nature knows no laws.
   For this was woman made.'

You *are* a fool, Smikrines. I'll quote you the whole speech from the *Auge*[11] if you still don't see it. [SOPHRONE *sees it, and dances with joy.*]

SMIKRINES [*to* SOPHRONE]: Your silly antics make me furious. *You* obviously know what he means.

ONESIMOS: Of course she does. The old girl got it before you did, that's for sure.

SMIKRINES: It's a shocking story.

1130 ONESIMOS: It's the greatest piece of luck ever!

SMIKRINES: If your story's true, then the child . . .

The end of the play is missing, but there cannot have been much more. Perhaps Charisios appeared, was reconciled with his father-in-law, and invited everyone into his house to celebrate.

The Rape of the Locks[1]

[Perikeiromene]

Introductory Note to *The Rape of the Locks*

The date of the play is quite uncertain, and a good deal of it is lost. But the confusion engendered by a combination of and variations upon the conventional themes of lost children and returning soldier is entertaining, and the treatment of the confused characters is sympathetic. Polemon is more human than most boastful soldiers, and the 'lost child with tokens' theme is enlivened by there being two children, only one of whom knows some of the truth, and who share between them the tokens which eventually reveal the truth.

CHARACTERS

MISAPPREHENSION, *a divine being*
POLEMON, *a professional soldier*
SOSIAS, *his servant*
GLYKERA, *his mistress*
DORIS, *her maid*
MOSCHION, *a young man*
DAOS, *his servant*
PATAIKOS, *an old man*
HABROTONON, *a guitar-girl*[2]

Polemon's servant, HILARION; *Moschion's adoptive mother,* MYRRHINE;
and PHILINUS, *a friend of Pataikos and possibly also Myrrhine's husband,
may also have appeared in the play: but they do not appear in the part which
is left to us.*

ACT ONE

SCENE: *a street in Corinth. There are two houses, one belonging to Myrrhine, the other to Polemon. Pataikos's house may have been shown, but it is nowhere necessary to the action as we have it.*

The beginning of the play is lost. A divine Prologue is necessary in this play, to give the audience the information they require: the whole action depends on the fact that the characters do not know all the facts, but the audience must know them. The divinity selected by Menander is Ignorance or Misapprehension. We clearly have most of her speech: its missing opening lines would have explained about Pataikos's wife's death in childbirth, the exposure of the twins, and their discovery by an old woman.

It is clear from the speech that this is a 'postponed prologue', that is, it is not the opening scene of the play. The most likely explanation of the missing scene is that it showed the meeting and greeting between Glykera and Moschion, with Sosias seeing it and reporting it to Polemon, who in a fury cuts off the girl's hair, possibly off stage. It then allows Menander to make a neat dramatic point, by demonstrating to the audience, via the prologue speech, that they have been under a misapprehension too.

MISAPPREHENSION: . . . she decided to keep the girl, but to give the other twin to a wealthy woman who lives here [*pointing*] and who was desperate for a son. So that was what she did. Some years passed, and the war got worse, and life in Corinth harder, and the old woman was pretty well destitute. The girl (whom you've just seen for yourselves) was now grown up, and a lover had appeared (the explosive man you've just seen). He's a native-born Corinthian, so she gave him the girl as her own daughter. She was 130 already failing and, mindful of the changes and chances of this mortal life, she told the girl the true story of how she'd found her, gave her the baby-clothes she'd been wearing, and explained about her unknown brother-by-birth, and who he was. She knew how chancy life is, and realized that he was the girl's only relative, if ever she needed help. She wanted to be sure, too, that they'd never, 140 through me – I'm IGNORANCE – enter without realizing it into a forbidden relationship. For he's rich and always drinking, and she's young and pretty – and the chap she was being left with is *not* reliable.

Well, the old woman died, and not long ago the soldier bought this [*pointing*] house. So she's living next door to her brother, but she hasn't breathed a word of what she knows – doesn't want to
150   compromise his apparent social standing, wants him to enjoy his good luck. But, quite accidentally, he saw her. He's a bold lad, as I told you, and he's always hanging about the house. Well, yesterday evening she happened to be sending her maid on an errand, and when he saw her at the door, he ran straight up and hugged and kissed her. Now, *she* knew he was her brother, so she didn't run away. But Someone Else[3] was coming up the road, and he saw what was happening. He's told you the sequel, how he marched off, saying he'd like a word with her 'when it was convenient', and
160   she burst into tears there, quite upset because she wasn't free to greet her own brother.

All this *Sturm und Drang* has been stirred up with an eye to future developments, to put him [*pointing to* POLEMON'S *house*] in a towering fury. He's not really like that, but I led him on, to get the process of discovery started, and to ensure that these young people eventually find their family. So if anyone here was shocked at the scene and thought it 'disgusting', just think again! When a god's at work, even evil turns to good, in the very act.

170   Goodbye, Ladies and Gentlemen. Be kind to us – and pay attention to what's coming.

[*Exit* MISAPPREHENSION, *left. Enter* SOSIAS, *right.*]

SOSIAS: Our swaggering ruffian of an hour ago, our Mighty Warrior (the one who won't let girls keep their hair), he's in floods of tears over his lunch. His friends have all rallied round, to help him bear up, and I've just left them at their meal. He's got no way of discovering what's going on here, so he's sent me to fetch his army cloak. The devil! He doesn't want the cloak at all, he just wants to
180   keep me on the trot.

[*Enter* DORIS, *from Polemon's house, speaking back over her shoulder. She does not see* SOSIAS.]

DORIS: I'll go and see, madam. [*She moves towards Myrrhine's house.*]

SOSIAS [*aside*]: It's Doris! How she's grown, how well she looks. These women live the life of Riley, that's quite clear. I'll be on my way.

[*He goes into* POLEMON'S *house.*]

DORIS: No one about. Better knock. [*Does so*] Any girl who gets involved with a soldier has my sympathy. No respect for the law, not one of them. You can't trust them an inch. What my poor mistress is suffering – done nothing to deserve it, either. [*Knocks again*] Door!

SOSIAS [*entering from Polemon's house and carrying cloak*]: He'll be pleased to hear she's in tears now. That's just what he wanted. [*He goes off, right.*]   190

DORIS [*as door is opened*]: Please tell . . .

Some seventy lines are missing, during which Glykera must have moved from Polemon's house to take refuge in Myrrhine's. At the end of the act, Daos is finishing a speech.

DAOS: . . . boys. Here comes a crowd of young lads, pretty merry too. Full marks to Mistress. She's bringing the lass to stay with us – that's being a real mother. Well, must go and find young master. If you ask me, this is the moment for him to come home – at the   265 double. [*He goes off, right.*]

FIRST CHORAL INTERLUDE

ACT TWO

[*Enter* MOSCHION *and* DAOS, *right.*]

MOSCHION: Many's the time, Daos, you've told me tales that weren't true. You're an abominable liar! If you're trying to gammon me now –

DAOS: Whip me immediately, if I am.

MOSCHION: Not enough!

270 DAOS: Then declare war, and give me no quarter. But if it *is* true, and you find the girl in the house, what about me then? *I* managed the whole thing for you, Moschion; *I* persuaded her to come here (and it took some talking to do it); and *I* persuaded your mother to take her in and to make all provision you could desire. How shall I stand *then*?

MOSCHION: Then think, Daos! What sort of life most appeals to you? Consider carefully, then tell me.[4]

DAOS: Be a mill manager, perhaps?

MOSCHION [*aside*]: He'll go to a mill, all right – the treadmill.

DAOS: No manual labour, now. Don't suggest it.

MOSCHION: I fancy making you Minister for Hellenic Affairs, or
280 CO of a regiment.

DAOS: Huh! They'll promptly cut my throat in an army camp, if I'm caught stealing.[5]

MOSCHION: But you'll be able to let out contracts and make a large profit.

DAOS: I'd rather keep a general store, Moschion, or have a stall in the market and sell cheese. I've no desire to be rich, none at all. But shopkeeping would suit me, and give me more pleasure.

MOSCHION: What a dreadful idea! You know the old saying, 'I hope no honey-seller ever turns virtuous in her old age'.[6]

DAOS: To have a full belly, that's what I like. And I say I've earned it for the services I've mentioned.

290 MOSCHION: Yes, you've done well, Daos. All right, sell your cheese, and good luck to it.

DAOS: 'That's my prayer', as they say. Now, open the door, sir.

MOSCHION: Yes, I must. It's my job now to chat her up, and to cock a snook at the goddamned five-star general.

DAOS: Sure it is.

MOSCHION: You go in first, Daos, go on. Spy out the lie of the land—what Glykera's doing, where my mother is, how they're likely to receive me. You're a smart chap, I don't need to spell it out for you.

DAOS: I'm on my way. [*He goes into Myrrhine's house.*]

MOSCHION: I'll walk up and down in front of the house and wait for you. Yes, she did show some sort of feeling when I went up to her   300
last night. As I ran forward, she didn't run away, but flung her arms round me and hugged me. I'm quite good-looking, they tell me, and quite good company, I do think. And (if I may say so without offence) the girls all like me.

DAOS [*emerging from the house*]: Moschion! She's bathed, and sitting there, all ready.

MOSCHION: The darling!

DAOS: Your mother's bustling about, busy with this and that. Lunch is ready, and by the look of things, I'd say they're waiting for you.

MOSCHION: Well, I've known for years now that I'm attractive! Did you tell them I was here?

DAOS: No, of course not.

MOSCHION: Well, go and tell them now.

DAOS: About turn! See, I'm on my way. [*Re-enters house.*]   310

MOSCHION: She'll be shy when we go in, naturally, and hide behind her veil. That's what women do. Now my mother—I must kiss her as soon as I go in, win her over completely, make sure she's on my side, be her 'own dear boy'. She's really shown very proper feeling in this whole business. Ah, here comes someone. [*Anxiously, as* DAOS *comes out*] What's wrong, boy? You look worried, Daos.

DAOS: I'm worried all right. It's most peculiar. When I went in and told your mother you were here, 'None of that!' she says, 'how did he get wind of this? Have *you* been gossiping, telling him that   320
because she was frightened, she's run for refuge to our house? Yes, that's it. Damn you,' she says, 'out of my way, boy, I'm busy.' The prize has been whisked away from under your nose. She wasn't a bit pleased to be told you were here.

MOSCHION: You rat, you've done me down!

DAOS: That's a laugh. It wasn't me, it was your mother —

MOSCHION: Was it really? But you told me she came of her own free will, *didn't you*? And that she came because of me? And that you persuaded her to come?

DAOS: *I* told you that I persuaded her to come? I never did! I'd never tell you a lie, sir.[7]

330 MOSCHION: Then you didn't tell me ten minutes ago that you had
persuaded Mother to take the girl in, for my sake?

DAOS: Well . . . you see . . . Yes, I did say that, I remember now.

MOSCHION: And that you thought she was doing it for me?

DAOS: Oh, I can't say *that*. But I was trying to persuade her –

MOSCHION [*grimly*]: I see. Come here.

DAOS [*nervously*]: Where? Not far, I hope.

MOSCHION: You'll find out.

DAOS: Tell you what, sir, I – [MOSCHION *grabs him*] now, just a
minute!

MOSCHION: You're making a fool of me.

DAOS: I'm not, honest I'm not. I wouldn't do a thing like that. If
you'll just *listen*. Perhaps she doesn't want the affair to develop in a,
you know, in a rush, all anyhow. Before you discover what's
happened, she wants to know what *you* have to say. Yes, that's it!

340 For she's not come here like a call-girl, or a common street-walker.

MOSCHION: Now you're talking.

DAOS: Try it out. You know the situation, of course. She's left her
home and her lover, I tell you no lie. If you want her
for three or four days, Someone will give you her devoted
attention. She told me so. And you should be told it now.

MOSCHION: Where can I deposit you in safe custody, Daos? You're
sending me round in circles. Lies a minute ago, now your bab-
blings make some sense.

DAOS: You don't give me any peace to *think*. All right, change your
tactics, go in – and behave!

MOSCHION: While you take off?

350 DAOS [*sarcastically*]: Well, of course! You can see how well provided I
am with foreign currency . . .

MOSCHION: If you come in, you could be of some assistance to me.

DAOS: I'll be glad to, sir.

MOSCHION: Right, you win. [*He goes into Myrrhine's house.*]

DAOS [*relaxing*]: That was close! I'm shaking like a leaf. This plotting's not as easy as I thought.

[*Enter* SOSIAS, *right, carrying cloak and sword. He does not see*
DAOS.]

SOSIAS: Back again I'm sent with cloak and sword, to see what's
doing, then go and report. For two pins I'd tell him I found his rival
in the house, to make him spring into action. But I'm sorry for
him. I've never seen Master so miserable, it's a real nightmare.

360 What a Welcome Home! [*He goes into Polemon's house.*]

DAOS: The General's home! That certainly makes things awkward.

And that's not to mention the nub – if *our* Master comes back from the country sooner than expected, there'll be a fine furore when *he* appears on the scene.

SOSIAS [*emerging from house and shouting back over his shoulder*]: You let her *go*, you sacrilegious swine, you let her *out*?

DAOS: Here he comes again, in a fine fury too. I'll just step out of his way. [*He lurks behind a convenient piece of scenery.*]

SOSIAS: Gone straight next door, I suppose, to her boy-friend, leaving us lamenting long and hard.   370

DAOS [*aside*]: The General has a prophet on his staff! He's not far off the mark.

SOSIAS: I'll go and knock. [*He moves towards Myrrhine's house.*]

DAOS [*moving forward*]: What the devil do *you* want? Where are you going?

SOSIAS: You live here?

DAOS: Perhaps I do. What's it to you?

SOSIAS: For heaven's sake, have you all gone mad? Keeping a free-born woman under lock and key, in defiance of her legal guardian's wishes. The effrontery!

DAOS: That's a filthy lie.

SOSIAS: Do you think we've got no guts, that we're not *men*?

DAOS: Oh, sure, real pound-an-hour men. And when he takes   380
command of a tuppeny-ha'penny lot like you, we'll easily beat you.

SOSIAS: This is an outrage! Answer me, do you admit you've got her?

DAOS: Go lose yourself, chum.

SOSIAS [*shouting*]: Hilarion! Oh, he's gone. This chap [*pulling a servant forward*] will be my witness. Now! You admit you've got her?

DAOS: No lodgers here.

SOSIAS: Some of you will be sorry before long, I'll see to that. Who do you think you're fooling? Tell me that! What's your game? We'll storm this 'bijou residence' in ten minutes, no bother. Go put the Great Lover on red alert.   390

DAOS: Poor man, I'm sorry for you. You're wasting your time, imagining she's with us.

SOSIAS: Our flying column – call them tuppeny-ha'penny chaps if you like – they'll dismantle the whole place before you can *spit*.

DAOS: Just a joke. You're really desperate, a cornered rat.

SOSIAS: This, in a civilized country!

DAOS: I tell you, we haven't got her.

SOSIAS: Huh! I'm a regular soldier, *I'll* show you.

DAOS: Oh, go to hell, you're off your head. I'm going in. [*Does so.*]

DORIS [*emerging from Myrrhine's house as* DAOS *goes in*]: Why, Sosias.

SOSIAS: Doris, if you come near me, I'll do you a serious injury. You're mainly to blame for this coil.

400 DORIS: For pity's sake! Tell him that she's fled in mortal terror to a woman friend.

SOSIAS: Oh? To a woman friend? In mortal terror?

DORIS: Yes, she's gone next door, to Myrrhine, cross my heart and hope to die.

SOSIAS: Oh, really? Where her honey is, here in this house!

DORIS: I know what you're thinking, Sosias, but it's not true.

SOSIAS: Oh, go away, go *away*. I don't want to hear any more lies.

About sixty lines of text are missing here, from the end of this act and the start of the next. Doris must have gone back into Myrrhine's house and Sosias clearly went off to fetch Polemon. Then would follow the choral interlude.

[SECOND CHORAL INTERLUDE]

ACT THREE

Sosias has returned with Polemon, and they are accompanied by Habrotonon and some servants. Pataikos, whether he came with them or arrived independently, is also on stage, and has clearly been counselling caution. Equally clearly, Sosias has been drowning his sorrows.

SOSIAS: He's been bribed by the other side, believe *me*. He's a traitor to you and your force.

PATAIKOS [*to* SOSIAS]: Go and sleep it off, friend, and give the war a rest. [*To* POLEMON] It's *you* I'm talking to; you're not quite so 470 drunk.

POLEMON: Not quite so – ? *Me?* I had no more than one glass. I saw all this coming – what a mess! – and I was taking precautions.

PATAIKOS: Good. Now, take my advice –

POLEMON: What do you want me to do?

PATAIKOS: A good question. As I was saying when I was so rudely interrupted –

SOSIAS: Habrotonon, sound the charge!

PATAIKOS: Before I start, send this fellow and his 'troops' into the house.

SOSIAS: Your tactics are terrible. [*To* POLEMON] He'll stop the war, when we could be storming the ramparts.

POLEMON: That's because he –

SOSIAS: Pataikos is a disaster. [*To his 'troops'*] We're leaderless! 480

PATAIKOS: For God's sake, man, go *away*.

SOSIAS: I'm going. [*He moves over to* HABROTONON *and the servants.*] I expected you to do something, Habrotonon. *You*'ve got plenty of siege-tactics, *you* can make a frontal assault, or encircle the target, *can't* you? [*She moves away, insulted.*] Where are you going, darling? The tart's blushing! You don't mind my jokes, do you?

[HABROTONON *sweeps off the stage, probably followed by the 'troops'.* SOSIAS *probably subsides into a corner to sleep it off.*]

PATAIKOS: Now, Polemon, if the sort of thing you've been telling me about had happened to your lawful wedded wife –

POLEMON: This is outrageous, Pataikos!

PATAIKOS [*mildly*]: It does make a difference.

POLEMON: I regard her *as* my lawful, wedded wife.

PATAIKOS: No need to shout. Who 'gave away the bride'?

490 POLEMON [*sulkily*]: She did.

PATAIKOS [*drily*]: Quite so. Perhaps she liked you then, and doesn't any longer. Now that you're not treating her properly, she's left.

POLEMON: Not *treating* her properly? *Me?* That hurts me more than anything you've said yet.

PATAIKOS: Oh, you're in love, I'm well aware of that. That's why you're behaving so stupidly. But what are you trying to do? Who are you trying to take by force? You have no legal standing, she's her own mistress. The only course open to a disconsolate lover, is persuasion.

POLEMON: What about the man who seduced her when I was away? Isn't he in the wrong?

500 PATAIKOS: Yes, he is, and you can charge him with it, if you ever come to conclusions with him. But if you use force and he takes you to court, you'll lose your case. His offence entitles you to charge him, but not to assault him.

POLEMON: Not even now?

PATAIKOS: Not even now.

POLEMON: I don't know what to say, damned if I do. I might as well go hang myself. Glykera's *left* me, Pataikos, left me – Glykera! Look, do you think you could – you know her, you've often talked to her – would *you* go and have a word with her, be my ambassador? Please!

510 PATAIKOS: Why, of course I will.

POLEMON: I imagine you know how to put a good case, Pataikos?

PATAIKOS: Pretty well.

POLEMON: But you must, it's vital! Everything depends on that. If I've ever treated her badly – if I don't from this day forth do all I can to love and cherish her – just come and see what I bought for her –

PATAIKOS: Oh, no need for that, thank you.

POLEMON: Do come and see, Pataikos, please! You'll have all the more sympathy with me then.

PATAIKOS: Oh, dear!

POLEMON: This way, come on. [*He pulls* PATAIKOS *towards his house.*] What a wardrobe she had! And how beautiful she looks
520 when she puts on one of these dresses! Perhaps you never saw her like that?

PATAIKOS: Oh, yes, indeed I did.

POLEMON: And she's so tall – a splendid sight! [*Pause*] I'm mad, raving on about her height. That's nothing to do with the case.

PATAIKOS: Nothing at all.

POLEMON: You think not? But you must see her wardrobe. This way!

PATAIKOS [*resignedly*]: All right, I'm coming. [*They go into Polemon's house.*]

MOSCHION [*entering from Myrrhine's house, and addressing their backs*]: Yes, go in and be damned to you. They've 'scuttled away with spears in hand before me'. That lot couldn't storm a swallow's nest, for all their malice. Daos told me they'd got a squad of mercenaries: the famous mercenaries seem to be just Sosias 530 here. [*Addresses audience*] Of all the unhappy devils now alive – and there's a fine crop of them all over Greece just now, God knows why – I don't believe there's a single one as miserable as me. When I went in just now, I did none of the things I normally do: didn't go and see my mother, didn't send for any of the servants. I went 540 straight to my room and lay down. I was quite calm, and I sent Daos to my mother to report that I was home, nothing more. He found them at lunch, and without a thought of me he stayed there, stuffing himself. And I lay there, saying to myself, 'Any minute now Mother'll be here, with a message from my darling, saying how we can meet.' I was rehearsing a speech . . . 550

The end of the act, about a hundred and sixty lines, is lost. By the time it ends, somehow, whether by eavesdropping or in a dramatic scene with Myrrhine or her husband, Moschion has discovered that Glykera is a respectable girl and a foundling, and that he is a foundling himself. There would follow the choral interlude.

[THIRD CHORAL INTERLUDE]

ACT FOUR

The beginning of the act is missing, and when the text resumes, Glykera and Pataikos are conversing.

GLYKERA [*defending herself from a charge of having pursued* MOSCHION *to his mother's house*]: My dear friend, what good would it have done me to run for refuge to his mother? You're not thinking straight! To get him to marry me? Hardly: he wouldn't marry a girl like me. To become his mistress? Then, you must admit, I'd have been anxious to conceal the fact from his family – and so would he. Instead, with apparent recklessness, he's established me in his father's house, and I've apparently been so silly as to antagonize his mother, and raise in all your minds a suspicion that could no longer be glossed over. I'd be ashamed to behave like that, Pataikos. Did you really believe all this tarradiddle? Did you come here with the idea that I was that sort of girl?

PATAIKOS: Heavens, no. I only hope that you can prove that what you say is true. *I* certainly believe you.

GLYKERA: Even so, you can go back and tell him to find some other girl to insult in future.

PATAIKOS: It wasn't so very dreadful, what he did.

GLYKERA: It was abominable! Making me look like a slut . . .[8]

Some fifteen lines are missing here. When the text resumes, Glykera is telling Pataikos that she is free-born, and has some tokens of her identity.

GLYKERA: I've got some things belonging to my father and mother. I always keep them by me, and look after them very carefully.

PATAIKOS: So what do you want me to do?

GLYKERA: I want you to fetch them from Polemon's house.

PATAIKOS: Have you deserted the poor chap altogether, then? Is that what you mean?

GLYKERA: Just do as I ask, please, and I'll be grateful.

PATAIKOS: It shall be done. But it's foolish. You ought to think of all that's involved.

GLYKERA: I know my own business best.

PATAIKOS: You're quite sure? All right, then, do any of the maids know where your things are?

GLYKERA: Doris does.

PATAIKOS [*to a servant*]: Then one of you fetch Doris out here. [*To* GLYKERA] Even so, Glykera, do make your peace with Polemon on the terms I now propose —

DORIS [*entering from Polemon's house*]: Oh, madam!

GLYKERA: What's wrong?

DORIS: This is terrible!

GLYKERA: Bring me out the little box, Doris, the one containing the bit of embroidery. [DORIS *looks bewildered*.] For goodness' sake, you know what I mean, the box I gave you to look after. Why are you crying, you silly girl?

[DORIS *fetches the box, and* PATAIKOS *looks with interest at its contents*.]

PATAIKOS [*to himself*]: Now that's queer, by God it is. Nothing's impossible in this life. (*Some seven lines are missing here*.) I've seen a piece of embroidery like that before. Wasn't the next figure a goat or a cow or some animal like that?

GLYKERA: Not a goat, my friend, it's a stag.   770

PATAIKOS: Something with horns, anyhow. And the third figure was a winged horse. This is my wife's work, my poor, dear wife.

[*Enter* MOSCHION, *right, not seeing them. They do not see him*.]

MOSCHION: It's not impossible, I have to face it, that my real mother had a daughter at the same time as she had me. If that's true, and Glykera is my sister, then I'm in the devil of a mess! [*Broods*.]

PATAIKOS: God, is something still left of my family?

GLYKERA: Go on, ask me anything you like.

PATAIKOS: Where did you get these things? Tell me.   780

GLYKERA: I was found wrapped in the embroidery, when I was a baby.

MOSCHION [*aside*]: Hold it! I'm being swept towards a crisis in my life.

PATAIKOS: Tell me, were you alone when you were found?

GLYKERA: Oh no, my brother and I were exposed together.

MOSCHION [*aside*]: That answers one of my questions.

PATAIKOS: Then how did you come to be separated?

GLYKERA: I *could* tell you the whole story, for I've been told it. But confine your questions to my own story: I've every right to tell   790 that, but I gave her my word not to mention the other.

MOSCHION [*aside*]: Another piece of clear confirmation! She gave her word to my 'mother'. I don't know whether I'm on my head or my heels!

PATAIKOS: Who found you, then, and brought you up?

GLYKERA: A woman brought me up, the one who found me.

PATAIKOS: Did she say anything about *where* she found you?

GLYKERA: She said there was a spring – yes, and that the spot was shady.

PATAIKOS: That's what the man who left you there told *me*.

GLYKERA: Who was that? May I know?

800 PATAIKOS: He was a servant. But the man who grudged you life – was I.

GLYKERA: You abandoned your own child. But why?

PATAIKOS: Life is full of mysteries, my child. Your mother died in childbirth, and the day before –

GLYKERA: What happened? You frighten me.

PATAIKOS: I lost all my money. And I'd had a good income all my life.

GLYKERA: In a day? What happened? Heavens, how dreadful!

PATAIKOS: I heard that the ship that provided our livelihood had foundered in the angry surge of the Aegean sea.

810 GLYKERA: That was a sad day for me.

PATAIKOS: I thought that for a beggar to bring up children who would be an extra burden on him, was an act of absolute folly.

Two badly damaged lines follow, which cannot be restored.

GLYKERA: . . . there were necklaces, too, and a small brooch set with stones, to identify the exposed children.

PATAIKOS: Show me that brooch.

GLYKERA: I haven't got it any longer. I presume my brother has it.[9]

MOSCHION [*aside*]: The man's my father, I do believe!

PATAIKOS: Can you describe the things?

820 GLYKERA: There was a crimson girdle –

PATAIKOS: There was indeed.

GLYKERA: – with a row of girls dancing on it.

MOSCHION [*aside*]: That settles it!

GLYKERA: And a fine, thin cloak, and a gold head-band. That's all.

PATAIKOS: I can't restrain myself any longer. My darling daughter!
    [*He embraces* GLYKERA.]

MOSCHION [*coming forward*]: And if I'm your son, could I not have a hug too?[10]

PATAIKOS: Heavens, who's this?

MOSCHION: Want to know who I am?

Between one hundred and two hundred lines are missing here, from the end of this act and the start of the next. Moschion must have been established as Pataikos's son, and there would be the choral interlude.

[FOURTH CHORAL INTERLUDE]

ACT FIVE

Glykera's relationship with Polemon has still to be resolved. Glykera's own feelings, Pataikos's championship of Polemon, and perhaps Moschion's opposition have clearly produced a change of heart and purpose. But Polemon does not know that, and his discovery of her real status has left him gloomily convinced that he has lost her for ever. The text resumes as he converses with Doris.

POLEMON: . . . to hang myself.

DORIS: Oh, don't do that.[11]

POLEMON: But what'll I do, Doris? How can I live without her? Life will be a desert.

DORIS: She'll come back to you –

POLEMON: In God's name –

DORIS: – if you behave properly.   *980*

POLEMON: I'd do *anything*. Oh, marvellous! Go in to her now. I'll set you free tomorrow, Doris. Just a minute, let me tell you what to say – she's gone. Oh, Love, you've stormed my citadel. It was her brother she was kissing, not a lover. But like a Fiend, a jealous Fiend, I didn't wait to ask questions, but fell into a drunken rage. Then I was for hanging myself – and quite right too. [DORIS *comes out.*] What's the verdict, dear Doris?

DORIS: Good news. She'll come.

POLEMON: She wasn't just teasing?   *990*

DORIS: Oh, no, she was just getting dressed. Her father was still asking questions. Now, you must celebrate the good news of her good fortune.

POLEMON: Yes, indeed, how right you are. The cook's already in the house. Tell him to kill the pig.

DORIS: But where's the basket, and all the other things we need?[12]

POLEMON: The basket can be prepared later. Get the pig killed. Better still, I'll do it myself. I'll get a garland from an altar, and put it on.

DORIS: Well, that'll certainly make you look much more   *1000* convincing.

POLEMON: Can't you fetch her out?

DORIS: I do assure you, she's just coming, with her father.

POLEMON: Oh, how can I face her father? [*He hears someone coming, and dashes into his own house.*]

DORIS: Really! You'd think it was a disaster to hear a door opening. I'll go in myself, and do what I can to help. [*She goes into Polemon's house, as* PATAIKOS *and* GLYKERA *emerge from Myrrhine's.*]

PATAIKOS: I'm delighted to hear you say you'll 'be friends again'. To accept an honourable settlement when you're in a strong position – that's proof that you're a true Greek. Boy! Run in and call Polemon, quickly now.

010 POLEMON [*emerging from his house*]: I'm coming. I was just getting ready to celebrate Glykera's good fortune. I hear she's found her father.

PATAIKOS: Yes, she has. Now listen to me. I formally give her to you in marriage, to bear legitimate children –

POLEMON: I take her.

PATAIKOS: – and a handsome dowry with her.

POLEMON: That's very generous of you.

PATAIKOS: And in future, my friend, forget you're a soldier, and don't make any more sudden assaults.

POLEMON: Good God, no! When it's nearly been the death of me this time, am I likely to do anything like that again? I'll never criticize
020 Glykera. Just say you forgive me, darling.

PATAIKOS: This time, anyway, your crazy action has been the start of happiness for us all.

POLEMON: Yes, true.

PATAIKOS: So you've got your forgiveness.

POLEMON: Come and help us celebrate, Pataikos.

PATAIKOS: Thank you, but I've got another wedding to arrange. I'm getting Philinos's daughter for my son. God . . .

The play is almost over, but the last few lines of the text are missing. Perhaps they contained an expression of gratitude to heaven from Pataikos.

The Shield

[Aspis]

Introductory Note to *The Shield*

This play has an (illusory) historical background. Kleostratos, we are told early in the text (ll. 23 ff.), has been fighting as a mercenary in Lycia (now part of South West Turkey), and those who, in Fragment 1, 'hold the citadel' are said to be in danger of assassination. Unfortunately, mercenary service, raids on Lycia and political assassination were only too common during most of Menander's lifetime, and the play cannot be dated.

Most of Acts One and Two, and the beginning of Act Three, survive. But the rest of Act Three is badly damaged, and only scrappy half-lines survive from Acts Four and Five. This makes criticism of the play difficult, for we cannot be sure precisely how Menander worked out his plot. That plot depends on an Athenian law[1] which declared that an unmarried daughter who was her deceased father's heir, was *epikleros*, that is, that she went with the estate. Her nearest male relative had the right to marry her (and the estate), if necessary divorcing his present wife to do so. If he did not wish to marry the heiress, it was his duty to arrange her marriage with someone else, and to provide a dowry for that purpose.

This situation provides Menander with the possibilities of a lively and complicated plot. The (postponed) prologue ensures that the audience can enjoy the plot's twists and turns, in full confidence that all will eventually be well; Kleostratos is not really dead, and Smikrines will get his come-uppance. The play contains several very lively scenes. But the characters seem to lack the subtlety, and the situations some of the irony, that we have come to expect from Menander; the plotting in Act Two is sudden rather than economical; the observation of human nature is less penetrating than usual, and the play seems to lack the depth that usually lies behind Menander's comedy. Perhaps he wrote in a hurry; perhaps he had an off-day; or perhaps we are judging him on insufficient evidence.

CHARACTERS

KLEOSTRATOS, *a young Athenian gentleman*
DAOS, *his former tutor*
SMIKRINES, *his uncle, a miser*
CHAIRESTRATOS, *another uncle, younger brother of Smikrines*
CHAIREAS, *a young man, stepson of Chairestratos*
A DOCTOR, *who is actually a friend of Chairestratos's in disguise*
A COOK
A WAITER
CHANCE, *a goddess*

ACT ONE

SCENE: *a street in Athens. There are two houses, one that of Smikrines, the other that of Chairestratos.*

[*Enter* DAOS, *left, carrying Kleostratos's shield, and accompanied by prisoners of war, and by mules carrying treasures which are the spoils of war. He apostrophizes his young master, whom he believes to be dead, and is overheard by* SMIKRINES, *who probably comes out of his house.*]

DAOS [*sadly*]: Oh, sir! Every day is a sad day for me now, and life's balance sheet is not at all what I hoped it would be when I set out. For I thought you'd come safely back from the war, a hero, and that you'd live the rest of your life in some style, with the title of General or Privy Counsellor. And your sister, for whose sake you enlisted,[2] would marry a man you approved of, when you'd come home to those who loved you. For myself, I thought there would be rest from long labour, as I grew old, in return for my services to you. Instead, you're gone, Kleostratos, snatched away by death against all expectation; and I, your tutor, have come home with this shield, which failed to save you, though you often brought *it* safely back from battle. For you were a brave man, bravest of the brave.

SMIKRINES: Ah, Daos, little did we think –

DAOS: It's a tragedy.

SMIKRINES: How did he die? What happened?

DAOS: For a soldier, Smikrines, finding Cause of Death is easy. It's survival that's difficult.

SMIKRINES: Still, tell me the story, Daos, please.

DAOS: Well, there's a river in Lycia called the Xanthos, and we'd been lucky there in a fair number of actions. The natives had been routed, and had abandoned the plain. It looks now as if continuous success is dangerous – when you've taken a tumble, you're more careful. Confidence made us careless, and led us into a trap. Many men had actually left the protection of the camp, and were looting the villages, burning crops and selling booty. Everyone came back with his pockets full.

SMIKRINES: Lovely!

DAOS: My master had a collection of some six hundred gold coins,

and a fair number of silver cups, and that bunch of prisoners that
you see over there. He was sending me over to Rhodes, and told
me to leave it all with a friend, and come straight back to him.

SMIKRINES: What happened then?

40 DAOS: I was on my way at dawn. But on that very day, the natives,
quite unbeknown to our scouts, occupied a hill in front of us, and
dug themselves in: they had heard from some deserters that our
forces were scattered. Well, when evening came, and all those in
the camp were in their tents, after returning from a countryside
that offered plenty of booty, the inevitable happened – most of
them were celebrating.

SMIKRINES: How shocking!

50 DAOS: Yes, it was, for there was a surprise attack, I think.

Three lines are missing or mutilated. Daos must have explained that he had
travelled some distance from the main camp and pitched his own.

DAOS: . . . then, round about midnight, when I was standing guard
over the money and the slaves, walking up and down in front of
the tent, I heard a noise – howling, running, wailing, men shouting
one another's names. That told me what had happened. Fortunately, there was a little hill there, a possible strong point. We all
60 flocked up to it, and a stream of wounded joined us – cavalry,
special assault troops and regular infantry.

SMIKRINES: How lucky for you that you'd been sent away!

DAOS: At dawn, we built a palisade, and there we stayed. And those
who'd been scattered in the raids I mentioned kept trickling back to
join us. After three days, we started out again, for we'd heard that
the Lycians were taking their prisoners to the hill-villages.

SMIKRINES: Did you find our friend among the fallen?

DAOS: It wasn't possible to identify the body with any certainty.
70 They'd been lying out for four days, and their faces were all
bloated.

SMIKRINES: Then how can you be sure that he's dead?

DAOS: He was lying there with his shield. It was all buckled, and I
imagine that's why none of the natives had appropriated it. Our
noble captain banned all individual cremations, for he realized it
would take too much time to gather every man's bones separately.
So he had them all heaped together and burned, then, after a quick
committal, he promptly broke camp. We slipped away to Rhodes
80 first, then after a few days we sailed here. That's the whole story.

SMIKRINES: You've got six hundred gold coins, you say?

DAOS: Yes.

SMIKRINES: And silver cups, too?

DAOS: About sixteen kilograms in weight, no more. Your inheritance.

SMIKRINES: You don't suppose that's why I'm so interested, do you? Heavens, no! Was all the rest taken?

DAOS: Most of it, except what I got my hands on first. There are some gowns and cloaks, and this group of captives here – they belong to you.

SMIKRINES: They're of no interest to me. I'd rather have Kleostratos *90*
alive.

DAOS [*sadly*]: Yes, indeed. We'd better go in and tell the sad story to those it will affect most.

SMIKRINES: I'll want a word with you, Daos, when you've time. [DAOS *and the attendants go into Chairestratos's house.*] And now, I think I'd better go inside too, to work out the most considerate way of dealing with the family. [*He goes into his own house.*]
    [*Enter, right, the goddess* CHANCE.]

CHANCE: Well now, if something unpleasant had really happened to these people, I couldn't be the next to appear, for I'm a goddess. But in fact they're mistaken, quite led astray, as anyone who pays attention to me will soon discover.[3] *100*

A few lines are missing here, but it becomes clear that Kleostratos had a friend, a fellow-soldier, who shared his tent.

When the natives attacked the camp, and the 'stand-to' was sounding continuously, everyone rushed out to the rescue with any arms that lay to hand. And that's how Kleostratos's tent-mate came to rush out with the shield you've just seen. He fell immediately. And with the shield lying there among the corpses, and the young man's body decomposing, Daos here made a mistake. Kleostratos fought in the defence with borrowed arms, and was *110*
taken prisoner. He's alive, and he'll come back safely, quite soon now.

    Well, you've been properly briefed now on that. The old chap who was asking all the questions just now, is Kleostratos's uncle on his father's side, and a real villain, biggest twister in the world. He takes no account of the claims of relatives or friends, never gives a thought to the wickedness of his life. He wants everything for himself. That's his one idea. He lives alone, with an old crone *120*
as his housekeeper. Where the servant went in next door [*pointing*], that's the house of Money-grubber's younger brother. He's the young man's uncle too, but he's a good man as well as a rich one.

He's married, with one daughter. When the young man went abroad, he left his sister in this uncle's care, and the two girls have been brought up together.

130   He's a good man, as I said, and when he realized that Kleostratos was likely to be away for a considerable time, and that they had little money of their own, he was going to arrange the girl's marriage to his stepson (that's his wife's son by a former marriage), and he was going to provide a substantial dowry. The wedding was to be today, but what has happened now will upset everything. Our villain, who heard just now about the six hundred gold

140 pieces, and got a look at the foreign slaves, pack-mules and girls, will want to have the heiress himself: and his age gives him a prior claim. But he won't succeed! He'll cause a great deal of trouble, and show the whole world what he's really like – and then he'll be back where he started.

    Oh, I haven't told you my name. I'm the Controller and Director of this whole story. I'm called Chance. [*She goes off, right.*]

SMIKRINES [*emerging from his house*]: To make sure no one can say
150 that I'm feathering my nest, I didn't check the amount of gold he's brought, nor the number of silver cups, didn't count *anything*, just stood aside and let them take it in here [*pointing to his brother's house*]. They're always casting aspersions on me. Well, the accuracy of the count is guaranteed as long as those transporting the goods are slaves.[4] In any case, I imagine that they will be willing to abide by law and justice. If they don't, they won't get away with it! This wedding they're arranging – I'm going to give them notice to
160 call it off. Perhaps it's pointless even to mention it, no one thinks of weddings when news like this has just arrived. Still, I'll just knock at the door and call Daos out. He's the only one likely to pay any attention to me.

    [*As he approaches Chairestratos's house*, DAOS *emerges from it, talking back over his shoulder.*]

DAOS: You have every excuse for behaving like this. But in the circumstances, you must try and bear what has happened like reasonable human beings.

SMIKRINES: Ah, Daos, it's you I've come to see.

DAOS: Me?

SMIKRINES: Yes, certainly. I wish Kleostratos were still alive; he would have been the right man to deal with the treasure, and be the
170 lawful heir of all my property after my death.

DAOS: I wish it too. So?

SMIKRINES: Well, I'm the eldest of the family. I'm always being

insulted, and seeing my brother put me down. But I put up with
it.

DAOS [*drily*]: Very sensible of you.

SMIKRINES: Well, but look! He's not even reasonable. He treats me
like a family servant, or a bastard, arranging this marriage, giving
the girl to God knows who; no consultation, never a word to me,
though I'm her uncle as much as he is.

DAOS: Yes?

SMIKRINES: I see all that, and it makes me cross. He's not treating me   *180*
as a member of the family. Well, I'll do the same. I'll leave no
property of mine for them to get their hands on. I'll take the advice
of some of my friends, and marry the girl myself. That's more or
less, I think, Daos, what the law prescribes. So you should have
been thinking, too, how to do this properly. After all, you're
involved.⁵

DAOS: Smikrines, I think the old saying 'know yourself' enshrines a   *190*
profound truth. Let me stand by it. Anything that concerns an
honest servant, you can refer to me and question me about.

*One or two lines are missing, and the next five lines are damaged. Daos seems
to be explaining the limits of his knowledge and helpfulness.*

. . . any seals, contracts he made when abroad – all that I can tell
you. If so instructed, I can explain them one by one, giving place,
occasion, witness. But property, and marriage to an heiress, and   *200*
family, and differences of relationship – heavens, Smikrines, don't
ever involve Daos in that. You're free men, you deal with that
yourselves.

SMIKRINES: For heaven's sake! Do you think I'm doing anything
wrong?

DAOS: I come from Phrygia. Many things that you Athenians
approve of seem shocking to me – and vice versa. Why ask for *my*
opinion? Yours is naturally better than mine.

SMIKRINES: What in effect you're saying is, 'Don't involve me'.   *210*
I see. I'd better go down town and see if I can find one of
them [*nodding towards Chairestratos's house*] – if there's no one at
home?

DAOS: No, no one. [SMIKRINES *goes off, right.*] Really, Chance, what
a master you're giving me, after the one I had. What harm have *I*
done you?

[*Enter* COOK, *from Chairestratos's house, with assistants.*]

COOK: Every time I get a job, either somebody dies and I have to
shuffle off without my wages, or one of the daughters produces a

baby that no one knew about, and suddenly the party's over and I
have to be off. Fine luck I have!

220 DAOS: Oh, go away.

COOK: What do you think I'm doing? Here, boy, take the knives,
smartly now. After ten days without work, I landed this three-
drach job, and this time I thought I'd got the money. Now a corpse
arrives from Lycia and steals the lot. [*To boy*] You useless object! A
tragedy like this happens to a family, you see women crying and
beating their breasts – and still you leave with an empty flask.[6] Just
230 remember the chance you had. No Spark you, it's a Sea-Green
Incorruptible I've got, an honest assistant. I'll see you get no
dinner. The waiter [*looks round*] – perhaps he's waiting for the
funeral tea. [*He goes off, right.*]

WAITER [*entering from Chairestratos's house*]: If I don't get my wages,
I'll be cut up as much as you are.

DAOS: Go on!

*Four or five lines are missing or damaged. The waiter seems to be asking
Daos about his return from Lycia.*

DAOS: Absolutely!

WAITER: Then be damned to you, if that's what you did. You're
240 mad. You had your hands on all that gold and slaves, and you
brought it all back 'for Master'? Why didn't you run away? Where
d'you come from?

DAOS: From Phrygia.

WAITER: Then you're no good, you're a queer. Only Thracians are
real men. Getans – God, what heroes! That's why the gaols are full
of us.

DAOS: Take yourself off, away from our door. [WAITER *goes off, right.*]
There's another lot coming here, I see, all pretty drunk. Well,
[*addressing them as he goes into the house*] you're very sensible. You
never know, with luck. Enjoy yourselves while you can.

FIRST CHORAL INTERLUDE

ACT TWO

[*Enter* SMIKRINES *and* CHAIRESTRATOS, *right, with* CHAIREAS, *who remains in the background until the others leave the stage.*]

SMIKRINES: Well, what do you say to that, Chairestratos?   250

CHAIRESTRATOS: My good brother, first of all I've got to make arrangements for the funeral.

SMIKRINES: That's as good as done. Afterwards, don't promise the girl to *anyone*. That's not your business, it's mine. I'm older than you, and you've got a wife and daughter. I must now get the same.

CHAIRESTRATOS: Have you *no* sense of decency, Smikrines?

SMIKRINES: What do you mean?

CHAIRESTRATOS: A man of your age, proposing to marry a young girl.

SMIKRINES: *My* age?

CHAIRESTRATOS: I think you're very old.

SMIKRINES: Am I the only man to marry later in life?   260

CHAIRESTRATOS: For heaven's sake, Smikrines, show some human feeling. Chaireas here, who's engaged to marry the girl, has grown up with her. Listen! You'll not be the loser. All the property that Kleostratos left, take it, every bit of it. It'll be legally yours, a gift from us. But let the girl find a husband of her own age. I'll provide a substantial dowry from my own pocket.

SMIKRINES: God in heaven! Do you think you're talking to Simple Simon? You suggest I take the property and let him have the girl –   270
so that, if she has a child, I can be brought to court on a charge of keeping the child's property?[7]

CHAIRESTRATOS: You think we'd do that? Forget it!

SMIKRINES: Think? I *know*! You send Daos to me. I want a full inventory of the goods he brought.

CHAIRESTRATOS: What's the point of that? What on earth should I have done . . .[8]

Three lines are missing here. Smikrines probably persisted in his attitude, and went into his house.

CHAIRESTRATOS [*to* CHAIREAS]: I always intended that you should marry her, and that Kleostratos should marry my daughter, and   280

133

I'd leave my property between you. I hope I may depart this life soon, before I see what I never thought to see. [*He goes into his house.*]

CHAIREAS [*sighing*]: Oh, well. First of all, Kleostratos, it's perhaps proper to express my pity and sorrow for your sad fate: and then for my own. Not one of your family has suffered as I have. I didn't *choose* to fall in love with your sister, best-beloved of friends; I did nothing rash, or out of place, or wrong; I asked for her hand in proper form, from the uncle you made her guardian and from my mother who is looking after her. I thought I was a happy man, I really thought I'd reached the boundary of bliss. And now I can't even see her again. The law gives her to another, and judges my claim null and void.

DAOS [*entering from Chairestratos's house and speaking back over his shoulder*]: Chairestratos, this isn't right. Get up! You can't just lie there in despair. Chaireas, come and comfort him, don't let him give way. The future of us all may depend on him. No, open the door, Chairestratos, and make an appearance. Don't let your friends down. It's not like you to behave like this. [CHAIRESTRATOS *is helped out to a seat.*]

CHAIRESTRATOS: I'm in a bad way, Daos, my boy. All this has made me very depressed. I swear I'm not in my right mind, I'm practically demented. My precious brother is driving me distracted by his scandalous behaviour. He's going to marry the girl himself.

DAOS: Did you say *marry*? Can he?

CHAIRESTRATOS: So says our fine gentleman, even though I'm offering him all that the boy sent home.

DAOS: The devil!

CHAIRESTRATOS: Devil indeed. I'll end my life, by God I will, if I see it happen.

DAOS: So how's the devil to be out-manoeuvred? It won't be easy, not easy at all. But perhaps it can be done.

CHAIRESTRATOS: Perhaps. It's certainly worth the effort.

DAOS: I tell you, if a man once starts . . .

The next five lines are missing or mutilated, but in them Daos apparently began to suggest a plan to outwit Smikrines.

. . . Give him the hope of getting more than you offered – that'll bring him down full-tilt, all excited and all on the wrong tack.[9] You'll see! And then you'll easily deal with him. He only sees and thinks about what *he* wants. He'll be a poor judge of reality.

CHAIRESTRATOS: So what do you suggest? I'm ready to do anything you like.

DAOS: You must put on a great tragic act. What you said just now 330
must seem to be true – that you've fallen into a depression because of what's happened to young Kleostratos and to his promised bride, and because you see Chaireas, whom you've always thought of as your son, sunk in gloom. So you've fallen into one of these sudden afflictions. Grief is a very common cause of illness, and I'm well aware that you've got a bitter, melancholic side to you. Then we'll send for a doctor, who'll display his learning and 340
diagnose your trouble as pleurisy, or phrenitis, or one of these quick-killing diseases.

CHAIRESTRATOS: And then?

DAOS: Then you're suddenly dead. We shout, 'Chairestratos is gone', and weep and wail outside the door. *You*'re locked up inside. Then a dummy, wrapped up to look like your corpse, will lie in state –

CHAIRESTRATOS [*to* CHAIREAS]: Do you understand what he's getting at?

CHAIREAS: Heavens, no.

CHAIRESTRATOS: Me neither.

DAOS: Then *your* daughter becomes an heiress, just like the girl whose case is at issue. But there'll be this difference: your daughter will have a larger fortune than your niece. And old Greedy-for- 350
Gain stands in the same relationship to both girls –

CHAIRESTRATOS: Now I get it!

DAOS: You're thick if you don't. He'll promptly be delighted to give your niece, before any number of witnesses, to the first man who asks for her hand, and he'll take your daughter –

CHAIRESTRATOS [*grimly*]: He'll live to regret the idea.

DAOS: He'll organize the whole house, go his rounds with the keys, fix seals on doors, in a perfect daze of a dream of wealth.

CHAIRESTRATOS: And what about my 'corpse'?

DAOS: There it will lie, and we'll all sit round it and make sure he 360
doesn't come too close.

*The next ten lines are badly damaged, but enough remains to give some sort of
sense. Chairestratos is being promised the chance to get his own back.*

CHAIRESTRATOS: Your scheme's great, Daos, just what I need.

DAOS: Well, you couldn't get your own back on the old villain more satisfactorily.

CHAIRESTRATOS: I'll make him pay, I swear to God I will, and pay 370 dearly, for all the trouble he's ever caused me. It's true what they say, 'The wolf's jaws are open, but he'll go away hungry.'

DAOS: Action's what we need now. Chaireas, do you know any foreign doctor who'll see a joke?[10] A bit of a quack?

CHAIREAS: Not one.

DAOS [*crossly*]: Well, you should.

CHAIREAS: Suppose I go and get one of my friends? I'll bring a wig and a cloak and a stick for him, and he'll do his best to talk with a foreign accent.

DAOS: Right. But be quick about it. [CHAIREAS *goes off, right.*]

CHAIRESTRATOS: And what do I do?

DAOS: What we planned. Have a good death!

CHAIRESTRATOS: Right. Don't let anyone leave the house. Stand guard, and keep our secret.

DAOS: Who'll be in the plot?

CHAIRESTRATOS: Only my wife and the two girls. They'll have to be told, or they'll be in floods of real tears. Let the rest of the household insult me when they think I am dead.

DAOS: Right. [*To servants*] Take him in again. [*They do so.*] Our 'tragedy' is going to provide fine fun and excitement, if it once gets going, and if our 'doctor' performs with some conviction. [*He goes into the house.*]

SECOND CHORAL INTERLUDE

ACT THREE

SMIKRINES [*emerging from his house and speaking sarcastically*]: Daos has been really quick about coming to see me with the inventory of the goods. Great consideration he's shown for me! Daos is on *their* side. Well, fine. He's done me a favour, for he's provided me with a most welcome excuse to scrutinize the list without any feelings of altruism, but looking only to my own interests. I'm sure there's as much again that he's not declaring. *I* know the ways of this tricky customer.

DAOS [*emerging from Chairestratos's house, and pretending not to see* SMIKRINES]: Oh, God! A really dreadful thing has happened. I'd never have believed a man could succumb so suddenly to such 400 an illness. It's as if a violent hurricane had struck the house.

SMIKRINES: What on earth is he talking about?

Five lines are missing or seriously damaged. Daos is striking tragic attitudes and uttering tragic quotations.

DAOS: 'No man alive e'er prospers over all.'[11] Again, marvellously true. Dear God, this is an unexpected and grievous blow. [*He moves rapidly right.*]

SMIKRINES: Daos, you devil, where are you going at such a trot?

DAOS [*ignoring him*]: Then there's this one: 'Man's life's not Provi- 410 dence, but Chance.'[12] How true. 'God plants guilt-sense in mortal men, when he will blight a house to all eternity.'[13] Aeschylus, of noble sentiments the –

SMIKRINES: 'Full of wise saws' – you miserable rubbish?

DAOS [*still ignoring him*]: 'Incredible, irrational, dire.'[14]

SMIKRINES: Will he never stop?

DAOS: [*finally condescending to see* SMIKRINES, *but continuing in tragic vein*]: 'Is there aught in mortal suffering that's past belief?' That's what Karkinos says.[15] 'For in one day can God bring happiness to misery.' Great truths, all of these, Smikrines.

SMIKRINES: What *are* you talking about?

DAOS: Your brother – O God, how can I tell you? – is near to 420 death.

SMIKRINES: But he was talking to me just now! What happened?

137

DAOS: Bile, grief, a mental spasm, choking.

SMIKRINES: God, how awful!

DAOS: 'There is no word so dread to tell, no suffering'[16] –

SMIKRINES: You're wearing me out.

DAOS: 'For tragedy, so God ordained, should strike unseen' – one's from Euripides, the other from Chairemon, not exactly your everyday poets.

SMIKRINES: Has a doctor seen him?

DAOS: No, Chaireas has just gone to get one.

SMIKRINES: Which one?

    [*Enter* CHAIREAS, *right, with the* 'DOCTOR' *and his attendants.*]

430   DAOS [*pointing*]: This one, apparently. [*To* DOCTOR] Dear sir, do hurry.

DOCTOR: I am hurrying.[17]

DAOS: 'The sick are helpless, and so hard to please.'[18]

    [*All but* SMIKRINES *go into Chairestratos's house.*]

SMIKRINES: If they see me, they'll say I've come at once because I'm pleased, I'm sure of that. And *he* won't want to see me either. But it would be odd if I didn't even ask . . .

Sixteen lines or so are missing, during which the Doctor and his attendants obviously emerged from the house, to report on Chairestratos's condition to Smikrines. The next thirty lines are damaged, but enough remains to give the general sense, and to show that the Doctor, like most Greek doctors, was (in his case, pretending to be) a Dorian Greek and, like most doctors in Comedy, speaking in stage Doric, the ancient equivalent of stage Scots. Roll the 'r's and broaden the vowels.

440   DOCTOR: . . . his bile . . . because of his present weakness.

SMIKRINES: I quite understand.

DOCTOR: His brain, in my opeenion, is inflamed. 'Phrenitis' we doctors ca' it.

SMIKRINES: I see. And the prognosis? Is there no hope at all of recovery?

DOCTOR: I maunna offer ye fause comfort. Sic' maladies are mortal.

SMIKRINES: No, no comfort, just the truth.

450   DOCTOR: He canna leeve at a', I tell ye. He's bringin' up bile, his sight's failin', he's foamin' at the mouth, he looks set for burial.

SMIKRINES: How awful![19]

DOCTOR [*to attendant*]: On oor way, lad. [*They move right.*]

SMIKRINES: Hey, you!

DOCTOR: Me?

SMIKRINES: Yes, you. Come over here, away from the door.

DOCTOR [*looking closely at* SMIKRINES]: Ye'll no' be long for this
world.

SMIKRINES: Rubbish! You should pray for a constitution like mine.
There are plenty of non-fatal diseases.

DOCTOR: Aye, laugh. But I ken ma ain trade, an' I think ye're no a   460
weel man. There's a consumption on ye, ye look just like death.
[*He goes off right, with attendant.*]

SMIKRINES: I suppose the women are looting in there, like soldiers
sacking an enemy city. Communication with the neighbours will
be by the water-channels.[20]

[*Enter* DAOS, *from Chairestratos's house.*]

DAOS [*aside*]: I'll stir him up! As I was doing . . .

*The rest of the act is lost, some two hundred lines of it. Daos clearly intends to
tease Smikrines, and Smikrines presumably decided to marry Chairestratos's
daughter instead of Kleostratos's sister — this being the object of the plot
outlined at the end of Act Two. There would then be the choral interlude.*

[THIRD CHORAL INTERLUDE]

ACT FOUR

Very little of this act remains, and what does is badly damaged. Smikrines seems to be agreeing to the betrothal of Kleostratos's sister to another – presumbly Chaireas. They leave the stage.

[*Enter* KLEOSTRATOS, *left* [21]]

491 KLEOSTRATOS: Beloved land! I thank heaven for my return. Here I am, looking at what I longed for. And if Daos got clear, then I'd rank myself the happiest of men. I must knock at the door. [*He does so.*]

DAOS [*inside*]: Who's there?

KLEOSTRATOS: Me.

500 DAOS [*inside*]: Who do you want? The master of the house is recently dead.

KLEOSTRATOS: *Dead?* How dreadful.

DAOS [*inside*]: You shouldn't be disturbing a house in mourning.

KLEOSTRATOS: My poor uncle. Open the door, fellow.

DAOS [*opening door*]: Go away, young man. [*As he recognizes him*] God in heaven, it's my master.

KLEOSTRATOS: What's this story, Daos?

DAOS: Let me touch you! [*They embrace, and go together into Kleostratos's house, where all will be revealed.*] At some point there would be the next choral interlude.

[FOURTH CHORAL INTERLUDE]

ACT FIVE

This is even more badly damaged. The ends of some twenty-nine lines only survive, and they suggest that someone – Daos? – is relating the betrothal of the two girls to the two young men; that perhaps the Cook is summoned back to prepare the wedding-feast; and that Daos and the Cook may have conspired to punish Smikrines, as similar characters do at the end of Old Cantankerous. *Certainty is impossible, but it can be safely assumed that, somehow, the Jacks got their Jills, and that Smikrines got his deserts.*

Five fragments of this play have come to us from other sources. None can be placed in the text with any certainty, and three of the quotations are of single words, and one of three words only. But one is worth quoting, from Stobaeus, Eclogues, *4, 8, 7. It is clearly occasioned by Smikrines' behaviour, and refers to political assassination, but the precise occasion and reference are beyond recovery.*

Fragment 1

O thrice unhappy men, what advantage do they have over others? What a wretched life they live, who guard the forts or hold the citadel! If they suspect that everyone can approach them so easily, dagger in hand, what a price they pay!

The Sikyonian[1]

[Sikyonios]

Introductory Note to *The Sikyonian*

Unlike *The Shield*, this play is much better preserved in Acts Four and Five than in Acts One to Three. The remains of the papyrus, used in the making of three separate mummy cases, came to light over a period of more than fifty years.[2]

Some of the details of the plot are obscure, and some of the names uncertain, but the general line is clear, and displays a variation on the standard theme of lost and later recognized children – here *both* hero and heroine have to be recognized as true-born Athenians before they can come together in marriage. Moschion (a name whose owner seems doomed to unsuitable, difficult or unsuccessful love – see Introduction pp. 12–13) is here found to be the hero's brother, and relinquishes the girl to him.

CHARACTERS

A GOD, *who speaks the Prologue*

STRATOPHANES, *a captain of mercenaries*

SMIKRINES, *an Athenian citizen, who proves to be Stratophanes' father*

MOSCHION, *Smikrines' son*

THERON, *a parasite[3] attached to Stratophanes*

PYRRHIAS, *Stratophanes' servant*

DONAX, *another servant*

MALTHAKE, *Stratophanes' mistress*

KICHESIAS, *an Athenian citizen*

PHILOUMENE, *his daughter, kidnapped in childhood*

DROMON, *Kichesias's servant, kidnapped with Philoumene*

BLEPES, *an Athenian democrat*

ACT ONE[4]

SCENE: *probably Eleusis, a town fourteen miles from Athens, and the centre of the Mysteries (secret rites) and the worship of Demeter. Two houses are required, for the home of Smikrines and the lodging of Stratophanes.*

A GOD: . . . his daughter, I say. And when they [the pirates] had all three persons in their power, they decided it wasn't worth their while to take the old lady, but they carried off the young girl and a servant to Mylasa, a town in Caria,[5] and there they put them up for sale in the market. The servant sat there with an arm round his young mistress. Up came an army officer[6] and asked the price. He was told, agreed, and bought them. Another man, a local character 10 who was up for sale at the same time and was sitting near the servant, said to him, 'Cheer up, mate. The man who's bought you is the Sikyonian, a very gallant captain, and rich, too.'

There follow five badly damaged lines, and a gap of some thirty lines, then five more mutilated lines, of which the last looks like the closing form·la of the Prologue.

You'll see in due course if you like – and please do like.[7]   24

Then line endings and beginnings, with gaps, indicate a conversation in which one speaker is a woman. There is mention of someone, presumably a parasite, who is a hearty eater; there is an indication of a plot to put up a false witness, perhaps to claim that a girl (?Philoumene) is free-born; and a reasonable inference can be made that Moschion heard or overheard from Dromon that Philoumene was a free-born Athenian and that Dromon planned to take her off and seek refuge at an altar, because her master had fallen in love with her. Then the text resumes. Stratophanes and Theron are in conversation. Theron is, like a true parasite, agreeing enthusiastically with his patron, who seems to be intent on preserving some property.

STRATOPHANES: Surely that's not –

THERON: Who?

STRATOPHANES: Pyrrhias. I sent him home to say we were safely 120 back, and would soon be there.

THERON: Yes, I know.

147

STRATOPHANES: So why on earth is he coming back here, and at top speed, too?

THERON: Very down in the mouth, too.

STRATOPHANES [*as* PYRRHIAS *comes in, right*]: Is anything wrong, Pyrrhias? My mother –

PYRRHIAS: Your mother's dead. Died last year.

STRATOPHANES: Oh, I'm *very* sorry. She was a great age. So she's gone.

PYRRHIAS: But you're going to be involved in some peculiar business that you didn't expect, Stratophanes. It seems that you were not her son.

STRATOPHANES [*bewildered*]: Then whose son am I?

130 PYRRHIAS: When she was dying, she wrote down your family history here. [*He produces a package.*]

THERON [*sententiously*]: On your death-bed, never grudge a favour to those who go on living. She wanted you to know about your family.

PYRRHIAS: There's more to it than that. When your father was alive, he apparently lost a case brought by some Boeotian –

STRATOPHANES: Yes, I know.

PYRRHIAS: And, given the treaty arrangements,[8] he was liable to pay a large sum of money.

STRATOPHANES: A letter about all this reached me in Caria. It also told me of my father's death.

PYRRHIAS: Your mother discovered from the lawyers that you and your inheritance were liable for this debt, so she took steps to

140 provide for you, and on her death-bed tried to restore you to your family. All very proper.

STRATOPHANES: Give me the papers.

PYRRHIAS: There. Apart from the written evidence there, I have tokens to prove your identity. The people who gave them to me said that before your mother died, she said they'd do that.

THERON: Lady of Athens, make him your own,[9] so that he can have his girl – and I can have Malthake!

STRATOPHANES: On your way, both of you. This way, Theron.

THERON: Aren't you going to tell me –

STRATOPHANES: No more talking. Forward march.

THERON: Oh well, if I must, I –

STRATOPHANES: You too, Pyrrhias, this way. You can bring the supporting evidence for my statement, and produce it immediately anyone wants to inspect it. [*They go off, right.*]

CHORAL INTERLUDE[10]

ACT FOUR

[*Enter (probably)* SMIKRINES *and* BLEPES.]

SMIKRINES: You're a common nuisance, a gasbag, a real pain, if you   *150*
  expect a man who weeps and pleads to be speaking the truth.
  Nowadays, such behaviour is a pretty fair indication that someone's up to no good. That's no way to establish truth: much better
  to use a small committee.

BLEPES: You're a real dyed-in-the-wool old élitist, Smikrines, by
  God you are.

SMIKRINES: You and your kind'll be the death of me. Why all the
  abuse?

BLEPES: I hate you and all your supercilious friends. Of *course* I'm a   *160*
  nuisance, but I might be of some use . . .

SMIKRINES: Never!

BLEPES: Oh, yes, I could.

*He proceeds, in five damaged lines, to make wild charges of theft against
Smikrines.*

SMIKRINES: Get lost!

BLEPES: You too. [*He moves away.*]

SMIKRINES: You're right to retreat. I'd have made you button your
  lip, just like an immigrant.[11] [*He moves towards his house.*]

BLEPES [*returning*]: Sir, wait – just there in the porch.

SMIKRINES: I'm waiting. Why the shout?   *170*

BLEPES: I want to give you a small hint –

SMIKRINES: I'm listening.

BLEPES: It'll be worth your while –

SMIKRINES: Tell me all.

BLEPES [*aping the delivery of a messenger in tragedy*[12]]: I happened to be
  on my way, not from the country, no indeed . . . when someone
  kindly told me about a debate. I thrive on other people's troubles –
  I'm a terror on a jury – so off I went, loudly greeting anyone I met,   *180*
  for I'm a democrat, part of the backbone of the country. Well, I'd
  just come back from Athens to meet the village man who'd got the
  job of sharing out a skinny little bullock[13] (and of being cursed by
  those who got a piece – I was one of them). I take my name from
  the sacred township – I'm Blepes the Eleusinian.[14]

I stopped when I saw a crowd at the Temple gate. 'Excuse me', I said, and got a place in the ring. Then I saw a girl sitting as a sup-
190 pliant. An assembly was convened right away to consider her case . . .

Seven or eight lines are missing, and the next three are damaged, but it is clear from what follows that Blepes is recounting how Dromon spoke on the girl's behalf, explaining that she was the daughter of an Athenian citizen, but had lost her family.

'. . . her present guardian is threatening her safety, and I too take my suppliant seat among you.' He did so, and we all roared out, 'The girl's an Athenian,' and it was difficult to quell the uproar and
200 restore silence. Then a young lad, pale-faced and smooth-chinned, went up to the servant and tried to whisper something to him. We refused to have this. 'Speak up!' someone promptly shouted, and 'What's *he* want? Who *is* he? What are you saying?' 'The servant here knows me,' he replied, 'in fact, I've been helping him for some time. I'm just asking him if he needs anything. I heard most of the story when he was talking just now to his master.' Then, blushing scarlet, he stepped back a bit. He wasn't utterly beyond redemption, but we didn't like him one bit; we thought he was out
210 to get the girl. We shouted . . .

The next twenty-one lines are damaged, but enough remains to give the general sense, as follows:

One of our people looked at the girl and spoke at some length to those beside him. Then a fine, upstanding man came forward, and two others with him. When he saw the girl at close quarters, he
220 suddenly let fall a river of tears, and with a passionate cry clutched at his hair. This astonished the onlookers, who said, 'What's up with *you*? Tell us, tell us.' And he said, 'Bless you, gentlemen, I've brought up this girl from childhood, and I hope to restore her to her father.

The text now resumes.

'This servant belonged to her father and is now mine, but I give him to the girl, I renounce any return for my expense in rearing her, I make no claims of any kind. Let her look for her father and her family, I'll place no obstacles in her way.' 'Good man!,' we said.
240 Then, 'Listen to my proposal, gentlemen,' he said. 'You are now her guardians, she has nothing to fear, at least from me. Take her to the priestess and let her look after the girl for you."

This suggestion naturally attracted much approval. 'Very proper,' everyone shouted, and 'tell us more.' And he said, 'I used to think that I was a Sikyonian. But this servant here [*indicating* PYRRHIAS] has just brought me my mother's will, and tokens of my birth. If I can trust the evidence of these documents, I think that I, like you, am an Athenian citizen. Don't rob me of this hope yet. If I can prove that I am a fellow-citizen of the girl whom I've brought safely back to her father, let me ask him for her hand in marriage, and make her my wife. And don't let any of my rivals take charge of the girl before her father appears.' 'Quite right', 'that's reasonable', 'certainly', came the cries, and, 'Take her to the priestess, take her now.'

Then the pale-faced chap suddenly jumped up and said, 'Are you asking me to believe that this man has suddenly now got hold of a will from somewhere, and that he's an Athenian citizen, and that when he gets the girl by means of this melodrama he'll let her go?' Then there was confused shouting – 'Kill the pansy!' 'By God you won't: stuff you, whoever you are!' 'No? On your way, poofter.' 'And damn the lot of you.' Then the soldier said to the girl, 'Come on, get up, you can go now.' 'She'll go,' said the servant, 'when you gentlemen tell her to. *You* tell her,' he said. 'Yes,' we said, 'you can go now.' She got up and went.

That's all I saw. What happened afterwards, I couldn't tell you, for I came away. [SMIKRINES *goes into his house, and* BLEPES *leaves, left.*]

[*Enter* STRATOPHANES *and (probably)* THERON, *pursued by* MOSCHION, *right.*]

MOSCHION: Kidnappers! I arrest you[15] –

STRATOPHANES: Arrest us? You?

MOSCHION: Indeed I do.

STRATOPHANES: You're out of your mind, lad.

MOSCHION: You've emerged very suddenly as an Athenian citizen. [*Ironically*] That's great! It's not possible . . .[16]

STRATOPHANES: How? I know of no such thing.

MOSCHION: You see? Quick march to the judicial inquiry.

Some twenty lines are missing here. Moschion probably went into the house to fetch SMIKRINES, *who was joined by his wife. It is not clear which of them is speaking as the (damaged) text resumes.*

?SMIKRINES' WIFE: . . . one half of a woman's dress was wrapped round you when I sent you off to the foreign woman, who was then anxious to have children.

The next passage is too mutilated for continuous translation, but it is clear from the surviving words that Stratophanes is recognized as Smikrines' son, by the robe in which he had been wrapped as a child.

STRATOPHANES: Then – Moschion is my brother, Father?

310 SMIKRINES: Yes. Come this way, we'll find him waiting for us in the house. [*They all go into Smikrines' house.*]

FOURTH CHORAL INTERLUDE

ACT FIVE

The beginning of the act is mutilated or missing, but from the words that remain, from the rest of the scene, and from a comparison with Plautus's Poenulus, ll. 1087–1119, it is possible to conjecture that Theron was trying to bribe an elderly and poor Athenian to pretend to be Kichesias, and to claim that Philoumene is his daughter and so a free Athenian girl. But, unknown to Theron, the old man actually is Kichesias, and Philoumene is his daughter. This situation produces splendidly double-edged dialogue, with Kichesias meaning one thing and Theron understanding another, while the audience appreciates both. It is typical of Menander's dramatic economy that he uses this entertaining scene to demonstrate, too, the characters of the speakers, and of his irony that Kichesias really is Kichesias and Philoumene's father.

KICHESIAS: You go to hell!

THERON: You *are* being difficult.

KICHESIAS: Damn you, go away. Did you really think that Kichesias would do such a thing, or take a bribe from anyone? It's disgraceful, it's immoral! *Kichesias?*

THERON: That's right, Kichesias Skambonides.[17] Good. You've got   350
it, then. Take your pay for this, then, and not what I mentioned earlier.

KICHESIAS [*bewildered*]: For what?

THERON: For being Kichesias Skambonides. Your suggestion is much better. You seem to have grasped the general idea. *You* become *him.* Fortunately, you're short and snub-nosed, as the servant described him.

KICHESIAS [*sadly*]: I have become the old man that I am.

THERON: Then say that you lost your daughter from Halai when she was four years old, along with Dromon, a servant.

KICHESIAS [*sadly*]: Yes, I did.

THERON: Good!

KICHESIAS: She was kidnapped by pirates. You have reminded me of sorrow and suffering, and of my poor child.

THERON: Splendid! Just go on like that, and shed a tear or two.   360
    [*Aside*] He's a great chap!
        [*Enter* DROMON, *left, talking to himself.*]

153

DROMON: Well, my young mistress is in safe keeping . . . [*Sees* KICHESIAS] Oh, sir!

A few lines are missing.

She's alive, and she's here in Athens. [KICHESIAS *faints*] Don't faint, sir. Get up! Theron, water, water, quick!

THERON: I'll run and get it, sure. And Stratophanes is inside, I'll send him out to you.

DROMON [*as* KICHESIAS *begins to revive*]: The water won't be necessary now.

THERON: Still, I'll go and get Stratophanes. [*He goes into the house.*]

DROMON: He's coming round. Kichesias!

KICHESIAS: What's wrong? Where am I? And *what* did I hear some- one say?

370   DROMON: Your daughter's safe and well.

KICHESIAS: Really safe, Dromon, or just – alive?

DROMON: She's still a virgin, no man has laid a hand on her.

KICHESIAS: Thank God!

DROMON: And you, sir?

KICHESIAS: I'm alive, Dromon, I can say that much. Beyond that, when you see a poor, lonely old man, you have to believe he's in a pretty bad way.

    [*Enter* STRATOPHANES, *from Smikrines' house, talking back over his shoulder.*]

STRATOPHANES: I'll be right back, Mother, when I've looked into this.

DROMON: Stratophanes, this is Philoumene's *father*!

STRATOPHANES: Who is?

DROMON: This gentleman here.

STRATOPHANES: How do you do, sir.

DROMON [*to* KICHESIAS]: This is the man who's kept your daughter safe.

380   KICHESIAS: Blessings on him.

STRATOPHANES: With your consent, sir, I shall be blessed, and happy too.

DROMON: Stratophanes, let's go and get Philoumene *now*, for heaven's sake.[18]

STRATOPHANES: You go on. I'll be right behind you, when I've had a word with the people in the house.

DROMON: Come on, Kichesias. [*They go off, left.*]

STRATOPHANES: Donax! Hey, Donax! Go and tell Malthake to transfer all my gear to the house next door – suitcases, rucksacks,

all the baskets and trunks . . . And tell her to come over here herself *390*
to my mother. The foreign slaves and Theron and the donkey-
drivers and the donkeys can all stay there with you. These are my
orders. I'll settle everything else myself with Philoumene's father
. . .[19] [*He goes off, left, as* MOSCHION *enters from Smikrines' house.*]

MOSCHION [*gloomily*]: As things stand now, Moschion, you mustn't
even *look* at the girl again. She's gloriously fair, Moschion, and
she's got lovely eyes – you're wasting your time, she's going to be *400*
your brother's bride, the lucky man. For just think – still at it, you
fool? . . . Well, I won't say it. I'll obviously have to be Best Man,
one of a trio with them. [*Despairingly, to audience*] Ladies and
gentlemen, I won't be able . . .

*The end of the play is lost. A few surviving half-lines have a reference
to a torch and garlands, clearly for a wedding – perhaps Theron's to
Malthake. Then a standard formula concludes the drama, though it is not
clear who speaks it.*

ACTOR: Speed our play with loud applause! And may laughter- *421*
loving Victory, daughter of a noble line, smile upon us all our
days.

*A few more short fragments of the play are preserved in quotations by other
authors, but they cannot convincingly be assigned to any particular scene.*

The Man She Hated

[Misoumenos]

Introductory Note to *The Man She Hated*

This play, about a professional soldier who acquires a girl by conquest, falls in love with her and is, until the last minute, refused by her as lover and husband, was very popular in antiquity. Eleven[1] pieces of papyrus, dating from the third to the sixth century A.D., preserve fragments of it. These fragments do not always connect, and some of the details of the plot remain obscure. The girl is found by her father, and freed; the soldier finally marries her; there is some lively and economical writing, and some interesting characterization which produces an interesting situation. But difficulties remain. The setting of the play is not clear, it may or may not be Athens; Demeas has come from Cyprus, where Thrasonides has recently been fighting, and where presumably both Krateia and the spoils were acquired. Among these spoils is a sword which she recognizes as her family property, and which causes the trouble, because the conclusion she naturally draws is that Thrasonides has killed its owner. Demeas too recognizes the sword, but whether (and if so, how) it had been given to his son, and whether Kleinias is that son, cannot be determined. It is possible to construct a scenario, but for the moment any such scenario can only be rated as 'possible'.

CHARACTERS

THRASONIDES, *a professional soldier*
GETAS, *his servant*
KRATEIA, *a girl, his captive*
DEMEAS, *her father*
KLEINIAS, *Thrasonides' neighbour*
AN OLD WOMAN, *Kleinias's servant*
KRATEIA'S NURSE
A COOK

The last two characters do not speak in the extant fragments.

ACT ONE

SCENE: *a street in a city, possibly Athens. There are two houses, one belonging to Thrasonides, the other to Kleinias.*

[*Enter* THRASONIDES, *from his house.*]

THRASONIDES: O Night, you are the god with the greatest share of love; at night most words of love are spoken, most lovers' cares conceived. Have you ever seen a man more miserable, a lover more star-crossed? Here stand I, at my own front door, and I pace up and down in this narrow street, although it's almost midnight, and I could be in bed and in possession of the girl I love. For she's in my house, and I have the right, and I want this as passionately as any raving lover – and I don't do it. I prefer to stand outside, in the winter air, shivering with cold and talking to the night!   A10

GETAS [*emerging from the house*]: God! This weather's not fit for the proverbial dog to be out in. But as if it were midsummer, my master's strolling up and down, debating like a philosopher. Look at him! He'll be the death of me. I'm not made of solid oak . . . [*To* THRASONIDES] Poor man, why aren't you in bed and asleep? [*He falls in behind him.*] You're wearing me out, walking up and down. Are you sleep-walking? If you're awake, wait for me!   A20

THRASONIDES: Have you come out to see what I'm doing? Did someone tell you to do this – I certainly didn't – or is this your own idea?

GETAS: Well, I certainly had no instructions, they're all sound asleep in there.

THRASONIDES: Getas, I think you're here to look after me!

GETAS: Come in now, do, dear sir.

THRASONIDES: You're always a good *aide-de-camp*.

GETAS: And *you're* shaking like a leaf . . . I[2] haven't had a chance to talk to you yet. You only got back home yesterday after a long absence.   A30

THRASONIDES: Well, when I set sail from headquarters, I was pretty stout-hearted. My assignment was to act as escort to the spoils, a mere dogsbody.

GETAS: So what's upsetting you now?

THRASONIDES: I've been grievously insulted.

GETAS: Who by?

THRASONIDES: By the girl-prisoner. I bought her, treated her like a free girl, as the lady of the house; gave her maids, gold trinkets, dresses; thought of her as my wife.

A40

GETAS: Then what? How are you being insulted?

THRASONIDES: I'm ashamed to talk about it. Things have gone all wrong.

GETAS: Still, tell me.

THRASONIDES: She hates me like poison.

GETAS: She's the Magnetic Stone . . .

THRASONIDES: No need for such an idea. It's quite normal and human.

GETAS: Even if she were her own mistress . . .

There is a gap in the text.

A50 THRASONIDES: I wait for the right moment,[3] for a real rainstorm at night, thunder and lightning, and I'm in bed with her.

GETAS: Then what?

THRASONIDES: Then I call out. 'My girl,' I say, 'I must go out at once to see a man.' 'What did you say his name was?' – that's what any woman would say – and 'Poor dear, in all this rain? Do wait a bit.'

Some twenty lines are missing or mutilated.

THRASONIDES: She's the one. Give me your heart, darling. If you neglect me, you'll make me jealous, distressed, a raving lunatic.

GETAS: You poor unfortunate man.

THRASONIDES: If she'd only call me 'darling', I'd make offerings to all the gods of heaven.

A90 GETAS: What on earth can have gone wrong? It's not even as if you were particularly disagreeable – not enough to speak of. Of course, you don't get much pay as a soldier, that's a drawback. But your face is very refined. Still –

THRASONIDES: Damn you! We must find out what the trouble is, demonstrate some necessary cause.

GETAS: Well, sir, women are a rotten lot.

There is a gap in the text.

GETAS: From what you say, sir, she . . . sucks up to you . . . hasn't

A100 she always got some plausible excuse?

The rest of the act is lost. Some minute fragments of the play, cited by later authors, supply the information that Thrasonides' boasting of his exploits had turned Krateia against him; that he asks for a sword (presumably to kill himself) and is refused it; that his recent soldiering has been in Cyprus; and that all the swords in the house have been collected and put safely out of sight in (as appears from l. 178) Kleinias's house. There would have been a choral interlude.

[FIRST CHORAL INTERLUDE]

ACT TWO

Some ninety very fragmentary lines remain of this act. There are indications of a conversation between Thrasonides and Getas, and of another between (possibly) the Old Woman and a 'stranger' who is presumably Demeas. He had come to the city for some purpose not connected with his daughter, but in the course of this conversation he discovers that a girl called Krateia is living next door. He apparently asks his interlocutor to get the girl out into the street, so that he can see if she is his daughter. Then there would have been the next choral interlude.

[SECOND CHORAL INTERLUDE]

164

ACT THREE

The act starts with a conversation between two people, possibly servants, one of whom may be Krateia's Nurse.

— . . . suppliant. Saying what?
— Oh dear, are you going to fight with me?
— Not at all, but . . . he's living a terribly miserable life.
— Oh?
— Why, when he was happy and envied – for that's what he was – why did she stop him?
— She knows her own business best.

Then, after two badly damaged lines:

— What's this? Whoever is it? This whispering's from a certain person, I'm sure. Off with you!   *140*

The next eighteen lines offer only scattered words. A ring is mentioned, and clothing, beating the ground, a libation to be made, suppliants, and a hope for heaven's favour. Someone finally says 'Let's go' and the stage is left empty for a soliloquy by (probably) Getas. The text is damaged, and some of the translation can be only approximate.

GETAS: . . . I left. A man sang, a fat-faced pig of a man . . . to watch   *160*
the woman from outside . . . is he . . . once the other one sang . . . well, heavens above, as the proverb goes, 'perfectly right and proper' for a man who's drinking to sing. [*Apostrophizing the singer*] You make good listening, you that's come to visit. But why are you still twisting and turning as you offer your contributions,[4] if you're not intending some harm to us? Nonsense! Shall I tell   *170*
Master to invite him back to dinner? For it's quite clear . . . I'll go now . . . and try to discover something of what's being said and done. [*He goes into Thrasonides' house.*]

OLD WOMAN [*entering from Kleinias's house*]: I never *saw* such a peculiar visitor, I really didn't. Honestly, what *is* he up to? When he caught sight of our neighbour's swords in our house, he told us to bring them out, and he spent ages examining them.   *180*

Several badly damaged lines follow, in the course of which Demeas emerges from Kleinias's house and asks where the owner of the swords lives.

165

DEMEAS: . . . knock at the door, please.

OLD WOMAN: Knock yourself. Why bother me? I'm off. I've shown you the house. Call him out and talk to him yourself.

DEMEAS: It's awkward. I recognize this sword as my own.

OLD WOMAN: Knock at the door.

Some ten mutilated lines follow, including the statement 'I've just had this thought' and then Demeas advances to Thrasonides' door.

DEMEAS [*knocking*]: Door! Door! Oh, I'll just move back here. [*He moves away.*] The door's opening, someone's coming out.

[*Enter* KRATEIA *and* NURSE, *from Thrasonides' house.*]

KRATEIA: I couldn't have put up with that a moment longer! . . .

210 DEMEAS: O God, what vision is this? The thought never entered my head . . .

[NURSE *whispers to* KRATEIA *and indicates* DEMEAS.]

KRATEIA: What do you mean, Nurse? Whatever are you telling me? My *father*? Where?

DEMEAS: Krateia, my child!

KRATEIA: Who's calling me? Daddy! Oh, Daddy darling, how marvellous!

[*She runs to him and they embrace.*]

DEMEAS: I've found you, my child.

KRATEIA: I've longed for you, and here you are. I thought I'd never see you again.

GETAS [*emerging from the house*]: She came outside. Heavens, what's this? What are you doing with her, fellow? Yes, you – what are you doing? I knew it! Caught in the act, this is the chap I've been looking for. Got you! He looks old, grey-haired and sixtyish, but

220 he'll still live to regret it. Hey, you, who do you think you're hugging and kissing?

KRATEIA: It's my *father*, Getas.

GETAS: A likely story! [*To* DEMEAS] Who are you? Where've you come from?

DEMEAS: I've come from . . . and I *am* her father.[5]

GETAS: Is he really your father, Krateia?

KRATEIA: Yes, he really is.

GETAS: Well! And this is your master, old Nurse? Have you come from home, sir?

DEMEAS: I wish I had.

230 GETAS: You are in fact away from home?

DEMEAS: I've come from Cyprus. And here I see my daughter, my most precious possession. Others of my household have clearly been scattered in different directions by War, the common enemy.

GETAS: That's life. That's how your daughter was taken prisoner and came to us. But I'll run and get Master for you.

DEMEAS: Do that.

[GETAS *goes off, right.*]

Six badly damaged lines seem to indicate a conversation about the possible fate of Demeas's son, whose sword he had recognized among those from Thrasonides' house.

?KRATEIA: If he's no longer alive, where does the story come from?

DEMEAS: My life is done.

KRATEIA: And what a bitter fate is mine. This is tragic, Father dear. He is dead.

DEMEAS: And dead at the hands of the last man who should have killed him.[6]

KRATEIA: You know who it was?   250

DEMEAS: I do.

KRATEIA: I was taken prisoner. I'm a servant now . . .

DEMEAS: Why, Krateia . . .

KRATEIA: The man who did this . . . But, Father . . . we must work out a plan . . . I've lived as I had to . . .

DEMEAS: How strange and sad is human life. [*They go into Thrasonides' house, as* THRASONIDES *and* GETAS *enter, right.*]

THRASONIDES: Krateia's *father* has arrived, you say. Now you will make me the happiest or most miserable of mortal men. For if he 260
won't approve of me and give her to me in lawful marriage, that's the end of Thrasonides. I hope not. But let's go in. No more guessing, we've got to *know*. I shrink and shake as I go in. My heart is prophesying some disaster, Getas. I'm frightened. But better get it settled once and for all, no more guesswork. The whole thing is very remarkable.

[*They go into the house, as* KLEINIAS *enters, right, with* COOK.]

KLEINIAS: Our visitor, that's one, Cook, and I make two, and the 270
third is a woman belonging to me (if she's actually arrived: for I'm in agony too). Otherwise, only the visitor. For I'll be running round the city, looking everywhere for her. Come on in, Cook. Quick action, concentrate on that. [*They go into Kleinias's house.*]

THIRD CHORAL INTERLUDE

ACT FOUR

[*Enter* KLEINIAS *from his house, talking back over his shoulder.*]

KLEINIAS: What's that? He recognized the sword, you say, the one left in our house, and went off to the neighbours when he heard it belonged to them? When did they bring it here? Why to us, woman? . . . There's the door. Someone's coming. I'll get the whole story properly now.

[*Enter* GETAS, *from Thrasonides' house, grumbling to himself. He ignores* KLEINIAS, *and walks agitatedly up and down.*]

GETAS: God Almighty, the heartlessness of these two! Extraordinary! Inhuman too, it really is.

KLEINIAS: Has our visitor recently called at your house, Getas?

GETAS: God, what a nerve! . . . to marry her . . .⁷

KLEINIAS: Am I to understand . . .?

GETAS: He says . . .

KLEINIAS: Is Demeas . . . ?

GETAS: . . . not a bit . . . 'For, as you see, Demeas,' says the Master, . . . 'and you're her father and legal guardian.' That's what he says, tears in his eyes as he pleads. [*Sardonically*] Might as well play a harp to a donkey.

KLEINIAS: I'll fall into step with him, I think. [*He does so.*]

GETAS: The only answer he gets is this: 'I want my daughter from you, I've come to ransom her, I'm her father.' 'And *I'*m asking permission,' [says Master,] 'to marry her, now that I've met you, Demeas.'

KLEINIAS: Our friend clearly *has* gone visiting. He's talking about 'Demeas'.

GETAS: For heaven's sake, could he not take what's happened like a rational human being? No: wild boar on the mountain, as they say. But that's not the real trouble. *She* looked away again as he said, 'Please, Krateia, don't leave me. You were a virgin when I took you prisoner, I had the name of being your first lover; I loved, I *do* love you, I adore you, Krateia darling. What have I done to offend you? I'll die if you leave me, and then you'll know.' She didn't even answer him.

KLEINIAS: What on earth's the matter?

GETAS: She's uncivilized, a she-lion . . .

KLEINIAS: Dammit, are you still ignoring me? I'd never have believed it.

GETAS: He's off his head, absolutely. *I* wouldn't have ransomed her, by God I wouldn't. 'It's a Greek custom and goes on everywhere.' We're well aware of that. But it's right to show compassion for one who pities *you*. And when you two don't show any to me, I won't pay any notice or heed to you either. You have none? Then there's nothing strange in my . . .[8] He'll rant and he'll plan to kill himself   320
as he comes to a standstill. His eyes flash fire. Not a word does she say, and he tears his hair. [*He bumps into* KLEINIAS.]

KLEINIAS: Hey, you'll knock me to pieces.

GETAS: Oh good-day, Kleinias. [*Aside*] Where's he sprung from?

KLEINIAS: My visitor seems to be causing some trouble with his visit to you.

The next thirty-four lines are almost illegible. All that can be discovered is that the conversation continues, at least one of the interlocutors leaves the stage, and Thrasonides emerges and soliloquizes.

THRASONIDES: All right, I'm in love, and there's a rock in my heart.   360
I'm hiding my sickness from my companions . . . how can I bear it? Drink will only strip the bandage from my wound that would rather not be exposed.

Twenty-four mutilated lines follow.

What's this? You've been well treated? Are you acting as her advocate? Tell me . . . If it was an accident, then I blame . . .   390

The rest of the speech is very fragmentary, but the words that survive show that Thrasonides is arguing with himself about his relationship with Krateia. There would have followed the choral interlude.

[FOURTH CHORAL INTERLUDE]

ACT FIVE

Only forty-seven badly damaged lines survive from this act. But the line of action is fairly clear: Thrasonides gets his wife, and the play ends with a marriage procession and an appeal for victory.

[THRASONIDES *is on stage when* GETAS *emerges from the house.*]

GETAS: Come away from the door, sir.

430   THRASONIDES: It looks promising . . .

GETAS: They are giving you your wife . . . I prayed for it . . . I wish you every happiness.

THRASONIDES: You're not playing tricks? . . . How did she say it?

GETAS: I swear . . .

THRASONIDES: The words, the very words . . . tell me quickly.

GETAS: He said, 'My dear daughter . . .' and she said, 'Yes, Daddy, I

440   really do want it.' I heard her, I really did. She was smiling as she spoke.

THRASONIDES: Marvellous!

GETAS: There's the door, someone's coming out.

[*Enter* DEMEAS *and* KRATEIA.]

DEMEAS [*to* THRASONIDES]: Step forward.

THRASONIDES: Oh, bliss!

DEMEAS: For the procreation of legitimate children, I give you my daughter, and a handsome dowry.

THRASONIDES: . . . just give me your daughter . . . what a piece of

450   luck . . . dinner for all . . . let's go in . . .

Six badly damaged lines follow.

Light the marriage torch, put on the garlands, on to the feast! [*To audience*] Ladies and Gentlemen, please give us a proper clap. And

465   may laughter-loving Victory, daughter of a noble line, smile upon us all our days.

[*All process into Thrasonides' house.*]

The Double Deceiver
[Dis Exapaton]

and

The Two Bacchises *by* Plautus
[Bacchides, 494–561]

Introductory Note to *The Double Deceiver*

This important fragment of a play, once known only by some six single lines (including 'whom the gods love dies young'), was first revealed and discussed by Professor E. W. Handley in his Inaugural Lecture at University College, London.[1] Any fragment of New Comedy that is restored to us is valuable and important, but the unique importance of this fragment is that it allows us for the first time to place part of a Roman comedy against a reasonable portion of its Greek source. For Menander's *The Double Deceiver* is the original of Plautus's *The Two Bacchises*, and a comparison of the two plays illuminates both Menander and Plautus for us. Plautus's play provides the basic plot which enables us to make sense of the Menander fragment, and the possession of even some fifty lines of Menander's play gives us valuable information about Plautus's originality and dramatic art.

Plautus alters the title of the play. This was not unusual: Plautus's *Boastful Soldier*, *Rope* and *Trinummus* (*Three-bob Bit*), as well as Terence's *Phormio*, all indicate a change from the original title. The reason here was probably to provide a more attractive title for the rather less sophisticated Roman audience. Bacchis would be recognized as the name of a *hetaira* (prostitute), and *Two Bacchises* would give promise of confusion and intrigue connected with love affairs. Plautus also alters some of the names. Moschos becomes Pistoclerus, Sostratos becomes Mnesilochus, and Syrus is transformed into Chrysalus. The names are still Greek, but they belong less to ordinary life, and are more obviously 'comic' in sound and meaning. He alters some of the metre, too. Only Mnesilochus's monologue (ll. 500–525) stays in the original iambics: all the rest of the passage is presented by him in the longer, more elaborate trochaic lines. Finally, he alters the structure of the play. Roman comedy, performed in a different context and a different tradition, made no use of the Chorus which for Menander provided a kind of living curtain between the acts of his play. Menander presents the episode of the handing over of the money and the explanation of the slave's trick, in two dramatic and realistic dialogues between father and son, the dialogues being separated by a choral interlude during which the transaction takes place off stage. Plautus cuts the dialogue scenes and the choral interlude, and replaces them with one long and one short monologue by Mnesilochus (the long one full of particularly Plautine jokes), between which Mnesilochus makes a purely conventional withdrawal lasting for four lines of the text, to hand over the money and to plead for Chrysalus. Some of the dialogue is elaborated, too, notably in the scene between the two young men, where there is much more 'moralizing' in Plautus than there is in the text of Menander.

All these changes combine to produce a difference in tone. Plautus is broader, more emphatic and elaborate in his comedy and his comic effects, playing for a laugh rather than an appreciative smile. Menander is more naturalistic in his characterization and dramatic action, and his effects are more subtle and economical. This we had expected, but it is agreeable to have it confirmed by the possession of a portion of parallel texts.

From a comparison of these parallel texts, we can produce the following summary of the action of the play. A young man (Sostratos in Menander/Mnesilochus in Plautus) is sent by his father (Unknown/Nicobulus) from Athens to Ephesus, to collect some money that is due to be paid. There he falls in love with a girl (Unknown/Bacchis), who is 'contracted' to an army officer and soon has to leave with him for Athens. Sostratos writes to a friend (Moschos/Pistoclerus), asking him to find the girl in Athens. Moschos finds her with her sister (also called Bacchis in Plautus), with whom *he* falls in love. His tutor (Lydos in both plays) strongly disapproves of Moschos's behaviour, and brings Moschos's father (Unknown/Philoxenus) to remonstrate with him.

At this point, Sostratos and his servant return with the money, which the servant manages to keep for the purchasing of the first girl's 'contract' by telling the father that they had been unable to collect it in Ephesus. The young man meets the father and tutor of his friend Moschos and, hearing their story, naturally assumes that his friend is deceiving him and decides to tell his father the truth and hand over the money. The father and tutor ask for his help in rescuing Moschos, and it is in the middle of this scene that our fragment of Menander's play begins.

It is clear from the Plautine play that the confusion between the two friends is quickly sorted out. But the problem of getting the money back remains, and it is for this purpose that the second deception of the father by the slave is required. All is eventually revealed, and the fathers are beguiled by the girls into allowing a happy ending for the two pairs of lovers.

CHARACTERS

SOSTRATOS, *a young Athenian gentleman*
HIS FATHER
SYROS, *his servant*
MOSCHOS, *another young Athenian gentleman*
HIS FATHER
LYDOS, *Moschos's tutor*
TWO SISTERS, *both called by the same name*

ACT TWO

The text begins towards the end of Act Two of the play.

SCENE: *a street in Athens, with at least two houses, one probably the home of the girls, the other that of Sostratos's father.*

MOSCHOS'S FATHER [*to* SOSTRATOS]: Get him out, tell him off to his face, save him and our whole family, for we are your friends. Come on, Lydos, let's go.

LYDOS: Suppose you leave me here too –

FATHER: Let's go, I said. He can cope.

LYDOS: Go for him properly, Sostratos, keep at him. He's lost all control, he's a disgrace to all who love him. [*They go off, right.*]

SOSTRATOS: Well, that does for Moschos. She'll hold on to *him.* (But you got your claws into Sostratos first, my lady.) She's a
20 fighter, and I know she'll deny it – and bring all the hosts of heaven into the act to back her. I only hope . . . oh, to hell with her. *Moves towards the door.*] Wait a bit; perhaps she'll beguile you, Sostratos. I'm completely her slave, but just let her try her wiles on a man with empty pockets! I'll give the money to my father. She'll soon stop making up to me when she finds that she's conversing, as they
30 say, with a corpse.² Well, I must go and find him. [*As he moves towards the house, his father emerges from it.*]

Some badly damaged lines indicate that they converse about the money, and that Sostratos contradicts the story previously told by Syros.

50 SOSTRATOS: Don't for a minute blame your good friend. I've brought it here for you.

FATHER: Then give me the money, boy, quickly.

SOSTRATOS: You'll get it. Take no notice of that silly story. No one did any close-anchoring or plotting,³ no one at all.

FATHER: Then the money wasn't deposited with Theotimos?

SOSTRATOS: What do you mean 'with Theotimos'? Your friend took the money and managed it himself, and his investments always pay well, Father.

176

FATHER: Yes, he's a good chap, he always did use his head. So what was Syros up to?

SOSTRATOS: Forget it. Come with me and get the money.

FATHER: Are you serious?

SOSTRATOS: Come and get it. 60

FATHER: All right, I'm coming. Just hand it over, and you'll have behaved properly, just as you should. I'm not going to quarrel with you before I get it. *That* matters to me more than anything. [*They go into the house.*]

SECOND CHORAL INTERLUDE

ACT THREE

[*Enter* SOSTRATOS *and his* FATHER.]

The beginning of the act is damaged, and the subject of their conversation is not clear until:

FATHER: I'm off to town, I'll deal with that. You've got something
90   else to do. [*He goes off, right.*]

SOSTRATOS: And now that my pockets are empty, I think I'd like to see my fine lady-love making up to me, and expecting – 'this instant', she says to herself – all the cash I'm carrying. 'For he's got it all right, and he's certainly generous – the very best – and I've earned it.' With her fine foot-work, she's certainly turned out to be just what I once thought she was. But Moschos is a fool, and I'm sorry for him; I'm furious with him, and yet I don't altogether
100   blame him for letting me down; it's *her*, the bold piece.

MOSCHOS [*entering from the girls' house, and speaking back over his shoulder*]: Then if he knows I'm here, where *is* he? Oh, hello, Sostratos!

SOSTRATOS [*curtly*]: Hello.

MOSCHOS: Why so glum and gloomy, for goodness' sake? There are even tears in your eyes. Has something else gone wrong?

SOSTRATOS: Yes.

MOSCHOS: Then tell me about it.

SOSTRATOS [*pointing*]: Inside there, of course.

MOSCHOS: What do you mean?

SOSTRATOS: You've always claimed to be my friend, but now . . . This is the first time you've ever let me down.

110 MOSCHOS: Let you down, Sostratos? God forbid!

SOSTRATOS: No, I didn't think you would have, either.

MOSCHOS: What *can* you mean?

178

THE TWO BACCHISES (ll. 494–561),
BY PLAUTUS

PHILOXENUS: Mnesilochus, please try and bring his passionate temper under control. Save yourself a friend, and me a son.

MNESILOCHUS: Yes, of course.

PHILOXENUS: Then I'm leaving the whole business in your hands. Lydus, come with me.

LYDUS: I'm coming. But much better leave me here with him too.

PHILOXENUS: He can cope.

LYDUS: Mnesilochus, take over, go and dress him down properly. He's a perfect disgrace to you, to me and to all his friends, with his dissolute behaviour. [*They go off, right.*]

MNESILOCHUS: I simply don't know which of them to think is now 500
my worse enemy, my old friend or Bacchis. Wanted him instead of me, did she? She can have him! That's fine. But I tell you this, she'll certainly pay for what she's done. Heaven help me, if I don't absolutely and completely – love her. I'll make sure she won't say she's found someone to laugh at: I'll go straight home and – rob my father. What I steal, I'll – give to her. Oh, I'll get my own back on her in all sorts of ways. I'll press her so hard that there'll be beggary – for my father. But I must be clean out of my mind, maundering 510
on here like this about what's going to happen. God! I'm in love, I think – as if I didn't know. But she'll never be a fraction of a feather's weight heavier from *my* money. I'd be the most beggarly beggar before that. Never, I assure you, never in her life will she make a fool of me. I've made up my mind: I'll pay over every penny of the money to my father, this minute. So she'll be making up to me when my pockets are empty and I haven't a penny, when it'll have no more effect than if she were prattling away at a dead man's grave. I've quite made up my mind to hand the money over 520
to my father: that's final. When I do, I'll ask him, as a favour to me, to let Chrysalus off, and not to be angry with him for fooling him over the money. He did it for me, and it's only fair that I should look after him, when it was to help me that he made up the story. [*To servants*] Come with me. [*They go into Philoxenus's house as* PISTOCLERUS *emerges from Bacchis's house.*]

PISTOCLERUS [*speaking back over his shoulder*]: I'll give your instructions top priority, Bacchis. I'm to find Mnesilochus and bring him to you immediately. In fact, I can't imagine what's keeping him, if he got my message. I'll call at his house here, and see if he's at home.

530 MNESILOCHUS [*emerging from the house*]: I've handed over all the money to my father. Now that my pockets are empty, now's the moment I should like her to approach me – my saucy Miss. Gosh, how reluctant my father was to let Chrysalus off when I asked him. But I finally persuaded him to keep his temper.

PISTOCLERUS: Isn't this my friend?

MNESILOCHUS: Isn't this my enemy that I see?

PISTOCLERUS: Yes, it is.

MNESILOCHUS: It is. I'll go and meet him.

PISTOCLERUS: Hello, Mnesilochus, glad to see you.

MNESILOCHUS: Hello.

PISTOCLERUS: We must have dinner, to celebrate your safe return from abroad.

MNESILOCHUS: I've no desire for a dinner that makes me sick.

PISTOCLERUS: You surely haven't caught some complaint as you arrive home?

MNESILOCHUS: I have indeed, a very severe one.

PISTOCLERUS: Where from?

MNESILOCHUS: From a man I thought was my friend, until now.

540 PISTOCLERUS: There are plenty of people like that. You think they're your friends, but they turn out to be false friends, unreliable. They're active talkers, but poor performers, and they're very likely to leave you high and dry. They envy everyone who's lucky and prosperous. *They're* never envied, their own indolence takes good care of that.

MNESILOCHUS: You certainly seem to have a very good idea of those gentry and their ways. But there's one thing you could add: their harmful nature brings harm upon themselves. They're friends to no one, but every man's hand is against them. They're really deceiving themselves, the fools, though they think they're deceiving others. Just like this man that I thought was as 550 fond of me as I am of myself. He bent all his efforts and took great pains to do me all the harm he could, and to cheat me out of all I had.

PISTOCLERUS: He must be a perfect villain.

MNESILOCHUS: Exactly my own opinion.

PISTOCLERUS: For goodness' sake, tell me, who is he?

MNESILOCHUS: Oh, a friend of yours. Otherwise I'd be asking you to do him what damage you could.

PISTOCLERUS: Just tell me who the fellow is. If I don't rough him up somehow, you may dub me an arrant coward.

MNESILOCHUS: He is a villain, but I assure you he's a friend of yours.

PISTOCLERUS: All the more reason for telling me who he is. I do not care for a villain's favour.

MNESILOCHUS: I see I'll have to tell you his name. *You*, Pistoclerus, you've ruined me utterly, though I was your friend.   560

PISTOCLERUS: *What?*

The Farmer

[Georgos]

Introductory Note to *The Farmer*

This play is of particular interest, as the major portion of what survives (ll. 1–87 of the Oxford Classical Text) was the first sizeable fragment of Menander's work to be discovered and published.[1] Three more tiny pieces of papyrus confirm or slightly extend our text, and there are also some short quotations from ancient authors. But the Geneva papyrus remains our major source of information. It starts in the middle of a monologue by a young man (who sounds like a Moschion), and reveals what is in many respects a standard situation of New Comedy. He has got his neighbour Myrrhine's daughter pregnant, the baby is due, he has not been able to arrange the marriage, and he is now faced with a different marriage arranged for him by his father. The dialogue which follows reinforces this information, and produces a further complication in the offer by Kleainetos (the farmer of the title) to marry the girl.

All this clearly comes early in the action of the play. There is an indication of an act division soon after the end of the dialogue: it is probably, though not certainly, the end of Act One. The confusion must have been resolved, and the desired marriage duly arranged, but we can only guess how this was done. Perhaps Kleainetos turned out to be Myrrhine's long-lost husband, and so the father of the girl? There is contrast in the play between relative riches (the Young Man and Kleainetos) and respectable poverty (Myrrhine and Gorgias – the same names and situation as, but very different characters from, those in *Old Cantankerous*), and some general moral reflections are drawn from that. But we need more information to produce any certainty about plot development. Meantime, the interest of the fragment is in its presentation of another variation on a theme and on character names.

CHARACTERS

A YOUNG MAN, *possibly called* MOSCHION
MYRRHINE, *his neighbour, perhaps a widow*
PHILINNA, *an old woman, perhaps a nurse*
DAOS
SYROS } *servants to the Young Man's father*
GORGIAS, *Myrrhine's son*
KLEAINETOS, *a farmer*
The Young man's FATHER *probably also appeared.*

ACT ONE

SCENE: *a street, possibly in Athens. There are two houses, Myrrhine's on the left, and that of the Young Man's father on the right.*

The Young Man is speaking. The beginning of his speech is lost.

YOUNG MAN: . . . I went to her mother,[2] did all the right things, without any qualms at all. I was no villain, and no one thought I was. But with the boy[3] still out at the farm, a blow fell which has finished me. I was off in Corinth on private business, and I come back in the evening to find a *different* marriage being organized for me – garlands being put on the gods, my father making the proper offerings inside.[4] My father himself is giving away the bride – she's   10
my half-sister, daughter of his present wife.[5] How to struggle out of this disastrous coil I have no idea. But the position's this: I've slipped[6] out of the house without a word, and abandoned the wedding – I couldn't do that to my darling. That would be unforgivable.

I've every intention of knocking at their door, but I've been hesitating for ages. I don't know if her brother's home from the farm now. I must be very careful. Well, I'll take myself off and   20
work out a way to dodge that wedding. [*He goes off, left, as* MYRRHINE *and* PHILINNA *enter, right.*]

MYRRHINE: You're sympathetic, Philinna, that's why I'm talking to you, and telling you all my problems. Well, that's where we are now.

PHILINNA: Heavens, my dear, as I listen to your story I can hardly stop myself from going to the door and calling out this deceiver and telling him what I think of him.

MYRRHINE: Please don't, Philinna. Let it be.

PHILINNA: Let it *be*? You can't mean it. Damn him, he's a villain. And is this scum to contract a marriage, after he's ruined our   30
girl?

[*Enter* DAOS *and* SYROS, *left, carrying branches of green leaves.*]

MYRRHINE: Here's Daos, their servant, back from the farm with all these branches he's been cutting.[7] Let's move over here a bit.

PHILINNA: Why should we worry about *him*? That'll be the day!
[*They move aside.*]

DAOS: I don't think anyone farms a piece of land with a better idea of its religious obligations. It produces myrtle, lovely ivy, such flowers! But plant anything else, and it gives a due and proper return, no surplus, just the average. Still – Syros, take all this stuff
40   inside, it's all for the wedding. [*As* SYROS *does so*, DAOS *sees* MYRRHINE.] Morning, Myrrhine.

MYRRHINE: Good morning to you.

DAOS: I didn't see you, madam. How are you? I want to give you a taste of good news or rather, God willing, of good fortune to come. I want to be the first to tell you. Well now, Kleainetos – where your youngster's working – when he was hoeing in his vineyard the other day, he gashed his leg. Right job he made of it, too.

MYRRHINE: Oh, dear.

DAOS: Not to worry. Just listen to the rest of the story. Two days
50   later, the old chap's groin was all swollen from the wound, and he was feverish, in a real bad way.

PHILINNA: Well, for heaven's sake! Is this the 'good news' you've come to tell us?

MYRRHINE: Don't interrupt, Philinna.

DAOS: So he needed someone to look after him. The servants – and he has no one else – are all foreigners, and they consigned him to the devil. But your son, treating him like his own father, did what was necessary. He put ointment on his leg, rubbed him down,
60   washed him, brought him food and cheered him up. The farmer looked to be in a pretty bad way, but your son's treatment got him on his feet again.

PHILINNA: The dear boy!

DAOS: Oh, yes, well done that man. As Kleainetos recovered at home and was able to relax, away from his mattock and his troubles – for the old chap has a pretty hard life – he asked about the boy's position (though perhaps he had some idea of it already).
70   Anyhow, the boy confided in him, and told him about his sister, and how you weren't well off.[8] The old man sympathized, as people do, and thought he must on all counts repay his debt for your son's attention. He's old and lonely, and he showed sense, for he plans to marry your daughter. That's the sum and substance of the whole story. They'll be here any minute, and he'll take her off to the farm. You can all stop your struggle with poverty – which is a stubborn, cantankerous beast, especially in the city. One should either be rich, I think, or live where there's no one to
80   witness one's misfortune. Country solitude's the answer to this

problem. Well, that was the good news I wanted to bring you.
Goodbye.

MYRRHINE [*faintly*]: Goodbye. [DAOS *goes into the house.*]

PHILINNA: What's wrong, my dear? Why are you walking about
wringing your hands?

MYRRHINE: Oh, Philinna, I don't know *what* to do.

PHILINNA: What about?

MYRRHINE: Her baby's due, my dear, any minute now!

*Only scraps remain of the rest of the scene (nine more lines). It is fairly clear
that Myrrhine and Philinna go into Myrrhine's house, and that there is a
Choral Interlude. The remains of the next act are even more scrappy, but
indicate a conversation between Gorgias and Philinna, and the cries that
signify the birth of a baby within. Apart from the following fragments, which
cannot confidently be assigned to any particular part of the play, that is all we
have.*

FRAGMENT 1

(?)KLEAINETOS: It's easy to treat a poor man with contempt, Gorgias,
even if his cause is absolutely just. For he's thought to be speaking
with one motive only – gain. Anyone with a shabby coat is
promptly dubbed 'twister' – even if *he*'s the injured party.

FRAGMENT 2

(?)KLEAINETOS or DAOS: The man, whoever he is, who's done
damage to your poverty, is heading for trouble. Because what he's
damaged is something that could one day be his own. Even if he's
very rich, high-living is not soundly based. Fortune's stream can
dry up very quickly.

FRAGMENT 3

(?)KLEAINETOS: The best man, Gorgias, is the one who can best bear
injury without losing his control. This quick temper and excessive
bitterness is simply a general indication of a poor spirit.

FRAGMENT 4

?)ANOTHER YOUNG MAN: Are you out of your mind? It's ridicu-
lous! You've fallen in love with a respectable girl, and you don't

speak for her. And for no good reason you ignore a marriage that's being arranged for you.

FRAGMENT 5

(?)KLEAINETOS: I'm a countryman, I'm not claiming otherwise, and I've absolutely no experience of city life. But the years have brought me a little extra wisdom.

Two more fragments exist, and a statement in Quintilian (11, 3, 91) which implies that in this play a young man quoted a woman's words, and did so in a quavering, effeminate voice. The rest is (so far) silence.

The Toady[1]

[Kolax]

Introductory Note to *The Toady*

What remains of this play, which was perhaps written in the last decade of the fourth century B.C., comes mainly from a papyrus which contains only selections from it (perhaps intended for recitation at a dinner party). We cannot therefore always be certain that lines as written were originally consecutive.

The plot clearly concerns the rivalry of Pheidias and Bias for the favours of the same girl, who is a *hetaira*, a prostitute. Terence used this play for his *Eunuch*,[2] but not necessarily as its main source, so we cannot assume coincidence of plot. The machinations of the *kolax* of the title must have been central to the plot, which perhaps ended with the young man and the soldier agreeing to share the girl's favours. From the papyrus, and from the quotations in ancient authors, the cast list overleaf can be constructed.

CHARACTERS

PHEIDIAS, *a young man*
DAOS, *a servant*
BIAS, *a soldier*
GNATHON, *a hanger-on*
STROUTHIAS, *perhaps another hanger-on, or Gnathon disguised*
A PIMP
A COOK
SOSIAS, *the Cook's assistant*
A SERVANT GIRL

The last two characters may not have spoken.

ACT ONE

SCENE: *quite uncertain. Perhaps the houses of Pheidias and/or Bias and the pimp.*

Of the first thirteen lines, only the second half of each line survives. But the passage looks like the opening monologue of the play, and it may have been spoken by Pheidias. After an initial (and conventional) piece of moralizing ('You never can tell in this life'), there are references to fathers and sons, to administrators (perhaps trustees) and provision for a son, to unhappiness, to action required, and to the provision of a dinner for fellow-members of a club. The next extract shows a conversation between Pheidias and (possibly) Gnathon. The text is damaged, but some approximate sense emerges from it.

GNATHON: Cheer up, Pheidias!

PHEIDIAS: Cheer *up*? 'Cheer up' when I'm so worried about this girl   20
of mine? Don't be silly. [*Prays*] O Lady Athena, save me . . .

Material missing.

PHEIDIAS: What do you mean, you miserable man?

GNATHON: I mean that heaven favours rogues. We who behave
properly never get any proper reward. Like the poor corporal,
sometimes shouldering pack, helmet, a pair of spears, a sheepskin   30
— as heavy a load as the poor old donkey carries . . . and then
suddenly, Bias.

PHEIDIAS: . . . I'm ruined.

GNATHON: He's touched down from somewhere after betraying a   40
city or a Persian Governor or an army camp. Well, obviously.

PHEIDIAS: How so?

GNATHON: No honest man ever got rich quick. He scrapes
and saves for himself, but the other type lays a trap for the
long-time saver, and scoops the lot.

PHEIDIAS: Life is unfair.

GNATHON: I swear to God, if the boy hadn't been walking behind
me with the bottles of Thasian wine (so raising the suspicion of
drunkenness), I'd have been keeping pace with him in the market-
square and shouting at him, 'Hey, man, last year you were a   50
beggar and a living skeleton, and now you're rich. Tell me, what

trade have you been practising? At least tell me this – where'd you
get this gear? Changing sides, are you? Why are you teaching us
evil ways? Why are you flaunting yourself as a rich rogue?'

*The next twenty lines are fragmentary or missing. Daos is indicated as one of
the speakers, and the pimp is mentioned. The next extract provides a
conversation between a servant (perhaps Daos) and his young master (almost
certainly Pheidias).*

DAOS: I tell you, sir, he's the one man responsible for this whole
business of yours coming to grief. I tell you again: any cities that
you've seen in ruins have fallen only through this factor, which
90   I've just now discovered through him. All princes who ever were,
every great leader, governor, garrison-commander, founding-
father or general – I mean of course those who have been utterly
ruined – nowadays come to grief because of one thing only – the
toadies. And their misery is caused by them.

PHEIDIAS: Strong words. But I haven't the least idea what you're
talking about.

DAOS: It would be bad judgement on anyone's part to assume the
goodwill of anyone who is plotting against you.

PHEIDIAS: And if he has no power?

DAOS: *Anyone* can injure a strong man if he's off guard. If Astyanax[3]
100   himself were lying flat on his back, you could break his nose with a
garlic-crusher:[4] but the hired professional, coming expressly to
attack him, wouldn't have an easy job if he was expected.

There follow eight or nine badly damaged lines.

[*He knocks on the door.*] Door! [*To* PHEIDIAS] Either he or you will
be utterly destroyed. You've convinced him, and as you seem to be
doing nothing that you actually are doing, you've got him off his
guard, out of the action and out of the house. You can arrange the
rest just as you want.

The next extract shows part of a speech by the Pimp.

120   PIMP: He's clearly a braggart.[5] They're hungry wretches, with
calluses in their hands, but nothing else: and my neighbour's one of
them. Still, if he gets wind of this, he'll arrive with sixty friends,
the same number Odysseus took to Troy, and he'll be bawling
threats, 'You'll be sorry, scum, if you've sold my girl to someone
with more money.' Am I likely to sell her? Certainly not, whatever
his threats. She's worth ten to me, bringing in three hundred
130   drachs a day from the foreigner. But I'm afraid they'll kidnap her in

the street, when they get the chance, and I'll have to go to law and a lot of trouble – witnesses, the lot – to get her back.

Two fragments are worth quoting:

FRAGMENT 1

The speaker is a cook, preparing dinner for a club which met each month to celebrate Aphrodite Pandemos (the goddess of Love who was 'worshipped by the whole people'), a patron of political unity.

COOK: A toast! [*To his assistant*] And you, follow me and serve the offal. Keep your eye on the job. A toast! Over here, Sosias. A toast! That's right. Let us pray to the gods in heaven, to all the powers in heaven – here, take the tongue on this plate – to grant us safety, health, every blessing, general enjoyment of all the good things here. Amen.

FRAGMENT 2

BIAS: Once when I was in Cappadocia, Strouthias, after dinner I three times drained a golden goblet which held four pints – and it was full every time.
STROUTHIAS: You've drunk more than King Alexander.
BIAS: No less, I swear it.
STROUTHIAS: A mighty feat

A few more short fragments survive in quotation, but they add little to our knowledge of the play.

The Harpist[1]

[Kitharistes]

Introductory Note to *The Harpist*

Some forty-five more or less complete lines, plus another fifty or so which preserve useful words and phrases, survive from this play, in addition to the nine short fragments cited by ancient authors. The quotations show that the play had a character called Phanias, who appears to be rich and unhappy, and one called Laches, who is probably someone's father. The papyrus confirms the existence of Phanias, and reveals that he is the harpist of the title.

The words that survive from lines 1 to 28 indicate that one of the speakers is a woman and the other a man, and that the conversation was probably about rape and marriage. When the text becomes relatively intelligible, the interlocutors are two men, one probably Moschion (he is named in l. 54), a name which usually indicates a young and somewhat irresponsible man. He is almost certainly the son of Laches, who in turn is probably the character who enters at l. 53.

CHARACTERS (so far known)

PHANIAS, *a harpist*
LACHES, *an old man*
MOSCHION, *his son*
ANOTHER YOUNG MAN
A WOMAN, *perhaps the girl's nurse or mother*

SCENE: *a street in Athens with (probably) two houses, one belonging to Phanias and the other to Laches.*

FIRST MAN (*perhaps the girl's father*): . . . you are jealous, you have brought your daughter here, and you consider that she alone has riches, while you yourself have none.[2]

SECOND MAN (?PHANIAS): I reckon that everything belongs to her alone, and my wife to me. She was a free-born woman, from a Greek city, and all this [*indicating his luggage*] I acquired by good luck. I don't need to go to a pimp for a woman.   40

FIRST MAN: Then what's bothering you? Didn't you bring the woman and her property here?[3]

SECOND MAN: I don't know where on earth she is.

FIRST MAN: She's not with you?

SECOND MAN: Not yet, and it's been a long time now. I think of everything – an accident at sea, pirates . . .

FIRST MAN: Don't talk like that.

SECOND MAN: I don't know. I'm depressed, and full of fears.

FIRST MAN: You have reason to be upset.

SECOND MAN: So come down town with me, and let me tell you the rest of the story. Then you can give me your advice.   50

FIRST MAN: All right.

SECOND MAN [*calling to servants*]: One of you take this luggage in at once, out of the way. [*They go off, right.*]

LACHES [*entering left*]: And what might *this* be about? It's not a bit like him. Moschion sends a message, asking me to come into town, when previously, if I happened to come here, he'd run away to the farm, and if I went there, he'd turn right round and come back here and get drunk. Well, fair enough: no father at hand to chivvy him. Not that I lost my temper – I was one of those myself, able to let money run through the fingers. My wife's not to blame – not for this, at least: he gets it from me. But he's certainly doing no good. Well, best go in. If he's not here, I'll go straight down to the square. I'll find him there, I imagine, where the gilded youth congregate.[4]   60
[*He goes into his house, as* MOSCHION *enters, right.*]

203

MOSCHION: I wonder if my father's arrived, or if I'll have to go out to see him. My business can't be delayed, absolutely not.

Only the beginnings of the next twenty-two lines survive. They show that Laches emerges from the house, and that he and Moschion converse. There is talk of marriage, and of a free-born woman, but no connected sense emerges. The text resumes.

MOSCHION: Listen to the rest of the story.[5] I visited Ephesus, and fell in love. In honour of Artemis of Ephesus, there was a procession of girls carrying offerings. I saw a girl there, daughter of a man called Phanias, from Euonymon.[6]

LACHES: Oh? Are there Euonymonians in Ephesus too?

MOSCHION: No, no. He was there to collect debts.

100 LACHES: Then is it the daughter of Phanias the Harpist you're so keen to marry? The man who's now our neighbour?

Here the papyrus ends. It is worth adding two of the quoted fragments, which appear to be connected. Speaker and context are unknown.

FRAGMENTS 1 AND 2

I used to imagine, Phanias, that rich men, who have no need to borrow money, never spent their nights moaning, tossing and turning, and saying 'I'm ruined', but slept sweetly and gently, unlike the poor. But now I see that you people who are known as 'well to do' have troubles just like ours.

There's surely some family connection between trouble and life. If life's luxurious, trouble's there too: if life brings fame, it brings trouble too: and when life's poor, trouble grows old along with it.

The Hero

[Heros]

Introductory Note to *The Hero*

For this play, we have a verse synopsis, a cast list, some fifty lines of the opening scene, another fifty badly damaged lines from later in the play, and some quoted fragments. The eponymous Hero (perhaps a family 'guardian spirit') does not appear in the surviving lines, but almost certainly spoke a postponed prologue, after the conversation between two servants which opens the play.

Synopsis

An unmarried girl had twins (as a result of rape), a boy and a girl, and she gave them to a foster-parent to rear. Then, later, she married the man who had raped her. The foster-father, not realizing the connection, pledged the twins to this man. A servant in the house fell in love with the girl, thinking she was a servant too. A neighbour had raped her, and the servant was willing to take the blame for that. Her mother, who did not know the true story, was furious. When all became clear, the old man recognized and found his children, and the man who raped her, willingly married the girl.

CHARACTERS

GETAS, *a servant of ? Pheidias*
DAOS, *a servant of Laches*
A HERO, *who speaks the Prologue*
MYRRHINE, *the twins' mother*
LACHES, *the twins' father*
PHEIDIAS, *a neighbour*
SOPHRONE, *a Nurse*
SANGARIOS, *a servant*
GORGIAS, *the male twin*

ACT ONE

SCENE: *a district of Attica, called Ptelea. There are two houses, one belonging to Laches, the other to Pheidias.*

[*Enter* GETAS *and* DAOS, *from their respective houses.*]

GETAS: Daos, you look to me as if you've committed some frightful crime, and are expecting any minute to be shackled and sent to the tread-mill. You're obviously in trouble – why else do you keep beating your head? Why do you stop and tear your hair? Why the groans?

DAOS: Oh, God.

GETAS: I knew it, you poor sod. Look, if you've got a few coppers put together, shouldn't you hand them over to me for a while, until[1] you get yourself sorted out? I'm your friend, and I feel for   *10* you.

DAOS: That's silly talk. I'm in trouble, Getas, real trouble.

GETAS: (*Line missing.*)

DAOS: Don't damn a man, please, when he's in love.

GETAS: In *love*? *You?*

DAOS: In love. Me.

GETAS: Your master's giving you more than double rations. A bad thing, Daos. Your diet's probably too rich.

DAOS: It's my *heart* that's affected, Getas, when I look at a young girl in our house, an innocent girl, a servant like myself.

GETAS: A servant, is she?

DAOS: Yes. Well, in a way. A shepherd called Tibeios, who'd been a   *20* slave when he was young, used to live here at Ptelea. He had these twins, he said – Plangon, the girl I love –

GETAS: Yes, I'm with you.

DAOS: – and the boy, Gorgias.

GETAS: Is that the boy who works with your folks now as a shepherd?

DAOS: That's him. Their father Tibeios, when he was getting on a bit, borrowed money from my master to help feed them, then borrowed some more when food was scarce, and then he starved   *30* to death.

GETAS: Perhaps when your master wouldn't give him a third loan?

209

DAOS: Maybe so. Well, after he died, Gorgias borrowed a little more, and gave the old man a decent funeral. Then he came here to us, bringing his sister with him, and he's staying until he works off the debt.

GETAS: And what about Plangon?

DAOS: She works with my mistress, spins, serves at table. She's quite young – Getas, you're laughing at me!

GETAS: No, no, of course I'm not.

DAOS: She's really ladylike, Getas, behaves very nicely.

40 GETAS: So what about you? What are you doing to help yourself?

DAOS: I've tried nothing sneaky – wouldn't dream of it – but I've spoken to Master, and he's promised to let her live with me when he's had a word with her brother.

GETAS: You're sitting pretty.

DAOS: Not so pretty. Master's been out of the country for three months – some private business in Lemnos. We're still hoping.[2] If only he'd come safely home.

GETAS: You're a good chap. I hope his journey abroad has been profitable.

There follows some talk of sacrifice and wood-carrying (perhaps for the sacrifice), and an indication of a choral interlude.

CHORAL INTERLUDE

The rest of the play is very fragmentary, but the fragments seem to indicate a scene or scenes at the beginning of the fourth or fifth acts. Laches and Myrrhine converse about Plangon's marriage.

LACHES: You poor woman.

MYRRHINE: *What?*

LACHES: Well, obviously, madam – [*aside*] Oh, devil take it.

70 MYRRHINE: You're mad. What a suggestion!

LACHES: What I shall do, what I've long made up my mind to do – she's sweating, she's quite confused – I tell you, Myrrhine, I was beautifully taken in by a bleating shepherd . . .

Myrrhine and someone else (? Sophrone, or ? Laches) converse about rape.

MYRRHINE: Sad's my fate, my sufferings are unique, and impossible to exaggerate.

(?)LACHES: . . . Did someone once rape you?

MYRRHINE: Yes, indeed.

80 (?)LACHES: Have you any idea who it was?

Laches and Myrrhine finally discover that they are the twins' parents.

LACHES: Tell me first, was this eighteen years ago?

MYRRHINE: I'm not the only one to whom such things happen. But yes, if you like.

LACHES: Things are getting clearer. How has your rapist never been identified? How come he deserted you? Exactly when . . . ?

There are also a few short fragments quoted from the play by later authors, but they are not very illuminating.

The Phantom

[Phasma]

Introductory Note to *The Phantom*

We know, from Donatus,[1] the situation but not the development of the plot of this play. The 'phantom' of the title was the illegitimate daughter (the result of rape) of a young man's step-mother. She had established the girl in the house next door, and organized a shrine at a hole in the party-wall, so that she could talk to her daughter while making offerings. The young man saw the girl at the shrine, and thought she was a phantom. But when he discovered that she was real, he fell in love with her, and eventually married her. How this dénouement was achieved is not clear. There were obviously two families, two young men and two girls (one of them the 'phantom') involved in the action. The 'phantom's' parentage must have been discovered in order to permit the marriage, but details of the plot development can only be speculative.

CHARACTERS

A DIVINE PROLOGUE
PHEIDIAS, *a young man*
(?)HIS TUTOR
A COOK
SYROS, *a servant*
ANOTHER YOUNG MAN
The two girls may or may not have appeared.

ACT ONE

SCENE: *a street in a city, with two houses, one belonging to Pheidias's father, the other where the girls live.*

DIVINE PROLOGUE [*quoting*]: . . . 'to bring to a conclusion . . . consider yourself a bridegroom . . . the girl's mother . . . in some other way to her brother . . . and for heaven's sake don't give them any grounds for suspecting you.' That's what he's doing. What else could anyone do? . . . she's not a phantom, but a real, live girl, established in the house of the bride. She was born before her *10* mother came here . . . her mother put her out to be fostered, and she's here in the house next door, being fostered, and guarded when the husband's at home. At other times, when he's out at the farm and there's less need for supervision, then she can leave the house. What a vision . . . [*To audience*] Perhaps you still want a clearer account of this. The mother has made a hole in the wall, and *20* created an opening . . . to see everything . . . covered it with garlands, so that no one coming up can see what it is . . .

Some lines are missing from the text, and it resumes with a conversation between Pheidias and (possibly) his ex-Tutor.

TUTOR: What's the price of wheat in the market today?
PHEIDIAS: I have no interest in that.
TUTOR: No. But, if I may say so, if it is expensive, you might be interested on my account, for I'm a poor man. Take a look at *30* yourself, Pheidias. Accept that you're a human being, and an imperfect one at that, and don't set your heart on things beyond your reach. You say you don't sleep well: will anyone looking at your life-style see any good reason for that? You walk around as you like, go in immediately if your legs get tired; you bathe luxuriously, then eat what you like. Your whole life is a sleep! In short, you've nothing to worry you, and your sickness is what you've described. A more vulgar expression occurs to me, young *40* sir: excuse me, but as the saying goes, you've not a corner left to ease yourself in, for all the good things around you. I'm telling you!
PHEIDIAS: You be damned!

217

TUTOR: It's the truth, I tell you. That's what's wrong with you.

PHEIDIAS: And yet I've no control over myself, and I'm *very* unhappy.

TUTOR: It's weak and silly —

PHEIDIAS: All right! You've worked it all out. What's your advice to me?

50 TUTOR: My advice is this, Pheidias: if you were really ill, you would have to look for a real cure for your illness. But you're not. So invent an imaginary disease and the imaginary cure for it, and imagine it is doing you some good. Let the women circle round you, wash you and purify you. Get yourself sprinkled with water from three springs, into which you've put salt and lentils.

The next fragment consists of some twenty mutilated lines, from which all that can be deduced is that a servant called Syros is addressed twice, that there is mention of marriage and a sister, and there is something to do with a cook. A passage in longer metre follows, with two speakers.

A: That's finished me.

B: . . . this chap's no Clever-Dick. They quite rightly suspected immediately . . . he met . . . then he rushed on her again . . .

A: I am unlucky in love.

B: You're one of those, young sir, who offer him a locked-up girl for food.[2] If the fit comes on him, perhaps he'll bite off the girl's nose.

A: God forbid!

B: Yes, indeed. Or her lip, while he's doing a bit of kissing. And perhaps this is all for the best. For you'll stop loving her if you see her then.

90 A: Are you pulling my leg?

B: Who, me? Of course not.

A: I'll go in and see my sister, and get the whole story sorted out. I think she's rather depressed by the projected marriage.

Parts of fifteen more lines survive, in which there is a conversation about rape, about a future conversation involving a woman, and about Brauron (where there was a famous shrine of Artemis). But neither the speakers nor the place of the fragments in the play can be determined.

The Girl Possessed

[Theophoroumene]

Introductory Note to *The Girl Possessed*

The 'possession' of the title is by a deity and not by a man – the girl is, or claims to be, in a frenzy inspired by a god. The eight fragments of the play which we know from quotation have now been supplemented by thirty lines (half of them badly damaged) from a papyrus. These lines clearly belong to the central scene of the play, the scene selected to illustrate it by the maker of the Mytilene mosaic (see Introduction, note 5). They are perhaps further supplemented by another twenty-seven half lines, which may stem from this scene. From the mosaic and the fragments, we can deduce that included in the characters were those listed overleaf. The details of the plot are still obscure, but the central issue of the girl possessed by Cybele, and of whether that possession is real or assumed, is clear.

CHARACTERS

PARMENON, *a servant*
LYSIAS, *a young man*
KLEINIAS, *another young man*
A GIRL
KRATON, *an old man, perhaps the girl's father*

ACT

SCENE: *unknown*.

PARMENON [*reporting a conversation*]: 'My gifts' – are you listening – 'they took my gifts from me,' says the girl. And he said,
'But what did you *get*, you gold-digging harlot? The man who
gave you the gifts – how do you know him? What about the 20
young man? Why are you walking about outside with a wreath on
your head? Are you mad? Then why don't you keep your madness
behind closed doors?'
KLEINIAS: This is nonsense. She's not just putting it on, Lysias.
LYSIAS: We can easily apply a test. If she's really divinely possessed,
she'll come rushing out here in front of the house. [*To flautist*] Play
a tune of the mother of the gods, or rather, of her devotees.[1] Stand
here by me, at the door of the inn.
KLEINIAS: Oh, well done, Lysias, very well done. That's what I 30
want. A beautiful sight!

*This passage was presumably followed by the appearance of the frenzied girl.
A passage of twenty-seven lines has been plausibly supposed to come from this
scene. It shows a mixture of comic and lyric metres, poetic vocabulary,
references to a 'Phrygian Queen', to Angdistis (an Asiatic goddess associated
with Cybele) as a 'Phrygian and Cretan' goddess, and to Lydians. It would
fit, but it cannot be proven. One major quoted fragment is worth translating:*

FRAGMENT 1

KRATON: If some god were to come to me and say, 'Kraton, after
death, you can have your life over again, and you can be whatever
you like – dog, sheep, goat, human or horse. For a second life
you've got to have – that's fixed by Fate. So make your choice', I
think I'd say immediately, 'Make me anything at all, except a
human being – they're the only living things with no justice at all in
their good fortune and bad.' An exceptional horse is exceptionally
well looked after: if you're a good dog, you're much more highly 10
valued than a bad one: a noble cock has special food, and a less
well-bred one is actually afraid of the better-bred one. But a human

223

being can be good, of noble birth and fine breeding, and it does him no good at all in the world today. Toad-eaters – they come off best of all, then blackmailers, with slanderers a good third. Better be born a donkey than watch your inferiors living more comfortably than you.

The Girl From Perinthos[1]

[Perinthia]

Introductory Note to *The Girl From Perinthos*

This play is known to us from the statement in the Prologue to Terence's *Andria*[2] that the plots of Menander's *Girl from Andros* and *Girl from Perinthos* were almost indistinguishable; and also from Donatus's commentary on Terence's play. The papyrus fragment comes from late in the play, where Daos, the cunning slave, has taken refuge from his master's anger on a convenient altar, and the master is trying to burn him out from its protection.[3] We can construct the list of characters shown on the following page.

CHARACTERS

LACHES, *an old man*

DAOS, *his servant*

PYRRHIAS
SOSIAS } *servants*

TIBEIOS
GETAS } *also servants, who perhaps do not speak*

LACHES'S WIFE

A MIDWIFE

LACHES'S SON

ANOTHER OLD MAN

(?)ACT FIVE

SCENE: *a street in a city, with at least two houses.*

LACHES [*to servant*]: And you come with me, and bring out the firewood . . . fire . . .

DAOS: Fire, too. Obviously. Hey, Tibeios! Getas! Is he really going to burn me up? You might let me go, Getas, and rescue your fellow-servant. It would be great if you let me go now. [*Pause*] Ignoring me, are you? Are we no longer friends? Here comes Pyrrhias — what a load he's carrying! This is the end. And behind him, Master with a lighted torch.

LACHES: Put it all round him, quickly. Now, Daos, show us your 10 low cunning. Think up some trick and get out of my clutches!

DAOS: Trick? *Me?*

LACHES: You, Daos. For 'deceiving an easy-going and empty-headed master is a piece of cake'.[4]

DAOS: Oh, help!

LACHES: And if the '*crème de la crème* of intelligence . . . [DAOS *winces.*]

SOSIAS: That registered, did it?

DAOS [*reproachfully*]: This is not like you, sir.

SOSIAS: The brazen rogue, the one who's just fouled himself here . . . the inheritance . . .

LACHES: Light the fire! 20

FRAGMENT 3

DAOS: There's nothing particularly splendid in a servant cheating a master who's easy-going and empty-headed, in outwitting someone who's never had any wits.

Title Unknown

Introductory Note to *Title Unknown*

The play from which these sixty lines come cannot be identified. It is clear that one young man has, in his father's absence, raped and then married a girl; and that his friend is spinning a yarn to the first man's father, in order to preserve the marriage. We can identify the characters listed on the following page.

CHARACTERS

MOSCHION, *a young man*
LACHES, *his father*
CHAIREAS, *his friend*
KLEAINETOS, *father or guardian of his wife*

There must have been other characters.

Our fragment clearly comes from near the end of the play.

FRAGMENT

SCENE: *a city street, with the houses of (probably) Laches and Kleainetos.*

CHAIREAS [*self-righteously and mock-tragically*]: He does me dishonour, though I've done him no harm. He always loved the girl, and was constantly badgering me, and when he failed to persuade me to give up the marriage in his favour, he worked his will by violence.

LACHES: Well now, are you refusing to have my daughter to wife?

CHAIREAS: And what am I to say, Laches, to those who formally betrothed the other girl?

LACHES: Now, do, please –

CHAIREAS [*theatrically*]: Oh, what shall I do?

KLEAINETOS [*entering from his house, or right*]: Who's making all this   20
noise outside my door?

CHAIREAS: Just the man I need! . . . What shall I do, Laches?

LACHES: Let's persuade him . . .

CHAIREAS [*theatrically*]: How formidable the force of rape! I am to persuade him to give away my girl, when *I'm* the wronged party!

LACHES: Be brave! Do it for my sake.

CHAIREAS: I defer to you, Laches . . . So listen to me, Kleainetos. Moschion has raped your daughter, and she is now his wife.

KLEAINETOS: My honour is defiled!

CHAIREAS: Don't *shout*. The marriage is legal, his father Laches confirms it. [*To* LACHES] *Don't* you?   30

LACHES: I do, Chaireas. I don't want . . .

Only odd words survive of the next five or six lines, in which Laches seems to be promising Chaireas his own daughter as wife – which may well be what Chaireas has wanted all along. Chaireas goes off to tell Moschion the news.

LACHES: . . . after freeing my son from his present fears.

KLEAINETOS: Well, we've long ago agreed to this. Moschion has married the girl, and he did so voluntarily, not under pressure. We expected you to be angry when you heard the story, but you've

235

taken it like a real worldly-wiseman. We've been lucky. Why should we complain?

LACHES: I don't understand.

50 KLEAINETOS: But I've just explained.

LACHES: Didn't you originally betroth the girl to Chaireas?

KLEAINETOS: Of course not.

LACHES: What? *Not* to Chaireas? To whom, then?

KLEAINETOS: This is nonsense. Weren't you listening? To your son, of course.

LACHES: You can't mean it?

KLEAINETOS: Indeed I do. And he is now father of a son.

LACHES: *Moschion* is? God in heaven, what a terrible coil.

KLEAINETOS: Are you mad? I congratulated you too soon, I think.

LACHES: And Chaireas hasn't been 'wronged' at all?

KLEAINETOS: 'Dear friend Chaireas' – not at all.

60 LACHES: Then why did he come here and create a disturbance?

KLEAINETOS: Perhaps he wanted –

LACHES: Oh, *did* he? You've all been in a plot against me. Oh, God.

KLEAINETOS: So? What are you going to do about it?

LACHES: I'll do nothing. But let me vent my fury in two or three good howls, for heaven's sake.

Some Longer Fragments[1]

From *Drunkenness* [*Methe*]

FRAGMENT 264

This fragment has a double interest for us. The name of Kallimedon in the last line, and the implication that he is still in Athens, dates the play to before 318 B.C., when he was condemned to death in his absence; and it is the only example so far of a direct attack on a contemporary political figure in the works of Menander.

Well, our fortunes and our offerings are very much on a par. Here am I, bringing to the gods a satisfactory little sheep that I bought quite cheaply. While flute-girls and scent and guitar-players, Mendian[2] wine, eels, Thasian[3] wine, cheese and honey – they come to quite a lot! Returns are in proportion: a small amount of credit if the gods approve our sacrifice, and deduct against that the money spent on these luxuries. That doubles the cost of sacrifice![4] If I were a god, I'd 10 forbid anyone ever to lay the rump on the altar, unless he dedicated his eel too, to secure the death of Kallimedon, one of his relations.

From *The Ship's Captain*[5] [*Naukleros*]

FRAGMENT 286

FIRST SPEAKER: Theophilos[6] has arrived, from the salty Aegean deep.[7] How lucky, Straton, that I am the first to tell you that your son is safe and well, and so is the golden vessel.
STRATON: Vessel? What kind of vessel? You mean the ship?
FIRST SPEAKER: You're really in the dark, my poor friend.
STRATON: The ship is safe, you say?
FIRST SPEAKER: I do. The ship built by Kallikles, and piloted by Euphranor from Thurii.[8]

239

FRAGMENT 287

A RETURNED TRAVELLER: O beloved Mother Earth, how holy and valuable you are to men of sense! If any man inherits land from his father and wastes its substance, he should promptly have to go sailing for ever, and never set foot on land, so that he can learn what a blessing he squandered when he had it.

From Anger [Orge]

This was Menander's first play, produced about 321 B.C.[9] Note the references to contemporary characters.

FRAGMENT 303

HUSBAND [*addressing his wife*]: Even I was once young, but I did not bathe five times a day: I do now. I didn't have a fine cloak: but I do now. I didn't use scent: but I do now. I'll get my hair dyed and my body-hair removed – oh, yes, I will – and in short order I'll turn into the monster Ktesippos,[10] and like him, I'll devour even stones wholesale, not just land.

FRAGMENT 304

Not a scrap different from Chairephon[11] is any man who, invited to a party 'when the setting sun makes a shadow twelve feet long',[12] sees the shadow cast by the moon and rushes off at cockcrow, thinking he's late – and arrives at dawn.

From *The Necklace* [Plokion]

Four fragments survive from this play, three of them discussed by Aulus Gellius (2, 23, 5 ff.) and compared with the Roman poet Caecilius's adaptation of the play. From the fragments, from Gellius's discussion, and from the Mytilene mosaic (see Introduction, note 5) of the play, an outline of the plot can be reconstructed:

Krobule is an heiress married to a relative (Laches), and she rules her household with a rod of iron. She has a son (Moschion) and a daughter. She has become suspicious of her husband's relationship with a pretty maidservant, and has made him get rid of her. The necklace may be a recognition token belonging to this girl. Next door to Krobule and Laches live a poor man and his daughter. The girl has been raped, possibly by Moschion, and gives birth to a child in the course of the play. (The necklace may perhaps be connected with her.) Presumably, in the end, Moschion marries the girl, but the details of plot development remain obscure.

FRAGMENT 333

LACHES: Now my fine heiress-wife can sleep soundly – on either side. She's done a mighty deed, won a famous victory: she's thrown out of the house, as she wanted to, the girl who was worrying her, so that the whole world may look on the face of Krobule, and know that my *wife* is the mistress of this house. And what a face she's got herself – a donkey among monkeys, as the saying goes. I'll say nothing about the night that originated dire disaster. I wish I'd never married Krobule: though she brought a   10 fortune with her, she also brought a nose as long as your arm. And her insolence – it's quite insupportable, by God it is. The little girl was certainly very attentive, and a quick worker. But let her go. There's no more to be said.

FRAGMENT 334

LACHES: Mine's an heiress, a real vampire. I've never told you this.
ELDERLY FRIEND: No, you haven't.
LACHES: She's mistress of the house and the land and everything . . .
ELDERLY FRIEND: God, how difficult.
LACHES: It's insupportable! She's a perfect plague, and not only to me. It's worse for her son and daughter.
ELDERLY FRIEND: It's a hopeless situation you're describing.
LACHES [*gloomily*]: I know.

FRAGMENT 335

LOYAL SERVANT: Not a chance has the man who marries poor and starts a family. How foolish he is who fails to keep watch over his nearest and dearest when, if he has bad luck, he can't use money to cover it up, as far as his public life is concerned. No, when the storm breaks, his life is exposed and vulnerable, he has his share of every misery, but of benefits – nothing. My concern is for one man, but my warning for all.

FRAGMENT 336

SERVANT: Any man who's poor and chooses to live in town, [13] is only likely to increase his depression. For when he looks at someone who lives soft and at leisure, then he can see what a wretched life he has. My master made a great mistake. When he lived in the country, he was never really put to the test, for he belonged to the class that has no standing, and he had open space to protect him.

From *Trophonios*

FRAGMENT 397

(?)SERVANT: The dinner party is to entertain a visitor.
COOK: Where does he come from? The Cook has to take that into account. For instance: these visiting types from the islands, brought up on all kinds of fresh fish – they're not at all taken by salt fish, they just pick it up in passing: but savoury stuffings and spicy sauces – that's what they go for. Your Arcadian, on the other hand, who knows nothing of the sea, is grabbed by the fishy dishes. A plutocrat from Ionia? Thick soup's what I give him, a savoury casserole – fine aphrodisiac dishes for fags.

From *The Changeling* [*Hypobolimaios*]

FRAGMENT 416a

I maintain, Parmenon, that the happiest man is the one who, after happily viewing these impressive phenomena – the sun which is there for all, the stars, the rain, the clouds and the lightning – soon returns to the place from which he came. Whether you live to be a hundred, or have a short life, you will never see these things change, and you will never see anything more impressive.

FRAGMENT 416b

Think of this time I speak of as a public festival, a visit to this world. Crowds, stalls, thieves, gambling – a sheer waste of time. If you leave early, you'll get better lodgings; if you've still got funds, you'll have no enemies when you go. The man who stays on grows weary, loses what he had, grows old and miserable and poor as he drifts around, makes enemies, falls prey to plotters, and has a miserable end when he finally departs.

FRAGMENT 417

You can stop applying your mind, human wit gets nowhere. Luck's quite different, whether Luck's divine or not. Luck controls everything, both upsetting and preserving, but human forethought is mere smoke and nonsense. Take my word for it, and you'll never say I'm wrong. Every thought or word or action – sheer Chance: we just append our signatures.

From *The False Herakles* [*Pseudherakles*]

FRAGMENT 451

FIRST SPEAKER: Cook, I think you're quite sickening. 'How many tables are we to set?' That's the third time you've asked me! One little pig we're sacrificing; setting tables, eight, two, one, what's it to you? Put it down here.

COOK: It isn't possible to make a savoury casserole, nor the usual rich sauce to go with it (with honey, fine wheat-flour and eggs). Everything's upside down nowadays. The *chef* makes cakes in a mould, bakes flat-cakes, makes porridge and brings it in *after* the smoked fish, followed by a fig-leaf and bunches of grapes. While the *kitchen-maid* posted opposite him roasts pieces of meat and thrushes – as dessert. When the diner's had his dessert, and put on his scent and his garland,[14] then he's served dinner all over again – honey-cakes with roast thrushes.

10

From Unidentified Plays

FRAGMENT 581

We should all – God, how we should – go about marrying as we go
about shopping, not asking pointless questions like 'Who was the
girl's grandfather? Her grandmother?', while never asking about or
investigating the character of the woman you're going to spend your
life with. It's folly to rush off to the bank with the dowry-money (so
that the manager can assure you it's not counterfeit), when it's not
going to stay in the house for more than a few months. But to ask no
questions about the temperament of the woman who's going to settle
down in your house for the rest of her life, and thoughtlessly to
acquire a wife who's silly and quick-tempered and difficult, and a
talker into the bargain! I'll parade my own daughter all round the city
– 'All potential suitors for this girl, come and talk to her, find out
beforehand what sort of pest you'll be marrying.' A woman's bound
to be a pest, but happy the man who gets the most tolerable pest.

FRAGMENT 612

SON:[15] 'Family' will be the death of me. If you love me, Mother, don't
talk about 'his family' every time I mention a man. It's people
without any good qualities of their own who rush for support to
memorials and 'family', and number off their grandfathers. But
everybody's got grandfathers! They couldn't have been born if they
hadn't. If they can't name them, because they've moved or lost
their friends, they're not necessarily worse than those who can. A
man with a good character is a 'noble' man, Mother, even if
he comes from darkest Africa. 'A Scythian? Oh, dear!' But
Anacharsis[16] was a Scythian!

FRAGMENT 620

The whole animal kingdom is happier – and has more sense – than
humankind. To start with, just consider the donkey: he's a poor
creature, we all agree – but none of his misfortunes is his own fault,
they're all gifts of Nature. But we, quite apart from our inevitable
troubles, bring extra troubles on ourselves. We're hurt if we're

ignored, angry if we're slandered: a bad dream terrifies us, and an   10
owl's cry frightens us into fits. Worries, fancies, ambitions, conventions – all these troubles are gratuitous additions to Nature's gifts.

FRAGMENT 740

OLD SERVANT or EX-TUTOR: My dear young man, if, when your
mother bore you, you were to be the only man to do as you liked
throughout your life, and always to be happy, and if some Divine
Power made this bargain with you, then you are right to be
aggrieved, for the Power has deceived you and done you down.
But if you 'drew the air which all men share' – to quote a phrase
from tragedy – on the same terms as the rest of us, then you must
bear this trouble more courageously, and be reasonable. The nub
of the matter is this: you're a human being, and no living thing   10
swings more quickly between the heights and the depths. And
quite right too. We are weak creatures, but we manage great
affairs. When we fall, we bring a lot that's good down with us.
Now you, young sir, haven't lost superlative blessings: your
present troubles are quite ordinary ones. So put up with the pain
which is also, presumably, ordinary.

Some Fragments Doubtfully
Attributed to Menander[1]

1. Papyrus Antinoopolis 15

The papyrus preserves part of the list of characters, as follows:

KRATINOS
LYSIPPUS
KANTHAROS
GORGIAS
PHILINOS
A SERVANT GIRL

We have the beginning of the play, a conversation between a young husband and a servant.

HUSBAND: Has anyone in the city suffered more than I? I'm sure they have not. I did what my father wanted, and I've been married for four months now. From the wedding night itself – Lady Night, I call you as a faithful witness to my words – I have never been for a single night away from my wife's bed . . . Enchanted by her   *10* generous nature and unaffected style, I fell in love with the woman who loved me. [*To servant who enters at this point*] Why are you bringing all these things to show me, when I'm sick at heart at the sight of them?

SERVANT: So that . . .

Several lines are missing here.

HUSBAND: . . . of my wife.

SERVANT: Your mother's . . . and if (s)he gave it to your wife   *20* and . . . her ring. Don't you see?

HUSBAND: Bring it here, so that I can see if she actually keeps something useful.

SERVANT: There.

HUSBAND: What is it?

SERVANT: Half a cloak, old and torn, almost eaten away by moths.

HUSBAND: That's all?

SERVANT: And a necklace, and an anklet.

HUSBAND: Bring the lamp and shine it here. Don't you see the little figures with writing on them? Here, open the lid.

SERVANT: Letters, yes they are letters, I see letters.   *30*

HUSBAND: What does this mean? This contains a child's recogni-
tion-tokens, and the mother was keeping them. Put them back
where they were, and I'll lock them away. This is certainly no time
to look for what's hidden away: it's nothing to do with us. I hope
we can come to some settlement of the present upheaval.

2. Papyrus Didot I

*This speech is by a wife whose father is urging her to leave her husband (cf.
The Arbitration). It might be by Menander, or by his close follower
Apollodorus.*

WIFE: You should be making the speech which I am making, Father.
For it is more appropriate for you to take thought than it is for me,
and to speak where speech is necessary. But since you have let the
occasion pass, it is left to me, I think, to do what has to be done,
and to say myself what has to be said.

If my husband has committed a serious offence, it is not for me
to judge and sentence him: if he has committed any offence against
me, I must have known of it. But I have no such knowledge, I
assure you. Perhaps I am a silly woman: quite possibly. But I
10 assure you, Father, however silly in general a woman may be, she
usually shows sense when it comes to her own business.

Suppose you are right: what harm is he doing me, pray? The
established rule for husband and wife is that he should always
cherish his wife, and that she should do what pleases her husband.
He has been to me all that I asked, and what he wants, I want,
Father. He is a good husband to me, but he's fallen on hard times,
20 and now you want, so you say, to give me instead to a rich man, so
that I shan't suffer the pain of poverty. But all the money in the
world will never give me as much happiness as my husband does,
Father. And it is surely right and proper for me to share his poverty
as I shared his prosperity?

Suppose this second husband I am to have – which God forbid, it
will certainly not happen with my consent and if I can prevent it –
30 suppose *he* loses his money: will you then marry me to a third? And
then to a fourth, if the same thing happens to him? How far will
you try to play Providence in my life, Father? When I was a young

girl, it was right for you to look for a husband for me: the choice then was yours. But now that I am married, Father, it is for me to make these decisions. And that is reasonable, for if I make a mistake, I shall be the one to suffer for it. That's the truth. So don't, I beg you by the god of hearth and home, rob me of the husband to 40
whom you gave me. I ask this as a favour,[2] Father, but it is a reasonable request for an act of human kindness. If that is not possible, you have the power to do what you will, and I shall try to bear my lot with proper dignity, and not disgrace myself.

3. Papyrus Didot 2

This is part of a monologue, from an unidentified play by Menander or one of his contemporaries.

We are alone, and no one will hear any words I speak.[3] [*He addresses the audience*] Ladies and Gentlemen, all my life until now, I've been as good as dead – take my word for it. Nothing was real,[4] not beauty nor goodness, holiness nor sin. There was always a sort of dark cloud which seemed to hover over my understanding, hiding and conceal-ing life from me. But now that I've come here, slept (so to speak) in the temple of Asklepios[5] and been cured, for the rest of time I'm 10
restored to newness of life. I walk and I talk and I use my wits. Ladies and Gentlemen, I have now discovered this magnificent sun! In the clear light of today, I now see you, the sky, the Acropolis and the theatre.

4. Papyrus Ghoran 2

This papyrus comes from the same site as one containing part of Menander's The Sikyonian. *It shows a conversation between two (ultimately three) young men and a girl's father, and represents a situation not unlike that in Menander's* The Double Deceiver. *One of the young men, Phaidimos, is in love with a girl whose father is against the marriage. During his absence abroad, Phaidimos leaves two friends, Nikeratos and Chairestratos, to look after his interests. For some reason, the girl has left home, and is probably in Nikeratos's house. But the explanation of this situation is not given to Phaidimos, who on his return from abroad misses Chairestratos and his message, and hears about the girl's situation from other sources. The consequent misunderstandings make for a lively comic scene, from a typical New Comedy play, which could be by Menander or Apollodorus.*

SCENE: *a street in Athens, possibly with the houses of Nikeratos and the girl's father.*

SERVANT [*probably emerging from a house and speaking back over his shoulder*]:

The text is damaged, but he addresses his mistress, refers to 'the girl's father here' and to 'what has happened', and then he sees Phaidimos, just returned from abroad.

. . . there he is! Welcome home, Phaidimos. I heard you'd arrived, and I came straight out.

80 PHAIDIMOS: Don't come near me.

SERVANT: Why ever not?

PHAIDIMOS: You can ask me this and look me straight in the face?

SERVANT: Yes, I can.

The next eighteen lines are badly damaged or missing. When the text resumes, the girl's father appears to be speaking.

FATHER: On whose authority?

100 (?)PHAIDIMOS: You brought it on yourself, by your own actions.

FATHER [*apostrophizing daughter*]: My God, child, what have you done to me? Now I understand what's going on. She's there now, I presume?

(?)PHAIDIMOS: Yes, she is.

FATHER: This is terrible, child. I'd never have thought it of you, child. Are you breaking with me entirely, child? [*He goes into his own house, as* NIKERATOS *enters, right.*]

NIKERATOS: I haven't found Phaidimos *anywhere*, so I've come back here. I may have made a grave mistake in sending Chairestratos to the harbour. [*Sees* NIKERATOS] Oh, *there*'s our friend. He's unmistakable.

110 PHAIDIMOS: . . . how to deal with this.

NIKERATOS: Welcome home, dear friend. Let me shake your hand.

PHAIDIMOS: What do I do now? We've been close friends for a long
time . . .

*The next eleven lines are fragmentary. Love, honour and demonstration of
friendship are mentioned.*

PHAIDIMOS [*grimly ironic*]: Your actions have gone beyond
all friendship . . . you've made your mark as a super-helpful
friend.

NIKERATOS: I don't understand.

PHAIDIMOS: You were looking after *my* interests?

NIKERATOS: That was certainly my opinion.

PHAIDIMOS: God! They are braver men, in *my* opinion, who can
look their friends in the face when they've done them down,
braver than soldiers in the front line. Soldiers share a feeling of   130
apprehension, and both sides assume they are doing something
splendid. But false friends – I've often wondered how their
conscience allows them such confidence.

NIKERATOS: What on earth is all this about?

PHAIDIMOS: It's sad. I've clearly missed out on real life. For life
holds no greater blessing for us than friends. If I haven't grasped
that, if I don't know how to see and judge men, but am deceived by
my friends – some scheming to do me down, others providing no   140
help at all – what's the point of living?

NIKERATOS: What *is* all this? What's upset you?

PHAIDIMOS: *You* ask me that?

NIKERATOS: I do. And I'm very surprised to find you so tense with
me.

PHAIDIMOS: Tell me, do you admit that I told you the whole story
of my love for the girl, keeping nothing back?

NIKERATOS: Yes, of course you did. Hold on!

PHAIDIMOS: Hold *on*? And when her father looked like refusing my
suit, you thought fit, it seems, to marry her yourself.

NIKERATOS: Good heavens, no!

PHAIDIMOS: Oh? You didn't intend to marry her?   150

NIKERATOS: Listen, my friend –

PHAIDIMOS: I *have* listened.

NIKERATOS: You don't understand –

PHAIDIMOS: I understand perfectly.

NIKERATOS: Before hearing the facts? How can you?

PHAIDIMOS: The facts accuse you of being no friend of mine.

NIKERATOS: For God's sake, Phaidimos! You're twisting the whole
business. I'm beginning to see why you suspect me. Because

you're in love, I can make some excuse for you – but you've got it quite wrong.

PHAIDIMOS: You're asking me to listen to a fairy-tale. [*Aside*] What on earth will he say?

160   CHAIRESTRATOS [*entering, left*]: I never got to the harbour. I met one of his fellow passengers, who told me that Phaidimos had left ages ago. So I came back.

NIKERATOS [*to* PHAIDIMOS]: I've saved your bacon. To prevent –

CHAIRESTRATOS: Oh, here's Nikeratos – and Phaidimos himself. Glad to see you, Phaidimos.

PHAIDIMOS: And I to see you, Chairestratos. You're just in time.

NIKERATOS [*to* CHAIRESTRATOS]: I'm having a bit of a rough passage with him.

CHAIRESTRATOS: Oh? He's surely not *still* labouring under the delusion that –

PHAIDIMOS: I take exception, Chairestratos, that a man who calls himself a friend of mine –

CHAIRESTRATOS: Stop! Not another word, Phaidimos.

PHAIDIMOS: Why not?

170   CHAIRESTRATOS: Because you'll very soon be sorry for it.

PHAIDIMOS: Well, I'd be glad to. It will be easier for me to change my mind once I understand. But Nikeratos –

CHAIRESTRATOS: I'm not going to stand here and let you say anything silly. I know all about Nikeratos. If you had three friends like him, you could do *anything* with confidence. But leave us alone, Nikeratos, so that I can tell him the story without embarrassing you.

NIKERATOS: All right, I'm going in. [*To servant*] Come with me. [*He goes into his house.*]

It looks as if Chairestratos and Nikeratos then go off right (the audience probably already knows the story and has no need to hear it again), and the act (? four) probably ends soon after this.

5. Papyrus Hamburgensis 656

Moschion, a young man, is in love with Dorkion, who needs money, perhaps to buy her freedom. A kindly woman provides the means.

WOMAN: But look, Moschion, at these clothes and this jewellery that I've got. You can pawn them for Dorkion, and get a thousand drachs for them.[6]

MOSCHION: Merciful heavens!

WOMAN: You can pay me back if things turn out right. If not, call it my contribution to keeping her safe.

MOSCHION: By'r Saviour, Madam, that's a kind and generous 10
action. I can't find words to thank you. A god from the Machine (just like a tragedy) has provided you with the necessary sum, Parmenon.[7] The future now looks feasible.

WOMAN: I'm going in here to see Dorkion. I promised her I would, just now.

MOSCHION: Then take all these goods with you.

WOMAN [*to maid*]: You take them, Doris, and come with me. [*To* MOSCHION] Wish me luck! [*She goes into the house.*]

MOSCHION: I'd like to go in and see her too, Parmenon.

PARMENON: Then go. Cheer her up and comfort her. 20

MOSCHION: That's my idea. [*He goes into the house.*]

6. Papyrus Petrie 4 *and* Papyrus Hibeh 5

Some four hundred lines survive of this play by an author about whose identity there is no agreement. But not many of the lines are complete. Two fairly complete passages are appended here.

(a) LIBYS (A COOK): I tell you, whenever I happen to watch a comedy with a cook in it, I often feel sorry for our profession and our tribe, if *that*'s the sort of thing we're stealing. They blame cooks for dividing a joint of meat in two, and for stealing slices from the middle of a sausage and then putting it together again, and for using sponges to draw off olive oil and mead; and they malign them for expensive thefts.[8] 10

SECOND SPEAKER: And what do *you* do, in the name of the god of kitchens?

LIBYS: Two from one, sure . . .

(b) *A servant, Strobilos, pretends to take an unidentified character (the second speaker) for a god.*

FIRST SPEAKER: Think of it as running in the Olympics. If you get clear, you're a happy man. [*He goes off. Enter* SECOND SPEAKER, *perhaps from a house.*]

SECOND SPEAKER: Heavens, what on earth is going on?

STROBILOS [*raptly*]: Now I'm quite sure that this is clearly the one holy place in the whole world, that here dwell all the gods, and that they are here now and were born here.

SECOND SPEAKER: Strobilos!

STROBILOS [*taking no notice*]: God in heaven, the scent of sanctity!

SECOND SPEAKER: Strobilos, you rogue!

STROBILOS [*still rapt*]: Who is calling me?

SECOND SPEAKER: *I* am.

10 STROBILOS: And who are you? O mightiest of gods, how splendid to see you!

NOTES

Preface

1. *Golden Oddlies* (Methuen, 1983), p. 25.

Introduction

1. Diogenes Laertius, 5, 79.
2. The translation is taken from the Loeb edition of Plutarch, edited by H. N. Fowler, vol. X (Heinemann, 1936).
3. From the Introduction to *Sheridan's Plays*, edited by C. Price (Oxford, 1975).
4. The opinions of Aristophanes of Byzantium, *Inscriptiones Graecae* xiv, 1183c and Syrian, *Commentary on Hermogenes* II, 23; Plutarch, *Table Talk* 7, 8, 3; and Quintilian 10, 1, 69.
5. See Charitonides, Kahil and Ginouvès, *Les mosaïques de la maison de Ménandre à Mytilène* (Antike Kunst 6, Bern, 1970). The mosaics, from the third century A.D., illustrate scenes from eleven of Menander's plays, and testify both to his continuing popularity, and to the continuing conventions of costume and mask.
6. For example, 'Whom the gods love dies young' Stobaeus, *Eclogues* 4, 5, 27.

Old Cantankerous

1. See Production Notice and note 4.
2. This verse summary is attributed in the papyrus to Aristophanes of Byzantium, the great scholar and librarian of the third century B.C. The uneven style, the faults in metre and the misunderstanding of the plot are against this attribution.
3. This probably is derived from Aristophanes of Byzantium, and based on official records.
4. An almost certain correction of the obvious error in the papyrus. Demogenes was archon (chief magistrate of Athens, elected annually, whose name dated the year) in 317–316 B.C. and the festival of the Lenaia would have been held in January, 316.

5. Otherwise unknown. Skarphe was a town in northern Greece, near Thermopylae.

6. It was neither polite nor politic to pass without greeting the statue or shrine of a god, especially the god Pan. (See l. 433.)

7. The shrine of Leos, in the Market Place at Athens, was a popular meeting place.

8. It is 'worth about two talents', and it was possible to live (frugally) on an estate worth about three quarters of one talent (pseudo-Demosthenes, 42, 22).

9. A district on the east side of Mount Hymettus.

10. This may be her daughter (see Act Five), or a maid.

11. The text is damaged, but the general sense is clear.

12. A fable of Aesop's (122, Hausrath's edition) tells of the gardener who climbed down a well to rescue his dog, and was bitten for his pains.

13. The *aulos* was a wind-instrument, a pipe (single or double), rather like our oboe.

14. Three badly damaged lines follow, in which Sikon starts to describe the party.

The Girl From Samos

1. The text is uncertain, but the point seems to be that Moschion, though adopted, was treated exactly as a son of the house.

2. According to the myth, Adonis was a beautiful boy, loved by Aphrodite, the goddess of love. After his accidental death, he was allowed to spend part of the year on earth, but had to return to the Underworld for the rest. The Athenian festival was held in the spring, and consisted of mourning for death followed by celebration of rebirth. Quick-growing seeds were planted in trays (the 'gardens'), symbolizing the renewal of life. The festival was an especial favourite of women.

3. The text is uncertain.

4. This contained barley, garland and knife, for the preliminary sacrifice.

5. The general sense of two damaged lines.

6. Amyntor was jealous of his son Phoenix's attentions to his (Amyntor's) mistress, and cursed him and sent him into exile. According to Euripides' *Phoenix*, he also blinded him.

7. A notorious hanger-on of the generation before Menander.

8. Nothing is known of him.

9. Moschion says he will go to Bactria or Caria, the two areas where a mercenary soldier of the time could most easily find employment. Bactria (on the borders of modern USSR and Afghanistan) was in

turmoil after Alexander's partial conquest, and Caria (now in south-west Turkey) was fighting off Persian claims to sovereignty.

10. There are a few small gaps in the text of the speech, but the general sense is clear.

The Arbitration

1. She was, in fact, a 'harp-girl'. Such girls were high-class courtesans, who provided music (and other amenities) for men's parties.
2. Not *vin ordinaire*, but not a really expensive vintage either. Smikrines is very careful with his money.
3. Twin sons of Tyro by the god Poseidon. They were exposed, rescued and finally recognized in time to rescue their mother. Several dramatists, including Sophocles, are known to have treated the story.
4. As, for example, in Menander's own *Rape of the Locks*, in Sophocles' *Tyro* and in Euripides' *Iphigenia in Tauris*.
5. Syros was a slave of Chairestratos, but obviously allowed to live and work on his own, provided that a certain proportion of his earnings was paid to his master. Such an arrangement was not uncommon.
6. Onesimos had told Charisios about his wife's having a child. See l. 903.
7. Literally, to 'carry Athena's basket'. The girls carrying baskets in the Panathenaic procession had to be virgins.
8. A festival of Artemis, celebrated in a village in Attica.
9. The last two lines are damaged, but the general sense is clear.
10. The verse endings are missing, but the general sense is clear.
11. The quotation comes from a lost play of Euripides, which told the (very apposite) story of how Auge was raped by Heracles during a nocturnal festival, bore a child, and recognized the father later by a ring he had left with her.

The Rape of the Locks

1. The Greek title means 'the girl who gets her hair cropped'. But I like the neatness and allusiveness of the title suggested by G. B. Shaw to Gilbert Murray (*The Rape of the Locks*, Allen and Unwin, 1942, p. 6).
2. See note 1 on *The Arbitration*.
3. Sosias.
4. The text of this, and of the next ten lines, is doubtful.
5. This may be a reference to a recent historical occurrence. One Alexander was murdered by his troops in 314–313 B.C.

6. Both the form of the saying, and its exact meaning, are doubtful.
7. The text of this line is uncertain.
8. The text is fragmentary, but the words that survive are significant, and the general sense is clear.
9. The text is damaged, but the general sense is clear.
10. See note 9.
11. Some line endings are damaged, but the sense is clear.
12. See *The Girl from Samos*, note 4.

The Shield

1. See A. R. W. Harrison, *The Law of Athens* (Oxford, 1968), pp. 10–12, 132f.
2. He wanted to win enough to provide for her dowry.
3. A few lines are damaged here, but the sense is clear.
4. Because they had no self-interest to serve. And as their evidence would be accepted only under torture, it was thought to be reliable.
5. Because Daos would also be inherited as part of Kleostratos's estate.
6. He has not stolen any oil. Cooks were proverbial thieves.
7. An heiress's inheritance had to be kept in trust for her children.
8. The text is damaged here.
9. An approximation of the sense, based on the words that survive.
10. The great medical schools of the ancient world were in areas where Doric, not Attic (Athenian) Greek was spoken. And doctors were old-established comic figures.
11. The opening line of Euripides' *Stheneboia*. See Aristophanes, *Frogs* 1217.
12. From Chairemon's *Achilles, Killer of Thersites*. See *Journal of Hellenic Studies* 1970, 22f.
13. From Aeschylus's *Niobe*. See Plato, *Republic* 380a.
14. The source is unknown, but the language is tragic.
15. A fourth-century tragedian. See *Hermes* 1954, 300f.
16. The opening line of Euripides' *Orestes*.
17. There is an indication only of a brief reply here.
18. Euripides, *Orestes*, 232.
19. A short comment of this kind is clearly missing from the text.
20. The exact meaning of the allusion is lost to us. But Smikrines' suspicious nature is clear.
21. Enough text remains to produce an approximation of the dialogue.

The Sikyonian

1. Sikyon was (and is) a town on the south side of the Gulf of Corinth. Until the action of the play begins, Stratophanes has thought himself to be a native of this town, and he is the Sikyonian of the title.
2. See Introduction, p. 15 and E. W. Handley in *BICS* 12 (1965), 38.
3. Literally, a man who eats at someone else's table. The parasite made a living by attaching himself to a wealthy man and, in return for small services and agreeing with everything his patron said, being fed at his patron's table.
4. The Prologue is damaged, but it is clearly spoken by a god (no human character could know all these facts) and its general tenor is clear.
5. Now part of Turkey.
6. Probably Stratophanes.
7. Cf. *Old Cantankerous* l. 46.
8. Various Greek states had agreed terms for the settlement of disputes between their nationals. Boeotia was the territory immediately north-west of Attica.
9. That is, an Athenian citizen.
10. Because of the gaps in the text, it is not clear which act's ending is indicated here. However, a numeral in the papyrus makes it clear that the next section begins with Act Four.
11. Resident foreigners in Athens clearly had to guard their tongues in the community that allowed them in.
12. The speech has links of style and content with that in Euripides, *Orestes* 866 ff. The first few lines are damaged, but the sense is clear.
13. The animal would be sacrificed, its entrails given to the god, and the rest eaten by the male members of the community.
14. 'The Eleusinian' distinguishes him from any other Athenian who might have the (relatively common) name of Blepes.
15. Any citizen had the right to arrest a kidnapper caught in the act.
16. The text is damaged from here to the end of the act, and only approximate translation is possible.
17. This was the 'family' name of one of the districts of Athens.
18. The text is damaged, but the general sense is clear.
19. The text is damaged here.

The Man She Hated

1. The latest (so far) of these was first published in 1977, and so does not appear in the Oxford Classical Text. My translation of it is based on

the text published by Professor E. G. Turner in *Proceedings of the British Academy* LXXIII (1977), 315–31.

2. A case can be made for either Thrasonides or Getas to speak these lines. Thrasonides would have been in charge of official spoils, Getas (like Daos in *The Shield*) in charge of his master's share. In any event, the recent arrival of that share is what has triggered the dramatic action.

3. This seems to be some sort of 'test' of Krateia's affections.

4. The meaning of this remains obscure.

5. This and the next few lines are damaged, but the general sense is clear.

6. Presumably Thrasonides (he had the sword). This may be why Krateia steadfastly refuses to have anything to do with Thrasonides. The son must later have been found to be alive (is he Kleinias?), in order to produce the dénouement.

7. The text of the next seven lines is badly damaged.

8. The text is damaged, and the translation is approximate.

The Double Deceiver

1. E. W. Handley, *Menander and Plautus: A Study in Comparison* (London, Lewis, 1968).

2. That is, she will be wasting her time. A corpse cannot hear.

3. In Plautus, *The Two Bacchises*, 277 ff., the servant's story is that the man who owed the money plotted with the crew of a pirate ship in Ephesus harbour to attack the ship in which the young man was sailing, and steal the money back from him.

The Farmer

1. The first edition was by J. Nicole (Basle and Geneva, 1897–8).

2. Parts of the first four lines are missing, and this is an approximation of the sense.

3. Gorgias, the girl's brother, appears to be the 'head of the family', and his consent would be necessary for her marriage.

4. Part of the ritual of a Greek wedding. See *The Girl From Samos*, Act Three.

5. This was quite legal in ancient Greece, provided the common parent was the father and not the mother.

6. The text of the next few lines is uncertain.

7. The text is damaged, but the general sense is clear.

8. The text is damaged here.

Notes
The Toady

1. A *kolax* was someone who made himself agreeable and useful to another man, and expected favours in return for services rendered.
2. Terence, *Eunuch* 30–32.
3. A famous Olympic champion all-in wrestler, of the fourth century B.C.
4. The text is damaged, but the sense is clear.
5. The text is very uncertain here.

The Harpist

1. The *kithara* was a stringed instrument, played by plucking the strings. It differed from the harp in having its strings of equal length. The harp is, however, our nearest equivalent.
2. Both text and meaning are uncertain, and the situation is far from clear.
3. Note 2 applies here.
4. The 'statues of Hermes' were in the market-place of ancient Athens, and seem to have been at this time the haunt of the rich and idle.
5. The text is damaged, but the general sense is clear.
6. A district of Attica, a suburb of Athens.

The Hero

1. The next seven lines are damaged, but the general sense is clear.
2. The lines that follow are damaged, and the sense can only be approximate.

The Phantom

1. On Terence, *Eunuch* 9.
2. Text and interpretation are uncertain.

The Girl Possessed

1. The Corybantes were the frenzied followers and priests of the goddess Cybele, the great 'Mother-goddess' of Anatolia, whose worship was known in Greece by the fifth century B.C.

263

The Girl From Perinthos

1. Perinthos was a town on the Sea of Marmara, some seventy miles from what is now Istanbul.
2. ll. 9 ff.
3. It was sacrilegious to remove anyone from sanctuary by force, but almost any indirect means could be used to prise the suppliant loose.
4. He is quoting Daos's words preserved in Fragment 3.

Some Longer Fragments

1. This is a selection of some of the passages preserved by quotation in other ancient authors, especially Athenaeus (second century A.D.), Aulus Gellius (from the same period) and Stobaeus (fifth century A.D.). The numbering is that of the Oxford Classical Text. The passages, all ten lines or more in length, help to extend our knowledge of Menander's use of conventional themes and character-names, and also illustrate the attitudes of the authors quoting them. Their preference for 'moralizing' leads them to select passages which, divorced from their dramatic context, sometimes sound banal. Fortunately, we now have a sufficient amount of continuous text to counterbalance this impression of Menander.
2. A white wine from Chalkidike, in northern Greece.
3. A popular wine from the island of Thasos, off the coast of northern Greece. All these things are the normal provisions for a party.
4. The text and the meaning are very uncertain.
5. Or ship-owner.
6. Probably the name of the ship-owner or ship's captain, who was conveying Straton's son.
7. An adaptation of Euripides, *Trojan Women* 1, and deliberately mock-tragic.
8. A town in the 'toe' of Italy.
9. Sources give 325–324, 323 and 321 as the date. They also differ about whether it did or did not win first prize.
10. He was the spendthrift son of a general, who sold even his father's tombstone to pay for his pleasures.
11. A parasite or hanger-on, well-known from references in pre-Menandrean comedy. See *The Girl From Samos*, 603.
12. A method of reckoning time. See Aristophanes, *Women in Assembly*, 652.
13. For the sentiment, cf. *The Farmer*, 79–81.
14. The sign that the meal was over, and drinking and conversation could start.

15. More likely to be a son than a daughter. Daughters in the extant plays seldom express themselves so vigorously.
16. According to tradition, Anacharsis from Scythia (South Russia) travelled in Greece in the sixth century B.C., was a friend of Solon's and was ultimately accepted as one of the Seven Sages.

Some Fragments Doubtfully Attributed to Menander

1. Some of these passages could well be by Menander, others (in the translator's opinion) are quite certainly not. But they are all parts of New Comedy, and therefore contribute to our understanding of the context in which Menander was writing and producing. The Greek texts of the fragments are published in the Oxford Classical Text of Menander.
2. He had the legal right to do what he proposed.
3. The tone, vocabulary and metre are para-tragic. The speaker takes himself and his situation seriously.
4. Text and translation are very uncertain.
5. Where the sick would sleep and (perhaps) be healed in a dream or vision.
6. The text is damaged, but the general sense is clear.
7. Parmenon, a servant, has clearly been charged with the task of raising the necessary funds.
8. The text of the last phrase is very uncertain.